DATE DUE   MAY 06

GAYLORD			PRINTED IN U.S.A.

On Seeing

Things Seen, Unseen, and Obscene

On Seeing

Things Seen, Unseen, and Obscene

F. GONZÁLEZ-CRUSSI

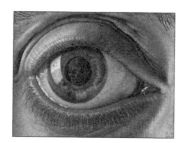

OVERLOOK DUCKWORTH

New York • Woodstock • London

First published in 2006 by
Overlook Duckworth, Peter Mayer Publishers, Inc.
New York, Woodstock, and London

NEW YORK:
141 Wooster Street
New York, NY 10012

WOODSTOCK:
One Overlook Drive
Woodstock, NY 12498
www.overlookpress.com
[for individual orders, bulk and special sales, contact our Woodstock office]

LONDON:
90-93 Cowcross Street
London EC1M 6BF
inquiries@duckworth-publishers.co.uk
www.ducknet.co.uk

Cataloging-in-Publication Data is available from the Library of Congress

Book design and type formatting by Bernard Schleifer
Printed in the United States of America
ISBN 1-58567-674-8 (hc)   ISBN 0-7156-3536-0 (UK hc)
ISBN 1-58567-838-4 (pb)   ISBN 0-7156-3586-7 (UK pb)

Contents

On Seeing
Things Seen, Unseen, and Obscene

Female Genitals:
Men's Foremost Visual Taboo

THE 17TH OF JULY OF THE YEAR 1791 WITNESSED A BLOODY
episode in the tumultuous history of the French
Revolution, the massacre of the Champ-de-Mars.
Curious to remark, it may have originated in a trivial incident
of voyeurism, if we are to believe Jules Michelet's account, who,
after all, was one of the most distinguished historians of the
period.

First, it is necessary to recall that the Champ-de-Mars is one
of the many sights that delight the tourist in Paris. It is a vast,
majestic expanse, terminated at one end by the École Militaire,
superb example of classical French architecture, and closed on
the other end by the Trocadéro, or hill of Chaillot. This huge
space is now a formal garden, but at one time it was simply a
very large esplanade where important events and ceremonies
took place. It was here that a physicist, J. A. C. Charles, in
1783, launched a hydrogen-filled balloon, thus inaugurating
the era of exploration of aerial space. Only one year later, Jean-
Pierre François Blanchard went up in a balloon himself, and
would later enter history by becoming the first man to cross the
English Channel in a balloon, in the company of an American
physician, John Jeffries. It was only natural that this large space
should have been chosen as a fit site for the ceremonies com-
memorating the storming of the Bastille.

One year after that feat, an extraordinary pageant took place here, whose lavishness and splendor left a profound impress in the popular imagination. No less ostentatious was the display planned for the second anniversary. An Altar to the Fatherland was erected, and no detail was spared that might enhance the pomp and brilliance of the projected extravaganza. The altar was in the center of the esplanade, on top of an immense, tall, quadrilateral structure supported by massive piers at each angle. These piers were joined to each other by stairs so wide that, in the words of an ocular witness, "a whole battalion of soldiers could climb marching side-by-side with each other." Colossal tripods at the angles increased the imposing appearance of the structure. From the platform to which the stairs led, rose a series of levels of progressively narrower surface, so as to conform a pyramid, at whose vertex stood the Altar to the Fatherland, flanked by a palm tree.

Grandstands were constructed, whence the public could watch the grandiose, patriotic spectacle. This fact gave certain fatuous and dim-witted men an idea that proved disastrous. For in the year 1791 the number of fatuous and inane men living in Paris had reached an all-time high. Mind you: this breed of men has never been scarce in the City of Lights, but there was a reason for their unbridled proliferation in the time of greatest revolutionary fervor. Many rich and powerful aristocrats, intimidated by the violence of the movement, which seemed to surge ever more menacing with no signs of ebbing any time soon, promptly absconded. And, as the *émigrés* increased in number, the masses of their dependent menials, now jobless, swelled out of proportion.

Consider that each aristocrat had a whole train of servants, subordinates, and parasites, whose livelihood heretofore had depended on the will and sponsorship of the master. They were gardeners, butlers, housekeepers, coachmen, valets, and assorted underlings, collectively designated by the pejorative French word *valetaille*, that is, the undifferentiated mass of valets or lackeys. Most pernicious among these were the kind connected with the furnishing of luxury and pleasure to their masters: jewelers, art dealers, dance masters, fashion designers, hair dressers, and the like. Needless to say, they were all perfervid royalists. Especially the hairdressers, for, as historians point out, they shared all the frivolousness and vacuity of their masters, without their polish, restraint, and education.

For centuries, hairdressers and wig-makers enjoyed a very high standing in the *Ancien Régime.* Imagine: theirs was the rare privilege of admission to the private rooms of the most exalted personages of the royal court. They could chat for hours with the exquisite ladies of the king's entourage, while these patiently endured the devices that curled their hair, or bleached it (Madame Du Barry, who passed for a blonde, lightened her hair with infusion of camomile), or the gums that held it still in the most extravagant shapes. And while the hairdressers waited with their patronesses, they could joke, or listen to gossip, or, less commonly, become privy to information of serious import. Indeed, some seem to have acquired a not negligible influence. When Queen Marie-Antoinette and her family made the ill-fated attempt to escape, she entrusted her diamonds to her *perruquier*, a certain *sieur* Leonard. This same man had a hand in the preparations for the escape; but his ability, outside of the procurement of hairdos and wigs, was apparently limited, and things went badly, as is well known, for the would-be escapees. Thus, Michelet is correct in stating that the most recalcitrant royalists in those dangerous times were not the noblemen, nor the priests, but the hairdressers.[1]

One of these, on the eve of the 17th of July, conceived an idea very much in keeping with his status as a vacuous, loose fellow in a state of forced idleness. This was, to introduce himself under the seats of a grandstand, in order to get a good view of the bodily parts hidden under women's skirts. And he sought the company of one of his friends, an incapacitated old soldier who had been an outspoken royalist, and was now a goatish old man, as lecherous, as dim-witted, and as jobless as himself.

The two go to the Champ-de-Mars at night, loosen the planks, and introduce themselves into the darkness, carrying with them a basket of food, bottles of wine, and other items to sustain themselves and their visual indulgence during the celebration, which was to last all day; for the pomp and circumstance of patriotic ceremonies of the period was not known for hastiness.

The pair of skittish friends anticipate great fun. They laugh at the possibilities: they would see just what kind of hidden assets had that woman who spoke at public gatherings, and passed for being a tribune of the people; and that other woman, a writer and a stern personality, little did she suspect that they would be canvassing at their leisure the parts of her anatomy that she most zealously concealed; and that other one, a hot-headed republican, they would know if the firmness of her political convictions was matched by that of her fleshy foundation . . . What a rich mine of ribald jokes, and jibes, and lusty fribbles! Just to think of what they could say in the *salons* already gave them fits of a laughter to split their sides. For, indeed, the tone of the conversations in the salons, all historians concede, was quite free; one cringes to note what kind of ribaldry and bawdiness was shown even in the presence of the Queen.

But these two jokers need to get a good, plain view. Accordingly, they set about drilling holes in various places of the grandstand, and they are still at it when the public begins to arrive. An old woman, a cake vendor, appears early to set up her wares. She hears a noise, looks into its provenance, and discovers with fright that there are two men busy doing she knows not what under cover of darkness. She runs to the police, who pay little attention to the old crone. But, as is now appreciated, old crones were not to be so easily dismissed in the French Revolution. She runs to the *Hôtel de Ville*, where she knows she will encounter short-fused, zealous patriots, finds them, tells them what she knows, and they all return to the ceremonial site armed with pikes, sabers, crossbars, and assorted implements fit to defend the revolution.

The two simpletons promptly realize they are in big trouble: a pair of fellows of the royalist persuasion hiding in the dark, in close proximity to the Altar to the Fatherland, forebodes ill. In vain do they confess their puerile, silly intent. They only make matters worse for themselves. The neighborhood is fertile in laundry women, a fierce race of females armed with sturdy canes and truncheons, with which they hit the bed sheets and tablecloths that they daily hang to dry in the sun. But they have been known to apply the same tools to less peaceful and tranquil employment; for they, the women, have often taken part in bloody revolt and murderous tumult. They are not amused when they hear the witless pair's confession: what they have done, say the furies, is an outrage to the dignity of women.

The affrighted pair stutter excuses, but it is too late. By now, a fast-spreading rumor has turned the basket of provisions into a powder keg. By now, the bottles of wine are said by everyone to contain kerosene, or some flammable liquid with which these two despicable traitors would set fire to the ceremonial structure. In vain the captives deny and implore: the jury is convinced: they planned to set fire to the Altar of the Fatherland! And as the rumor spreads, the captors' miens become ever fiercer, their tone more violent.

At last, the people's wrath cannot be contained. They literally pluck out the two suspects from their hideout; the guards that had come out to quell the disorder are unable to protect them. The women pounce on the two men with their truncheons, the wild-eyed sans-culottes with their pikes, and halberds, and daggers, and the two unfortunates breathe their last. In no time the two severed heads are at the end of respective pikes, making the royalists who see them turn white as sheets.

Meanwhile, the National Assembly is host to heated debates. The royalist party is still strong: four hundred years of absolute monarchy cannot be brushed aside easily. In spite of his disloyal conduct, the person of the king is deemed sacred. Thus, when reports of the disorder reach the Assembly, a royalist deputy declaims: "Two honest citizens have just perished . . . They enjoined the people to respect the laws. They were hung." The royalists' reaction is swift: their sacred cause is threatened, and now a crime has been committed: the stage is set for repressive measures to be enacted.

At the Champ-de-Mars, the people form groups; there is much shouting and yelling; they discuss the urgency of changing a decree that bolsters the inviolability of the king's person. In view of the recent incident, in which no few patriots see a royalist conspiracy, the people want to take their petition to abrogate the decree directly to the representatives of the people. The excited group, including many women and children, advance toward the Assembly, the two severed heads held aloft, like banners.

The deputies hear that "fifty thousand brigands are getting ready this very minute to march toward the Assembly." A detachment of soldiers is sent for what today might be called "crowd control." The rest is official history: someone shoots at the soldiers, and the cavalry charges against the crowd, amidst terrible clamoring and cries of pain. The fleeing citizenry is persecuted by saber-wielding dragoons; those who try to escape through the side of the Champ-de-Mars opposite the river, encounter the tips of the bayonets of soldiers who close this exit. On the stairs of the platform that supports the Altar to the Fatherland run rivulets of blood; and both stairs and platform are strewn with dead bodies, among them many women and children who wrongly assumed that this sacred site would be respected.

This is the story of the massacre of the Champ-de-Mars. Strange as it seems, the sexual desire of two insignificant churls, whose names history does not preserve, was its trigger. But it may be said that, in a way, fate rescued them from anonymous vulgarity by inscribing their action alongside the name of those who endured great personal misfortune on account of an irrepressible desire to see what should have been covered to them, the intimate anatomy of Woman. The archetype of such victims is Actaeon, as recounted in Greek mythology and reproduced in innumerable works of art.

In the well known myth, Actaeon is a hero and a great hunter. He hunts in the woods at Orchomene, when he falls upon a densely treed valley, where there is a grotto that hides a pond. He does not know that this pond is sacred to Diana, the divine and beautiful Virgin-Queen, whose attributes are the crescent moon, the silver bow, and the hunting-dog. She is also the Murderous Maiden: destined never to know the embrace of man; terrible because chaste and alluring at the same time. That day, she has come with her attendant Nymphs to bathe in her pond. To Cocale she hands her saffron hunting tunic with a red hem that reaches down to her knees; while Nephale, Hyale, and other Nymphs tenderly arrange her hair, bring her a mirror, draw water from the pond with their urns, or look after their mistress' hunting dog.

Actaeon parts the foliage to get a better view, and is dazzled by Diana's incomparably beautiful nakedness. But the Nymphs detect him, scream, and try to cover the exposed body of the goddess. She is irate, and would have slain immediately the impudent looker-on, but her quiver and arrows are on the other side of the pond, away from her reach. No matter: she is a goddess, and her destructive power is not subordinate to material tools. With her bare hands, she splashes water on Actaeon's face, and straight away he is seized by panic. He flees, but, lo!, as he runs his arms become legs with hooves, and so do his feet, and his whole body is gradually covered by a thick fur, and antlers sprout from his skull: he has been transformed into a stag. Alas, his own dogs attack him, since they no longer recognize him.

The wretched Actaeon wants to scream, to stay the powerful jaws that rend his limbs and tear his body apart, but instead of a shout, only a piteous bleat comes out of his throat.

It is a powerful image, this poor man transformed into a bleeding mass of ragged flesh, who dies amidst untold sufferings under a pack of vicious hounds with bloodshot eyes, ceaselessly barking, baying, and foaming at the mouth. And what can this myth represent, if not the expression of a male's subconscious fear, a fear that arises from seeing what he is forbidden to see in the body of Woman? Psychoanalysts have had much to say in this respect: they spent torrents of ink describing the labyrinthic ways in which this obscure preoccupation actuates the behavior of men. One may choose to believe their conclusions, or regard them with skepticism; but the inescapable fact remains that men evince a strong obsession for the sight of female reproductive anatomy. "Fascination" is an apposite term, for it is compounded of attraction and repulsion; it is a little like the emotion that overtakes many who stand on the edge of a cliff: they perceive a danger whence they would soon be removed; but they also feel a pull, as if they were sucked by a vacuum where they would fain plunge.

This obscure idea that lives in the murky depths of the male mind, has been brought to the surface in modern films. In a film by the Spanish director Pedro Almodóvar, entitled *Hable con Ella (Talk to Her)*, there is a silent movie sequence, which is very much an integral part of the film, in which a man is shrunk to a few inches in stature, and then, in a "pornographically surreal scene," as a critic dubbed it, we see the miniaturized man enter whole into a woman's vagina. The lady is presumably his sweetheart, and there is no question of malefic, injurious, or ghoulish womanly intent. But the atavistic, irrational idea of being engulfed, eaten up, cannibalized,—the fear of the *vagina dentata*, or *"le sexe mangeur,"* is barely adumbrated, lurking underneath. A 1999 French film directed by Bruno Dumont, entitled *L'Humanité*, also shows a close-up of a woman's vagina, but the context in which the camera exposes this part of the female anatomy is much harsher than that of the aforementioned film. The action takes place in a bleak Northern French town, and the grim, oppressive tone of the work is perhaps more propitious to a negative representation of the female genitalia.

It is hardly surprising that affected litterateurs should have gone so far as to say that to look squarely into Woman's sex is tantamount to "confronting the absolute prohibition," and therefore, in a sense, like looking at the face of Medusa, she of the head of hair made of writhing snakes, or, in this case, she of the face that is all mouth, a mouth that is all shade and unfathomable abyss. The image may seem extravagant, distasteful or antipathetic to one's sensibility, but it has the power to portray the complex reaction of the male mind to the forbidden sight. As when seeing Medusa, the perceiver sees the allurement of the feminine, commingled with the horrid fascination of death.

That such a powerful image was not fully exploited in traditional painting is probably due to the very severe social taboos and interdictions against the unimpeded pictorial figuration of female genitals. If we are to believe the various interpreters of artistic expression, in traditional painting such sexual images were sublimated into symbols, such as bivalve shells, oysters, half-moons, spindles, or objects such as the mandorla, whose almond shape resulting from two intersecting circles, and usually drawn vertically, more directly recalls the shape of the vulva. However, there was a painter who, in the generally prudish European nineteenth century, dared to make this subject the central theme of one of his paintings.

The painter was Gustave Courbet (1819-1877), leader, in his native France, of a school of Realism that broke with the affectation of the Romantic movement, and the artificial, controlled sentimentality of Neoclassicism. Thrice his work was rejected by the official Salon of the Royal Academy, on account of his unconventional style and the boldness of his chosen subject matter: Courbet was a socialist, and often made his art a means of expressing his social and political ideas. The striking painting in which a woman's private parts constitute the very center of the work was executed in 1866, when the painter had achieved widespread recognition. The name of the painting is *L'Origine du Monde* (*The Origin of the World*), and perhaps it is not difficult to see why. One is reminded of a statement by Nicolas Venette, 17th century physician, that a woman's pudenda were called (in his time) "Nature, because we all come from there;" and he added that "all our pleasures as well as all the misfortunes that occur in the world, and continue to occur, come therefrom."[2]

Courbet met the American-born painter James MacNeill Whistler, and was utterly taken with his work. Unfortunately for their friendship, he was no less taken with Whistler's beautiful model and mistress, Joanna Hiffernan, an Irish woman familiarly referred to as "Jo," whose flaming red hair Courbet praised effusively from the start of their acquaintance. Whistler had expressed unbounded admiration for Courbet's work, of whom he is said to have exclaimed enthusiastically "A great man!, a great man!" shortly after having first met him. Courbet, in turn, had the highest respect for Whistler's work, and even told his mother, erroneously it seems, that the American was his disciple. As luck would have it, Whistler decided to travel to South America, because, out of remorse for being away from his native country during the Civil War, he wanted to fight for Chile's independence from Spain (actually, Chile had recently ceased to be a colony of Spain, but a punitive and repressive action of the colonialist powers, Spain included, was in the making). Whistler returned to Paris having seen no military action—the fight was really quite brief and subdued—but was shocked out of his wits, as if he had just witnessed the most brutal carnage, when he saw Courbet's *L'Origine du Monde*.

Whistler realized that Joanna had been the model for that painting (the face is not shown, but he must have been sufficiently familiarized with the lower region, for him to be so sure of the incriminating identification). He could not conceive that a woman would be so reckless as to pose for a male painter,

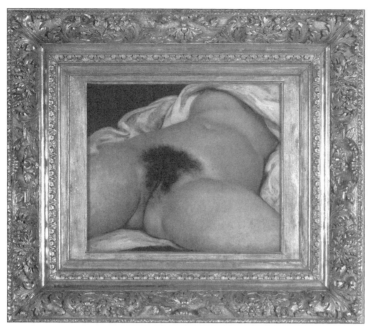

Figure 1. *The Origin of the World*, by Gustave Courbet (1866). Oil on canvas measuring 46 x 55 cm. The lavish, elegant frame enhances the theatricality of the presentation, a characteristic attached to this painting since its creation.

alone, in the seclusion of his study, and while uncovering the most intimate parts of her anatomy, without at the same time having the forwardness to surrender her whole person to the painter. In a word, he was sure he had been betrayed. Art historians unanimously speculate that the origin of the acrimonious breakup that followed between Whistler and Courbet was traceable to earthy, carnal jealousy, more than to airy discussions of esthetics, as some pretended. Whistler said that he "did not complain of Courbet's influence [on his own work]," because "it had not any." And he lamented ever having known him, wishing instead he had met and been influenced by Ingres, the classicist master.

The history of *The Origin of the World* is not without interest. For a long time, very few people knew of its existence.

It was bought by a wealthy Middle Eastern diplomat (some say Turkish, others Egyptian) named Khalil-Bey, who had commissioned a painting to Courbet. The work commissioned was a copy of some classical-style rendering of a mythological theme, Venus chasing Psyche, which we can imagine full of naked bodies with a surfeit of evoked rosy flesh and trembling rotundities. Khalil-Bey, for all his good taste and art expertise, seems to have been somewhat of a sybaritic fellow, with a tendency to collect erotic pictures. Courbet refused: he was not in the least inclined to produce copies. Instead, he suggested another mythological theme, Sleep. His patron agreed, and gave him complete freedom in the execution.

In Courbet's completed work, the viewer sees a segment of a woman's body, from the mid-chest (which is depicted in foreshortening) to about the middle of the thighs, which are, of course, spread apart to present a full genital view. The body lies in a position of abandonment that suggests sleep, although other, lewd interpretations may naturally come to mind. The white sheets that serve as background enhance the body's contours and reaffirm the suggestion that the model is lying on a bed. Khalil-Bey kept the easel in a back room of his house, in the company of other voluptuous images of feminine nakedness, such as Ingres' *The Turkish Bath*.

When this first owner took possession of the painting, he kept it covered by a board, in the manner of a triptych's volet, on which was painted a snowy landscape. A special mechanism allowed him to remove the board, displaying the limned shocker underneath, always to great effect upon the onlookers. After the owner passed away, the whereabouts of the painting were unclear until about 1910, when it reappeared in the possession of a Hungarian collector, Baron Batavy, who kept it in Budapest through World War II. Then, in 1955, it was acquired by two French citizens, actress Sylvia Bataille and the renowned writer and psychoanalyst Jacques Lacan. The latter kept it in his country home near Marnes-la-Jolie.

Lacan had an important surrealist artist, André Masson, paint on a board an abstract rendition of his painting, and this board was again used to cover the work, securing it in place by a contrivance furnished with lock and key. Note the effort to preserve the theatrical effect. The unsuspecting viewers approach the covered painting, and are asked what do they see. The superimposed board shows an abstract painting, in which a few elegantly curved white lines stand out over a brown background, with a darker central spot. Are these mountains around a treed valley? Stylized birds in flight over a pond? Then, the board is drawn aside, and the hills become a woman's spread thighs, and the central valley a densely hirsute vulva, that is, *The Origin of the World*.

It was by virtue of certain clauses in the French tax laws that the painting found its way to the famous Orsay Museum of Paris, where it arrived under the guise of a so-called "donation." Today, viewers can see it there at their leisure, minus the gizmos that once enhanced the theatricality of the exhibit. Art connoisseurs, whose erudition does not necessarily preclude a little prurient streak, argue whether the model in *The Origin of the World* is really the same Joanna Hiffernan who posed for *Symphony in White # 1: The White Girl* (kept at the National Gallery of Art, Washington, D.C.), *Symphony in White # 2: The Little White Girl* (the Tate Gallery, London), *Caprice in Purple and Gold: The Golden Screen* (Freer Art Gallery, Washington, D.C.), and other productions of Whistler's now famous oeuvre. Points of contention are, among others, whether the color of the model's hair is the same in the head of the personages of the portraits, and in the pudenda of the woman in *The Origin of the World*. Their debates revolve around the possibility that the patina of time may have altered the hair's hue in some paintings more than in others; and that the color of hair in red-headed girls may not be precisely the same in the private parts as in the head. Personally, I should think these discussions are carried into the realm of the unbecoming by an excess of finesse. But then, again, true connoisseurs are always splitting hairs.

The boldness of this production was recently matched by a provocative counterpart, the creation of a female artist. The name of the work is *L'Origine de la Guerre* (*The Origin of the War*), and the artist goes by the name of Orlan. She has been extremely difficult to categorize. Although she claims adherence to feminism, prominent feminists have criticized her severely, as contributing to the objectification of the feminine body. She uses her own body in the pursuit of what she calls "carnal art," presumably an effort to obtain "rebirth" by subjecting herself to plastic surgery in operations that are highly publicized and sometimes televised. Her idea is not to conform to the standards of beauty generally propounded by bourgeois society, but to "deconstruct" her face, which she wishes to resemble an inharmonious computer-generated composite of ideal features. On November 1993, during one of the nine operations to which she has subjected herself, a surgeon implanted silicone devices, such as those used in reconstructive procedures to raise cheekbones sunken because of trauma or congenital deformity, on her forehead. The implants form striking protrusions that are part of her facial "deconstruction."

In her *Origin of the War*, this original artist and odd, controversial individual reproduced the exact posture of the model in *The Origin of the World*, using computer-assisted photography. She sought to obtain exactly the same format, achieving a work that has the identical measures (54 cm. x 46 cm.); the difference being, her model was a man. Therefore, what the gaze encounters is a rather hirsute masculine body, in a position of abandonment on a white sheet, thighs spread out to reveal an obtrusively erect male genital organ (!). Critics have noted the apparently symbolic aggressiveness of the artist's representation. In effect, what she did was to suppress or erase the female body, and, thanks to the mathematical precision of modern electronics, superposed the body of a man on the vacated space, as if this male body had been a collage that filled exactly the void left by the preceding, female form. And to further accentuate the satirical intent of parody, she used a highly ornate, baroque frame for this photo, as one would expect for a classical painting at the Louvre Museum.

If literature and the plastic arts have approached this scabrous representation, might not the theater have done it, too? This seems to me very unlikely. In ancient times, actors on the stage, especially the Roman stage, probably had no qualms in "mooning" their public. For reading the bawdiness and ribaldry of some ancient comedies (for a long time expurgated by prudish translators or overzealous censors), one can scarcely avoid the conclusion that the disportment of theater people in ancient times was seriously at variance with current notions of decorum. But even then, all that the spectators of, say, Aristophanic comedy may have perceived, was a brief flash of a derriere, and, more often than not, the "shameful parts" of a male clown. Full and sustained exposure of the outer generational organs of a woman is quite another matter. Following classical antiquity, each successive age has had its own reasons for enforcing the ancestral prohibition: religious law, common notions of decency, received ideas of politeness or decorum, scruples of modesty, and perhaps not least, the atavistic male dread of female sexuality.

It is a reflection on present mores—encouraging or disheartening, I cannot say—that our times witnessed the arrival of the ultimate female exhibitionism to the theatrical stage. Together with plentiful live spectacles of full "frontal nudity," as is customarily said, and of successful plays with such titles as *The Vagina Monologues* and *The Penis Puppetry*, the end of the twentieth century and beginning of the twenty-first also saw in America the unabashed display of female genitalia. At least once, this was made the central theme of a theatrical event, although it can scarcely be called a "play." This, in a theater hall that was not mainstream, but cannot properly be considered "underground" either, although entrance to the show was restricted to adults. I am referring to the 1991 Chicago performance of Annie Sprinkle (her *nom du guerre*; née Ellen Steinberg), former prostitute, photographer, and porno star, turned pro-sexual rights activist, stage performer, and guru of human sexual behavior.

The name of this show was, humorously enough, *A Public Cervix Announcement*.[3] Its description is as follows. Miss Sprinkle demonstrates to the predominantly—but not exclusively—male public some diagrams and drawings of the internal female reproductive organs, making some humorous remarks along the way, and engaging the audience in exchanges. She then proceeds to give herself a vaginal douche in full view of the spectators. Having declared that women's fashion has progressed from absurdly long dresses to the miniskirt, she proudly announces: "This is the next stage," while pointing to a vaginal speculum that she is holding in her hand. Without further ado, she sits on an armchair, spreads her legs wide, inserts the speculum into her own genitals, faking that the maneuver is sexually pleasurable. Once thus accoutered, she invites the members of the public to come and inspect her private innards at close range.

It is mostly men who come to the stage. An assistant hands them a flashlight, and they take turns to come very close, in order to get a peek at Miss Sprinkle's rosy *cervix uteri*. (She has learned to so place the bills of the speculum as to ensure that the cervix of the womb is fully displayed.) While each gazer is at it, Miss Sprinkle approaches a microphone, asking him to describe what he sees and to make some comments. This, for the benefit of those who stayed in their seats or who don't get a turn at peeping; for gynecological examination is, of necessity (and in the absence of closed-circuit television and monitor), an individual task that must be performed one at a time: the field of view is very small and narrow.

It would be impossible to defend the proposition that this

show is "educational." Miss Sprinkle, who seems to be an intelligent woman, noted that she wished to show others what they had never seen. And it is true that outside of the medical context few people, men or women, have seen the cervix: some parts of the body, including this one, have been utterly "medicalized." A trend within feminism enjoined women to remove all fears connected with their own bodies, to de-mystify those areas of their own anatomy that are surrounded by feelings of inhibition and shame, and which are passively surrendered to the care of experts. To the extent that some women (a distinct minority in Miss Sprinkle's show) and some men may be able to overcome the fear of the unknown; and to the extent that seeing the performer use the speculum with nonchalance and disinvolture helps some women to get rid of the thoughts that associate medical examination with unbearable pain; to that extent the show may be said to be of some didactic value. We must own this is not much.

As to the men who stand in line, flashlight in hand, waiting for their turn to see, what draws them thither? What is this never-assuaged desire to see, to look, to watch the body of woman? It is a facile explication to say it is the spur of sexual attraction. It may be equally plausible to argue that it is the fear of sex itself. Roland Barthes noted that the most allegedly sensuous spectacles created by men may have an anti-sexual significance. Thus, the arrays of strip-tease performers—gloves, large plume fans, veils, exotic attires of Oriental princess, odalisque, and so on—of which the women pretend to divest themselves little by little, transform them into beings that fall outside of the sphere of common reality or daily experience, and turn them into romantic personages of fable or beings from a remote land, withdrawn from us and thus from the possibility of human usage. And even when she drops one by one the ritual objects that covered her, it is as if these left their magical imprint upon her. For the stripper who first appears on the stage decked in a very luxurious mink fur, and then sheds it and goes naked, is an essentially improbable woman. Hence, it follows that her nakedness is just as unlikely. Therefore, affirmed Barthes, strip-tease is founded on the paradoxical premise of de-sexualizing Woman at the same time as one undresses her.

The anecdote that opened this chapter is not of purely historical interest. The mentality that inspired it is not much changed, even though today's voyeurism takes on a technological slant, very much in keeping with the rapid advances of science and technology that characterize our times. A new word has been coined, "upskirting," to refer to the taking of pictures with a hidden camera that is placed in a shopping bag, a box, or otherwise artfully concealed, and then directed upward under a woman's skirt. This has been relatively common in American shopping malls and changing rooms of department stores. The variations are multiple: the current astounding miniaturization of photographic equipment has made it possible for voyeurs to resort to new underhand tricks, likely to evade detection. There are reports of palm-sized or smaller video cameras dissimulated or camouflaged in attaché cases, backpacks, or shopping bags, under stacks of towels in locker rooms, in bathrooms behind windows, and innumerable other strategic sites; all with the aim of obtaining images of men and women in various states of undress, or while engaged in physiologic functions whose discharge is normally attended with a reasonable expectation of privacy.[4]

Another new term, "downblousing," is sufficiently graphic to need no further explanation; it is the ignoble corollary and complement to the vile and perfidious "upskirting" misdeed. And, as linguists have had to create new words for the novel infamies, legislators have had to frame new laws, and set up the penalties with which these infractions must be met. This was not easy. The so-called Peeping Tom legal statutes that regulate this activity in most American states refer to the inappropriate sighting that takes place in homes and private spaces, where by universal agreement individual privacy must be zealously defended. But the laws say little or nothing about peering in *public* spaces, since the assumption has been that legal protection does not extend to those sites. However, this is precisely where women's victimization is commonest, as the videotaping up skirts is most often done in shopping malls, fairgrounds, parks, and other public places.

In recent years, complaints about technology-mediated voyeurism having increased, legislators in the United States grew sensitive to the problem, and enacted various measures to keep up with technological "progress." Laws now exist in some states that punish severely the unauthorized, surreptitious or unsuspected capturing of images for "lewd and lascivious" purposes.

But the male thirst for seeing has no end. Seeing what? Once every possible exterior hallmark of feminine genital anatomy has been inspected, looked upon, well canvassed, one wonders if men would like to continue seeing. What else is there to see? Peel off the vaginal epithelial walls, look at the pudendal nerves, arteries, veins . . . But even this may not suffice. For it may be that what they are really looking for is a way to exorcise their own neuroses. Which ones? Among others, an obscure, ancestral fear of a sex that seems to them mysterious, hidden, intricate, and puzzling. Again, it would be too simplistic to reduce the complex male reaction to a simple fear, even if it is ennobled with a term of Freudian terminology, and we say "fear of castration."

There is perhaps fear, such as the unknown commonly inspires, but it is admixed with reverence, fascination, admiration, and morbid attraction. Man senses in Woman the insatiability of the ocean, the mystery of night, and the unfathomableness of infinity. Man senses here the ineffable power of the Giver of Life, who shall become, unavoidably, chief mourner and Lictor of Death, our death. He senses all this and would like to lose himself in the immensity of the unknown, to plunge in the unfathomable mystery, like the miniature man who, in a work of the symbolist German artist Alfred Kubin (1877–1959), appropriately entitled

Leap of Death, dives headlong into a gigantic vulva. It is no coincidence that the same idea bubbles up from the recondite male imagination, whether it be in a film director, a fiction writer, or Kubin, a tortured, clinically insane painter—all stand in awe of a mystery in which they see Womb and Tomb at the same time.

Eyes on Privities

FOR THE LIFE OF ME, I NEVER UNDERSTOOD THE BRASHNESS OF those who would expose every aspect of their lives to the universal curiosity. It puzzles me that people appear on national television, and, in pert defiance of the principles of modesty, beam their most private secrets to the whole world. Even the most extrovert, I used to think, ought to keep a corner of their life-experience well guarded from public scrutiny. But just where one must trace the frontier between intercommunity and privacy, is difficult to say. Sex, birth, death, or the discharge of those physiologic functions for which even animals seem to prefer seclusion, most human beings would loathe to expose. Yet, into these shaded recesses of private life some would shine the brightest light, and of things which are best concealed they make an ostentatious display. Thus, I know of artists who have filmed the death of a friend or a relative, in their immoderate desire of capturing "live" the power of real drama. (I attended a viewing of a documentary recording the death of the photographer's father, which shows that filming of this sort is rarely meant to be kept strictly private.) And there are many men who, without the excuse of artistry, wish to film the birth of their children.

Birth is unquestionably a momentous occurrence for all of us, since it marks the time of our independent existence. But apart from its rich metaphysical significance, we must admit it is a rather messy affair. From my brief stint as resident physician in obstetrics, I learned this much. I never fully empathized with fathers who insisted on filming the event, when others could not bear the sight of the routine goings-on in the obstetrical suite. Indeed, for some men the wife's labor and delivery are very trying: they can scarcely observe them without fainting. The husband or companion who manifests solidarity and affection by accompanying his loved one in this difficult pass, deserves our sincere plaudits and unreserved praise. Less straightforward is the motivation of one who divides his attention between encouraging the spouse and making sure the lighting is adequate, the viewing angle appropriate, and the film in the camera in good order. Such a one seemed to me suspiciously parted between grossly discrepant concerns: conjugal tenderness and movie-making. In case an unexpected calamity supervened, I could not help wondering, would preoccupation for the well being of the mother and child or for the *mise en scène* of the motion picture take the upper hand?

As to the esthetic qualities of the production, these are debatable. Birth is a mini-drama, and undoubtedly a most powerful one. But the chief protagonists, mother and child, are likely to be shown in an unflattering light. The mother is tossing, sweating, moaning. She may be prey to intense pain, the kind that Jessica Mitford says (in her excellent book, *The American Way of Birth*) was first described to her as comparable to "having a large grapefruit pushed up her nostril." Or else, heavily anesthetized and sedated, she is not quite herself. She is tired, exhausted, her eyes are glazed; her awareness is perturbed; she is not her usual self. To capture her countenance at this time smacks of malice aforethought.

And the baby? It was for him, or her, that the floodlights were on, the reflecting screen was placed behind the obstetrician, and the camera was rolling. He, or she, has the leading role. But I suspect that, if the newborn could choose, he/she would turn down the part. For look at the newly born: stark naked; red with the blood of his mother; sometimes soiled here and there with repugnant maternal excreta; daubed with the unctuous sebum of fetal skin; still wet with amniotic fluid, as if he were just coming in from outside, where he had been caught unprotected in a downpour; weakly flailing his arms; and at the same time emitting a feeble wail, a cry uttered out of cold, pain, surprise, confusion, and defenselessness. A newborn baby is taken to symbolize an upsurge of vitality, and life's strength and endurance as manifested in the perpetuation of the race. But every time I looked at the just born, instead of conjuring images of triumphant life, I thought of a foot-soldier in a defeated army, a pitiful survivor in a catastrophic retreat, dragging himself painfully amidst the wreck and bloody devastation that follow a terrible battle, which he fought and lost.

The spectacle of childbirth, which by a strange volition some men insist on recording, had to be watched—by order of the law—in some instances. I mean the birth of kings in past eras. The royal succession was a serious matter. Any suspicion of a possible substitution had to be suppressed. To this effect, a strange ceremonial was implemented in the French court, called the *gésine* (probably from French *gésir*, Latin *jacere*, to be lying down), by which the process of childbirth was obligatorily witnessed by some influential individuals. As soon as the queen experienced the pains that seemed to announce an imminent labor, the Princes-of-the-Blood and other members of the aristocracy had to be called in. We have vivid descriptions of royal births, such as that of Louis XIII, in the chateau of Fontainebleau, on the 27th day of September of the year 1601, the day of St. Cosmas and St. Damian in the Catholic calendar.

A large tent of rich Holland fabric was built inside the queen's bedchamber; and within it is the delivery bed in crimson velvet. In those times, people used to sleep in the sitting position, not lying horizontally as today.[5] Therefore the bed is also an obstetrical chair, since it was then common for women to deliver in the sitting position. It is provided with lateral wooden bars, which the queen could hold when bearing down during the labor contractions; it also has a transverse bar to rest the feet. In a second tent, in front of the first, there is a table on which are exposed the relics of St. Margaret, known intercessor for women in labor. Here, two nuns of St. Germain-des-Près are praying constantly. Here, too, the witnesses of the birth will be assembled.

The queen, Marie of Medicis, had been duly admonished by her relatives on the historical importance of ensuring the dynastic succession. Her uncle, the Duke of Tuscany, advised her, on the day she left the refined Italian court for the then coarser and inelegant French lodgings: "Make little sons in any way you can." Dutifully, she complied: nine months and four- teen days after the consummation of her marriage, here she was, expecting to give birth at any moment. But she is twenty- seven years old, this is her first pregnancy, and she cannot avoid being apprehensive. The king warns her: as soon as the con- tractions increase in intensity, the Princes-of-the-Blood must be summoned into the bedroom. Such is the custom, and she must consent, because of her rank. She says she is willing to do what- ever pleases her royal husband. The king rejoins: "I tell you this because I know that you are naturally shy. I am afraid the sight of persons present here may retard your delivery, if you do not decide this on your own accord."

The king, Henri IV, waits impatiently in his bedroom, adjoining the queen's. He comes in and out. When the princes are called, he comments: "If ever three princes were seen to be together in distress, these three shall soon be so; the three are soft-hearted, and seeing my wife suffer they shall wish they were far away . . ." The three come, and stay for some time, but it is a false alarm. They must be sent back to their apartments, with instructions to hold themselves in readiness for immediate return on short notice. Meantime, the five officially appointed court physicians are called in to examine the queen and give their opinion; thereafter they withdraw to a small room close by. However, the whole day goes by without appreciable progress. It is then that the judicious intervention of a midwife saves the day.

Her name is Louise Bourgeois. She was chosen by Marie of Medicis as her midwife for no other reason than "she had a good face," a conclusion the queen reached after looking at her "for the duration of a *pater noster*," just before climbing into her carriage on her way to a dinner. And it was just as well, considering the state of backwardness of the science of obstetrics in those benighted days. As it turned out, it was a good choice. Midwives had all the practical knowledge that doctors of medicine shunned: the pedant medical men felt obstetrical practice was beneath their status.

The midwife's memoirs contain vivid details of the royal birth narrated with undeniable accents of authenticity. The king was an unrepentant womanizer; no French historian of the period fails to comment on his sexual exploits. When he came back from a trip, and found her residing in a room close to his (midwives were allowed to live in the royal household when the delivery approached), Louise Bourgeois tells us that the monarch whispered to her we know not what salacious, ribald remarks. Imagine! His royal spouse is in the throes of giving him an heir, when the royal monarch is already thinking the kind of immodest thoughts that seem to have occupied him for most of this waking life. But the midwife is quick to excuse him, remarking that the king knew nothing of midwives; that he had been influenced by the common misconception that all women of that profession were wanton and unchaste; and that this was natural, since those who came to the royal house before fitted the description very precisely. Moreover, Henri IV gave explicit orders that the advice of the midwife should be followed above all others. "Nowhere in the world did I enjoy greater peace of mind than here," writes a grateful Louise, "thanks to the good order imposed by the king, and the assurances that I received from the queen." In effect, if nothing else, the withholding of sundry suspicious remedies had a beneficial effect; herbs, poultices, suppositories were suggested by apothecaries, physicians, and well intentioned friends and ladies-in-waiting of the queen's Italian retinue. They were accepted uncritically, and may have done more harm than good. Louise Bourgeois discontinued their use, and Marie of Medicis delivered after about twenty-two hours of labor.

She chose the sitting position. The Princes-of-the-Blood sat squarely in front of her, that they could get an unobstructed, frontal view of the proceedings. When the moment came, she felt a strong desire to scream, but made a big effort to retain it. Perhaps the presence of witnesses was a strong inhibition. The midwife advised her not to suppress the urge, "for fear that her throat might swell." The king reiterated the advice, saying: "My friend, do as the midwife tells you, scream, so that your throat does not swell."

But, alas, all is not well. The royal baby lies unresponsive, "afflicted by a great feebleness," limp and semi-asphyxiated, probably on account of a prolonged and difficult labor. The spectators in the bedroom look at each other in consternation. Anxious looks are directed to the midwife. She has asked for a bottle of wine and a spoon. The king seems to question her anxiously with his eyes, and she says: "*Sire*, if this was any other baby, I would put some wine in my mouth, and would give it to him, for fear that the weakness may last too long." And the king, pressing a bottle of wine against her mouth, replies: "Do as you would do with any other baby." Upon which, the midwife takes a sip of wine into her mouth, and blows it into the baby's. The infant, in her words, "at that very moment came to, and even seemed to relish the drink that I had given him." A good vintage, no doubt, whose appreciation in France starts rather early.

Ladies of the court had vied with each other to be the first to tell the king the happy news. Some preferment might result, they figured, from breaking the good news to the monarch.

Accordingly, they had pressured the midwife, using all manner of blandishments and stratagems, to let them know the sex of the newborn by a preconvened sign. The sign was given, and two ladies ran to inform the king. When at last he became persuaded of the truthfulness of the reports, he was truly moved. Tears "the size of big peas" ran down his cheeks. There had been no Dauphin in France, he kept saying, for the past eighty years.

At last, all was well. As the good news were diffused, more and more courtiers came in, until the room was crowded with over two hundred persons, all of them making an effort to appear conspicuously jubilant.

The king lifts the baby in his arms above the crowd, and exclaims in a loud voice: "This child belongs to everyone!" In the back of the room, some cynical, rakish courtiers nudge each other on the ribs with a sly smile on their faces. There are rumors of the queen's infidelities, and the courtiers make fun of the king's exclamation, which they interpret literally.

All who can get close to the infant praise his features. This one extols the delicate conformation of his hands, that one the strength of his little fingers, which prevented the midwife from cutting the umbilical cord for a long time, so firmly did the baby grasp it. One praises this, another lauds that. Madame de Bar, the king's sister, after hearing the eulogies and finding that everything in the infantile body was already extolled, "fixed her sight on those parts that made him Dauphin," according to a royal physician's memoirs, "and turning toward Madame de Panjas, her lady-in-waiting, told her that he was very well equipped, indeed." Her words were received with a guffaw of laughter from those who heard them.

This was the prevailing coarse ribaldry and crass unsophistication of the court of Henri IV of France, at the close of the sixteenth century and beginning of the seventeenth. With the passage of time, there came a progressive refinement of uses and customs, but the tradition of witnessing the royal childbirth was not deleted. Kings, potentates, rulers, emperors, are, in the felicitous expression of a contemporary historian, "idols of the tribe." Idols are objects of worship that must be constantly displayed. They must be kept constantly within view, if they are to allay the collective fears, and to incarnate the aspirations of the group that raised them to their high station. Thus, after the French court moved to Versailles, the custom of witnessing the royal childbirth did not disappear. We have a description of Marie Antoinette's labor and delivery, by her loyal *femme de chambre* and memorialist, Madame Campan (1752-1822).[6]

Marie Antoinette's pregnancy came late. She married Louis XVI in 1770, but he proved to be an inattentive husband. The queen was not seen to be with child until the summer of 1778. The royal court had moved to the splendiferous chateau of Versailles. Here, the royal family made it a custom to come out for a stroll in the gardens, at night, to make the summer heat a little more bearable. Sycophants noted that the outings were forming a habit, and arranged for a group of musicians to play on a scaffold, behind some trees. Lighted candles on earthenware pots on the parterre, and pitchy wood torches on suspended cressets, illuminated the alleys. The whole royal family would be seen sitting on a bench until late at night, while the musicians sounded their instruments. The king, however, was seen there once or twice only. There was no way to make him change his custom of retiring to bed early.

Because many courtiers attended the promenade, there was plenty of occasion for malicious rumors. Madame Campan assures us that these outings remained innocent, but undoubtedly they contributed to Marie Antoinette's reputation of frivolity. For instance, a young and handsome officer once pretended not to have recognized the queen, and under this pretense allowed himself a lively exchange with her, full of witty remarks, which would have been out of the question under normal circumstances. The queen seemed elated at the opportunity of being approached so uninhibitedly, and to discourse so freely, supposedly by remaining incognito. On another occasion, an officer of the guard of Monsieur (the king's brother) saw the queen sitting on a bench, and addressed her, saying how happy he considered himself for being able to implore from Her Highness, and to solicit . . . But as soon as the word "solicit" was uttered, says Madame Campan, the queen, the princesses, and Madame Campan herself sprang up from the bench and entered the chateau precipitously. One of the princesses, irate, wanted to denounce the officer to his commander, and to have him punished for his impertinence. (I gather he was neither as young nor as handsome as the one who faked not to know that he talked to the queen.)

These nightly jaunts gave a sure footing to courtly intrigue. They permitted the development of the notorious "diamond necklace affair," in which the queen was unjustly accused of having a love affair with a cardinal, rendered worldwide famous by a novel of Alexandre Dumas. It was also in these promenades that the queen's pregnancy first was noticed by the courtiers. There was all manner of public celebrations, and the *Te Deum* was sung in all major churches. Then, in December of 1778, the first contractions appeared, and the queen moved to a chamber of the palace next to the apartments of the Princes-of-the-Blood. They would have to be present to witness the childbirth.

On the 19th of December of that year, the court's official accoucheur announced loudly, according to tradition: "The queen is going to deliver!" and all readied themselves for the coming event. For the custom of watching the queen's parturition was now so liberally observed that almost every courtier counted on being admitted to the delivery room. There were so many, in fact, that they made the place unsafe. The night before, the king had ordered that the large, heavy tapestry-covered screens in the chamber be secured with ropes. Without this precaution, the screens would have been toppled over her majesty. One could hardly move there. The crowd was so dense, and so rambunctious, that the place looked really like a public plaza.

Imagine the poor queen suffering the pains of delivery, while a veritable crowd mills around her in the room, everyone trying to catch a glimpse of the birth of a Dauphin. It is a show, a public spectacle. In the first row sit the most exalted personages, those convoked by ancient tradition, such as the Princes-of-the-Blood. But behind them are aristocrats of lesser rank, and behind them others of still lower importance in the hierarchy. The fact is, almost anyone whose employment happened to emplace him in the bedchamber's surroundings feels entitled to come in and take a peek. Our memoirist says that two guards actually climbed on top of nearby tables so they could watch better.

Little wonder that things started to turn bad. The queen felt as though she were being smothered. Suddenly, consternation sets in. Her majesty's breathing turns labored, her face is flushed, and her mouth deviates to one side. Whether the excessive crowding in the room robbed her of air, or whether fatigue and intense emotion have overwhelmed her, no one can say. The princess of Lamballe, her confidant, tries to tell her the sex of the newborn child, but the queen seems to be having a seizure. There are cries of "Air!, Air!" and "Let her breathe!" The accoucheur, alarmed, asks for hot water, saying that he must bleed the queen (the hot water presumably to help in dilating the vein that was to be lanced).

The windows of the room were well fastened, glued, and secured with strips of paper; but the king, "with a strength that only his tender feelings for the queen could communicate to him," succeeds in forcing them open. The queen needs air.

Meantime, the basin with hot water does not arrive yet. The accoucheur, impatient, turns to the first surgeon, already at the bedside, and tells him to go ahead and lance *à sec*, that is, on dry skin. The cut is performed, and "as soon as the blood spurted strongly, the queen opened her eyes." The room now resounds with joyous exclamations, seeing that mother and child evinced a state of good health, so quickly following the mortifying minutes of alarm that had preceded. Writes Madame Campan: "Count Esterhazy and Prince Poix, to whom

I first announced that the queen was able to speak, embraced me and flooded me with their tears in the middle of the room, surrounded by all the nobility." The effusions of mirth are now as immoderate as those of rue moments ago, when the Princess of Lamballe had to be removed from the room, unconscious, through the agglomeration and the empressements of the crowd, under the shock of sudden worry.

The next problem is to tone down the expressions of collective happiness. Unregulated mirth appears to be as much a threat to mother and child as was unbridled woe. The *valets de chambre*, assisted by gentlemen ushers, toil to clear the room. They are obligated to grab many a laggard by the lapel, and literally to eject them from the room. All this while the queen, recovering from the ominous recent episode, still half-dazed, asks her attendants why there was a linen bandage tied across her leg. Marie Antoinette had no awareness of her recent bleeding.

It strikes us as the height of indelicacy and boorishness to make a public spectacle of a parturient queen. But kings, too, were constantly watched. People seemed to have thought that *someone* had to keep the Idol of the Tribe within view, out of the irrational fear that to let him escape from the visual field was to allow him to disappear from existence; just so were some thinkers of the idealist persuasion convinced that the world existed only so long as some mind conceived it, but that objective reality would dissolve into nothingness, if no conscious thoughts of it ever arose in anyone's mind.

Therefore, kings are ceaselessly surrounded. Guards, attendants, valets, innumerable followers watch their most trivial acts. They are observed when they wake up, then when dressing up in the morning—in fact, the royal getting-up became an elaborate ceremony—and when they undress to retire in the evening; and the interval between getting up and going to bed is one of uninterrupted observation. Past ages thought nothing of following the monarch into the room where he relieved himself, since chroniclers report conversations between the ruler and some high dignitary while the former was sitting on the *chaise percée*, that is to say, the toilet. Henri IV conversed with his minister Sully while moving his bowels; and one wonders, with a sense of revulsion, how many peace treaties, alliances, invasions, or declarations of war were planned amidst disgusting noises and malodorous emanations. Voltaire comes to mind, for somewhere he quips with his usual sharp wit about the destiny of nations being linked to the regularity or irregularity of their king's intestinal evacuations.

In this context, the Orient sets the example of ritualistic and ceremonial elaboration. We know how some of the Chinese emperors lived in the fabled Forbidden City, behind walls twenty-two feet-high, painted the color of dried blood. Someone was always watching, so that details of the private life of those exalted personages has come down to us. Vivid descriptions exist of the life of the Manchu empress dowager in that mysterious environment.[7]

She shared that space with guards, officers, and countless silk-robed attendants. She had a veritable army of eunuchs (two to three thousand lived there at one time), who entered her service after being apprenticed to older, more experienced retainers for as long as it took them to learn the very complex palace routines; and it must be said that it was no easy task to become familiar with the complex, unperspicuous lines of official power and unofficial preferment, in that vast hierarchy. The empress stood at the pinnacle, like the true Idol of the Tribe. She sat, hieratic, unperturbed, amidst volutes of incense, truly like an idol on her throne, in a luxurious central hall within the Forbidden City.

This magnificent complex of pavilions and halls housed the richest collection of Oriental art that ever existed: ancient bronzes, delicate porcelains, superb jades, plus numerous paintings and exquisite carvings in ivory and wood. No effort was spared for the comfort of the inhabitants. The huge audience halls were kept cool in the summer by storing blocks of ice in an underground system of tunnels and caves. Through vents that could be opened and closed, an ingenious precursor of "air conditioning" systems, waves of cold air would come up and attenuate the heat of the summer. By the same token, live coals provided heat in the winter, whose inclemency was also diminished by hanging heavy, padded drapes on walls and windows, and sealing the latter air-tight with strips of paper. Anyone of importance was also protected by wearing lovely fur-lined vestments. But in the midst of this magnificence there are no bathrooms, no toilets, and no piped running water.

When the Manchu empress hears the call of Nature, which she usually detects in the Hall of Concentrated Beauties, after taking a few morsels cooked in the Manchu style, she gives an order to a lady-in-waiting, who passes it on to the eunuch in charge of bringing the House of the Mandarins. The eunuch, upon a mere nod of his mistress' head, takes off running through the corridors of the Forbidden City. He runs silently, sliding like a shadow—part of the laborious learning for his job was to master the art of inconspicuousness, almost to the point of self-annihilation—and returns carrying on his head a very large bundle wrapped in silk with embroidered dragon figures. He stops at the threshold of the hall where sits the Idol of the Tribe, and there he kneels. Normally, he would be expected to kowtow to the ground nine times, touching the ground with his forehead as a sign of humility and complete subservience. But he is excused this time, because he is carrying a large bundle on his head.

A lady of the court takes the bundle from him, and unwraps it. The House of Mandarins is the imperial chamber pot. Only this is no ordinary chamber pot. It is a work of art. The finest, most talented artisans and sculptors exerted their artistry to produce this mythological lizard, or gecko, carved in the finest wood. Its chine is incurved, and may serve as a handle to transport it; its open mouth serves as a repository for the toilet paper. The mythological animal is depicted in an artistic pose of great dynamism, as if it were about to jump on a prey. The exquisite carving seizes the imagination; it is of the most admirable workmanship. The empress wished to be buried with it, in order to make it "a guest of heaven," an honor reserved to the most cherished possessions. The toilet paper, of a light yellow hue and the texture of soft cotton cloth, is manufactured in the city of Hangzhou. It is moistened and ironed flat by court ladies just before use.

The doors and windows are shut. Behind some screen, the empress has now removed her lower garments, below the waist, and she sits astride the gecko, in view of her closest female attendants. The belly of the animal is, of course, the receptacle for the imperial feces. A fine sandalwood sawdust covers the bottom of the recipient, so that the excreta are immediately buried in it, and no disagreeable odors are perceived. When the empress has finished, a discreet sign summons the servant, who, head lowered and in the kneeling position, receives the chamber pot, covers it with a padded cloth lined with silk with embroidered peonies and phoenixes, and disappears running silently; every move is accomplished in silence; the remarkable noiselessness of the palace is a feature that courtiers remembered long after the emperors and empresses were no more, and the Forbidden City had ceased to be the residence of the Son of Heaven.

There is no cesspool, and no sewer system. The chamber pots must be cleaned right away. Lesser mortals use ordinary, inelegant chamber pots: no fragrant sandalwood dust for them; they simply use ashes. The Gate of Spiritual Valor is opened at regular intervals, and menials dispose of the accumulated excreta. Where do they go? The chroniclers do not say, but we know that human feces were used as fertilizers from time immemorial.

The elegant ladies of the court are not concerned with these lowly matters. One of the ladies-in-waiting reminisced wistfully, after the collapse of the empire, of the many tranquil scenes that she had seen in the Forbidden City. Deeply engraved in her mind was the image of her mistress, supreme ruler of the heavenly empire, riding her gecko, at the same time that she toyed, inimitable in her grace, with the toilet paper that the beast held in its mouth.

A fine reminiscence, indeed: the melancholy memento, for the lady chronicler, of times forever disappeared. But, to be frank, I should not like to be remembered that way. The need to eliminate repugnant excreta is one of the Great Levelers of the human condition. No matter how beauteous, intelligent, or powerful we may be in the opinion of the world, defecation sounds a reiterated reminder of our transient and fundamentally putrescible corporeality. A famous Italian movie director had the idea of depicting Casanova, the famous lover, in his advanced old age. With an earthiness for which Italians are justly renowned, he pictured Casanova (played by Marcello Mastroiani), oblivious to the charms of an incredibly voluptuous woman, and preoccupied chiefly with sitting at the toilet. The eye of the camera becomes the eyes of us, the film viewers, who follow the former philanderer into this private space. To see the old man sitting at the toilet has a strangely saddening effect. This spectacle makes us aware that, for the man who had enjoyed the supreme delights of seduction and sensuality, bodily pleasure is now largely reduced to a good nap, digestible sops, and a successful bowel movement.

Sex, the carnal act itself, has also been turned into a public spectacle. Not only by pornographers, pathologic peeping-toms, or seedy entrepreneurs, but by austere ecclesiastics and magistrates. Indeed, the law of several European countries throughout the sixteenth century sanctioned the so-called "trials by congress," in which the carnal act was performed in front of witnesses.[8] These bizarre judicial trials were abolished as late as 1677. A wife could sue for annulment of her marriage, under the allegation that her husband was impotent. If he contested the allegation, he could submit to the trial. A judge had legal power to enforce the performance.

In a previously selected house, usually not the domicile of the estranged spouses, the concerned parties were gathered. The site chosen was often the place of a *baignueur*, a sort of public bath and lodgings, in which the well-off in the seventeenth century would find all the amenities that are offered today by luxury hotels. Husband and wife were ordered to disrobe. A doctor and several matrons carefully examined the naked body of the wife, from head to toe. The naked husband underwent a similar examination. The idea was to prevent any cheating, for the possibility of fraud should never be discounted in any conflict between human beings: the man could have some instrument that allowed penetration; the wife could use astringents that hindered penetration; or she could be hiding a talisman in her hair (for in superstitious times many believed that there were charms or amulets of which a woman could avail herself to put a spell on a man and render him impotent).

Having ensured that the proceedings were free of cheating, the naked spouses climbed into bed. Several matrons were admitted into the room as witnesses. The officers of the law would leave, but the matrons stayed in the room. The curtains were drawn, but the matrons were just beyond, and I suppose they could see much of the proceedings through thin, translucent curtains. Friends and relatives waited in the adjoining room, with the justice delegates. The door of the room remained ajar. In the course of these activities, it was not uncommon for altercations to arise between estranged married couples: he complained loudly that the woman was not cooperating; she countered that he accused her unjustly, blaming her for his incapacity, and added that all he could attempt was strictly fingering work. As is well known, these quarrels are strongly inhibitory for the male, who under such circumstances was likely to come out the loser party.

After about two hours, the experts came back into the room, and there was a new, detailed inspection. Everything was canvassed: what was the state of the genital organs of the litigants; whether there had been an emission, and if so, of what characteristics (for a man could lose his case if the secretion was deemed too serous or somehow defective). The various experts and witnesses then rendered a report to the judge, who was at the same house.

One of the most famous cases of "trial by congress" was that of the Marquis of Langey and his wife, Madame de Langey, née Marie Saint-Simon. The celebrated affair started in the late 1650s.[9] The Marquis de Langey was a handsome man. When his wife accused him of impotence, a contemporary lady exclaimed: "Alas, who is to be trusted these days?" Although we do not know what complex motivations may have started the affair, the authorities ordered a "visit," *i.e.*, a preliminary legal inspection of the bodily conformation of the contending parties. The Marquis was found to be strong, handsome, and with no visible malformation to support the allegation leveled against him by his wife. When he appeared in front of the judges, a market woman in the public was heard to exclaim: "Would that God grant me a husband like that man!" The chronicler of these facts tells us that, had our man let things continue the way they were going, there is little question he would have won the case. Unfortunately, he was vain as a peacok. His pride had been wounded. Instead of letting things rest, he demanded "the congress."

The woman was made to suffer all sorts of indignities in these proceedings. However, Madame de Langey seems to have remained unperturbed. The preliminaries in the Langey case lasted two years. The inspectors of the "visit," especially the women, appeared to have some partiality for the Marquis. They doubted the assertions of Madame, whom they thought no longer a maiden. But he was unwise, and insisted on "the congress." The whole of Paris talked about the scandalous affair. Each of the litigants had supporters and adversaries. Female relatives of Madame de Langey, who had been present at the inspection, commented on the report that adjudicated the husband's sexual anatomy to be "well formed": "Yes, we did find it well formed, but not *animated*." Of two male witnesses,

Aimonon and Gache, who testified in favor of the husband, jokesters said that they had proved to be valuable "testimonies" for the Marquis, that Aimonon was the right, and Gache the left testimony. Needless to say, the joke was hinged on the pun of the word "testimony," whose etymology should be clear to the reader. Through it all, Madame de Langey kept her cool. When some friends wished to comfort her, she replied: "I shall win. I know whom I am dealing with."

When the day of reckoning finally arrived, the vain man made all sorts of macho displays. He ordered two raw eggs served to him before getting to bed, "so I can make her a son at the first shot." But with all the stress of the ceremony, the presence of witnesses, and the drugs he had ingested in an ill advised attempt to fortify himself with aphrodisiacs, his much-vaunted virility flagged. The more he strained, the farther he was from the desired goal. He sweated so much that he had to change his shirt twice. Enraged, frustrated, irate, he knelt and started to pray: divine intercession was his last recourse. His wife looked at him disdainfully, and said curtly: "You didn't come here for that." That was the *coup de grâce*. He was undone. When the experts came into the room, he exclaimed most dolefully: "I am ruined."

The sequel is of little interest to us. The wife remarried, to a man that our chronicler qualifies as "stupid." However, this time her married life coursed uneventfully. The Marquis wanted a second trial, which gave rise to a good number of jokes and scurrilous epigrams in Paris. He claimed he had been bewitched. Later, he had an opportunity to prove himself a normal, functioning male, when he gave a half-dozen children to a mistress. He applied for revokement of the order that prohibited him from marrying again, and obtained it. But he was the butt of ridicule for years. He even tried to change his name. When his grandmother died, he inherited some land and tried to change his name to Marquis de Teligny. Langey, says our chronicler, he remained for many.

I. Corollary

What are we to think of these ladies and gentlemen of old, whose lives are consigned in dusty tomes that, save for generations of moths and spiders, are hardly visited by anyone any more? Do their lives have any relevance to our daily experience? It may be, it may just be, that their ideas comport with at least some aspects of our ways of looking at the world.

Kings, queens, princes, and potentates were, as we have noted, "Idols of the Tribe." They were fetishes in the sense defined by most dictionaries: objects of superstitious awe, regarded by large numbers of people with admiration, sometimes with genuine worship. The possessors of vast powers, they were thought to commune with supernatural forces, and this only increased their public esteem. They were also symbols of the nation to which they belonged. Upon their persons the people projected all the qualities which they wistfully associated with their country. But as fetishes endued with these admirable features, they had to be kept constantly within view. A high symbol cannot simply depart from the collective visual field. Imagine the holy Ka'bah suddenly disappearing from Mecca, or the most sacred shrine of Christianity vanishing from sight. Would the Pope abruptly remove himself without notice to an undisclosed location? That is inconceivable, a scandal that the faithful undoubtedly would deem an exorbitant, outrageous occurrence.

Nowadays there are no absolute monarchs, and the few remaining vestiges of ancient nobilities have been reduced to a chiefly decorative role. But the place that the disappeared aristocracy left vacant is occupied by those we are in the habit of calling "celebrities," such as movie actors and actresses, singers, rockers, outstanding athletes, and other persons of great fame and notoriety. These are the new fetishes, the modern Idols of the Tribe. Upon them the vast anonymous masses project their deepest yearnings and desires. Obscurely, the undistinguished feel that the glory of the exalted somehow reflects on themselves. But the Idols must be kept always visible. As did the old generations, the new maintain an unremitting vigilance on their adored symbols. The eyeing of the fetish must be unwavering. To preserve its power undiminished, the idol must never be left out of sight.

Hence the complaints of the new fetishes. Oblivious to the fact that they are not "like everybody else" (since they, of course, are idols), they complain of the aggressive intrusions into their lives. Fans, paparazzi, admirers, and assorted lookers-on feel compelled to know every detail, and to watch every incident, down to the most trivial, of their lives. This, argue the irritated objects of contemplation, exceeds all bounds. When Princess Diana, the consort of the Prince of Wales, died in an automobile accident in Paris, many blamed the tragedy on some overeager paparazzi who, riding motorcycles in order to obtain some photographs, recklessly pursued the car in which the Princess was traveling.

Similarly, overzealous reporters and photographers hound cinema and television personalities day and night, so persistently that a House Committee on the Judiciary held hearings in the late nineties. The aggrieved celebrities presented a vehement testimony of their hurtful experiences with harassment and stalking by reporters. A Hollywood actor, Richard Masur, then president of the Screen Actors Guild, an organization of considerable political influence in the United States, whose members numbered almost 100,000 across the country, emphasized the high respect that personal privacy had always merited in the laws of this country; and he added that "no one, no matter how their notoriety came about, should be seen as consenting to reckless endangerment or trespass."[10]

This sort of ringing statement has great emotional appeal: it evokes the most cherished principles ensconced in libertarian pronouncements. Individual freedoms are adamantly shielded by the Constitution of the United States, and no less vigorously in the founding documents of most modern democratic states. Under the pressure of the powerful actors' lobby, the governor of California signed into law a piece of legislation that was distinctly partial to the plaintiffs.

By this law, those who capture visual images, sound recordings, or "other physical impressions" of a person who has "a reasonable expectation of privacy," are guilty of a "physical trespass," even if they were not physically present inside the plaintiff's property, but captured the image by means of a "visual or auditory enhancing device." In other words, paparazzi using cameras equipped with powerful telescopic lenses could no longer photograph a famous person without being liable to serious criminal charges. The penalties for infringements of this law were quite severe, and to these were added punitive sanctions that would make most reporter-photographers think twice before securing an image potentially capable of inciting litigation in the courts.

It was not by sheer coincidence that the draconian measures were first implemented in the state of California. Hollywood is there; and this is where the largest number of film actors and television personalities may be found. These facts notwithstanding, the mentioned legislation has been sharply criticized on various grounds.[11] Firstly, its wording was imprecise: a "visual enhancing device" may mean any photographic camera, even the most rudimentary. Indeed, the simplest camera may be construed as constituting in some ways an enhancement over vision with the unaided, naked eye. Secondly, there is a taint of elitism in a law that tends to protect a privileged class. It is likely that the poor, lacking the ability to mobilize the legal machinery, would not be defended as efficiently from infringements to their privacy as would the "celebrities" who caused the laws to be created. Thirdly, conscientious reporters who might have a chance to publicly expose the wrongdoings of venal politicians, swindlers, and assorted criminals may feel hampered from doing so out of fear of legal suits. In other words, although the legislation aimed originally to curtail impertinent and intrusive acts, its effects spill over to other areas or social life whose rigorous checking is not as desirable.

But, most importantly, the application of stringent, unsparingly drastic laws against paparazzi (whose acts, after all, are devoid of intrinsic criminal intent, and are carried out in order to make a living), imperil the process of collection and diffusion of news. The freedom of the press, and the right of the public to be informed, suffer some detriment. Legislators must weigh the protection of individual privacy against the right to have a free press and a well informed public opinion. This is a delicate balance. It is not to be expected that all legislators will be able to summon the wisdom needed to make the right choice.

Paparazzi activities will continue. It has been said that the application of federal criminal and civil penalties to these activities will only drive the price of newsworthy photographs still higher. The public's thirst for "intimate," compromising, or somehow suggestive images of their admired idols is not going to cease. If it becomes riskier to obtain those images, their monetary value will naturally rise.

The complaints of the photographed subjects will increase accordingly. Compassion, leniency, and sympathetic understanding will inspire us to agree that "one should not treat others in ways one would loathe to be treated oneself." But a moment's reflection, and a dash of congenital cynicism, might bring forth the contrary sentiments of aloofness, mercilessness, and implacability. And thus armed, we may conclude that the "do unto others" implies the conviction that the others are equal to ourselves. But "celebrities" are not our equals. They are the Idols of the Tribe, who must be untiringly, ceaselessly watched. In their capacity as symbols, idols, or talismans, they are granted great wealth, public reverence, and boundless admiration. They, in turn, must understand that this is in payment for their being displayed implacably, tirelessly, conspicuously, and eternally.

The Body as Will and Representation

I. The Body, Viewed from Inside

T HIS I KNOW VERY WELL: NOT ONLY DO WE SEE SOLELY WHAT we are prepared to see, but we see what we want to see. The gaze carries with it the double ballast of our preconceptions and our desires. This postulate is perhaps no more strikingly illustrated than by our different ways of looking at the body. Historians of science have wondered why the systematic study of anatomy did not originate sooner than it did. And as puzzling as the when, is the *where* of its origination. Several ancient cultures left proof of keen intelligence and extraordinary powers of observation. Many learned men in ancient times performed dissections on cadavers or somehow became acquainted with the interior of the body. Yet, knowledge of anatomy, as we now understand it, remained unexplainably rudimentary.

The Aztecs of Mexico, who wrote exquisite poetry and made astonishingly accurate astronomical observations, left absolutely nothing to indicate that they had any notion, nay, any interest, in the structure and function of the heart, which they tore out of the chest of sacrificial victims. Ritual sacrifices awoke no interest in the arrangement or disposition of the organs of the thoracic cavity, even though their priests had to split open the rib cage, and to look inside, before avulsing the hearts of their unfortunate victims. Clearly, the desire to look was lacking. Observation of organs—as objects in themselves— was deemed banal, unimportant, or idle. The overwhelming concern was to stave off the end of the world and the extinction of the sun, catastrophes that they believed would surely happen if they ceased to supply their horrific deity with human blood. Compared to these enormous, cataclysmic events, what interest could they attach to the shape of the cardiac cavities?

By the same token, the ancient cultures of Mesopotamia reached a very high level of civilization. The opulent power of Babylon is nearly legendary. Here, people emerged from prehistoric primitivism in a harsh land, and in a few centuries developed a script, built up a strong economy, and created a mighty empire that for a long time reigned unique and unchallenged in the whole of the Middle East. The realism of reliefs in their monuments is extraordinary. The scenes of the hunt, in which the game appears pierced by arrows, powerfully convey the tense, strenuous effort of the persecuted beasts, down to the twitching of their leg muscles, convulsed in the tremor of agony. In a well known relief, a lion has just been hit by arrows that protrude from its chine, and the two hind legs are hyperextended, poignantly and faithfully portraying the spastic paralysis that is caused by the traumatic severance of the spinal cord. Strangely, this power of observation was not directed to the interior of the human body.

In ancient Mesopotamia, *extispicy* (from the Latin *exta*, a term originally denoting the thoracic viscera, but later extended to viscera in general, and *specere*, to look at), or divination by looking at entrails, was a millenarian practice. So was divination by observation of the liver (hepatoscopy).[12] Systems of divination were made into a sophisticated scholarly activity. The diviner was a specialist who underwent a long and difficult formation; he had to go through voluminous compendia in order to interpret the forecasts or omens of the viscera adequately. The corpus of texts referable to extispicy surpasses those devoted to any other form of divination. Many tablets have survived that prescribe the meticulous order in which the viscera had to be arranged in order to interpret the omens correctly.

By the light of these facts, one might think that anatomical observation was highly developed in Mesopotamia. No such thing. The people did not want to look. In some instructional tablets, rough sketches are made of the alluded anatomical part. Only a coarse representation is resorted to, such as a coiled line for the loops of intestine. Mesopotamian three-dimensional models of the liver in clay are kept in the British Museum. Anatomical detail in these productions remains unsophisticated, even childish. Their purpose was not to teach the anatomical arrangement, but to facilitate instruction or the explanation of omens to the king or to other persons of rank.

The people of ancient Mesopotamia left behind impressive codes of law, admirable literary productions, myths of creation, legends, and a hefty corpus of magic and divinatory texts, but no anatomical treatise. They did not want to look at the body's inside. Or, rather, they looked beyond the anatomical organs into the divinatory or ominous qualities that they thought they saw inscribed in the viscera. The nonscientific approach is reflected in the mystical, esoteric terms applied to inner organs, a fact that complicates the task of modern specialists. Thus, there is no pharynx or intestine, but "the palace door" or "the path," and so on.[13]

As with the interior, so with the body's exterior. Human beings were believed to carry inscribed on their bodies fateful signs that, correctly interpreted, could foretell the future course of the bearer's life, or proclaim the person's nature. Today's Assyriologists study ancient tablets that they call "physiognomic omens," whose topic is the shape of the nails, the color of the hair, the size or characteristics of various parts of the body, with much attention devoted to "birthmarks" or skin discolorations—i.e., moles, vascular blushes, pigmented cutaneous lesions—on account of their important predictive value. But nowhere have experts found evidence that ancient Mesopotamians paused to consider bodily form and structure as such, for their own sake, divorced from magical or divinatory implications.

Thus, for the Aztecs, the heart was a device for storing and liberating energy: a force so massive that it could propel the sun along its orbit. The heart-avulsing sacrifice was the Aztec version of the modern cyclotron: the means to free enormous amounts of energy. As to the Mesopotamians, extispicy was to them what DNA and the genome have become to us. The viscera were a series of coded signals: whoever could read the visceral code would be able to predict future events. Other ancient cultures looked at the body without seeing anything, save what they wanted to see. More than a thousand years later, Europeans of the Middle Ages had their own style of distorting the sights of the body's interior, as the following story makes clear.

Sister Clara de Monfalco died in odor of sanctity inside a convent of the followers of the Second Order of St. Augustine, in the year of the Lord 1308. The European Middle Ages did not look benignantly upon the practice of cutting up dead bodies. But exceptions were made now and then, and autopsies were performed under certain well defined circumstances. The need to ascertain the existence of evidence of sainthood was sufficient reason to permit the post-mortem examination of the blessed Clara. Mind you, it was the sisters themselves who carried out the procedure. Nor is this to be wondered at. The deceased had been a woman of unsullied virtue and immaculate purity. She had died a virgin, and no man would be allowed to touch her body, even after her death.

The dutiful sisters proceeded to open the body, and with characteristic diligence and order went on to place the viscera in carefully prepared jars. The heart received a special treatment. There was much expectation when they came to it. For some remembered that, before passing away, Sister Clara had declared, with genuine earnestness of manner and perfervid accent, that "she carried the crucified Christ in her heart." Thus, the sisters gather around the table on which the cardiac viscus is deposited; one of them sinks a knife in it and cuts it open. Marvel of marvels! To the gasping admiration of the congregated servants of Our Lord, they discover a "nerve" in the shape of the cross upon which the Redeemer of Mankind had been crucified.

What did they "really" see? The inner surface of the heart's ventricular cavities is coursed by numerous fleshy bands (*trabeculae carnae*), which stand more or less detached from the walls of the organ, and impart to it a highly irregular appearance. It would not be surprising if, somewhere in this anfractuosity, a cross-shaped structure was discovered by eyes inflamed in religious fervor and predisposed to seeing the beloved symbol. But this is not all. Looking at the heart with careful attention, another sister discovered a structure that was quite like the whip with which the body of Jesus Christ was flagellated.

Again, one may wonder what was seen. Those familiar with cardiac anatomy know that stringlike fibrous tendons (*chordae tendinae*) are normally present, that serve to anchor the cardiac valves to the muscular walls of the heart. These strings, or tendons, may uncommonly rupture under the injurious effect of some cardiac diseases. When this happens, the affected fibrous string is agitated at its free end by the turbulence of the circulating blood. In the circulatory torrent, the torn string is agitated with motions that are veritable "whiplashes." But it should not be necessary to resort to such complex explanations of pathology to account for what the sisters saw. The fact is, religious fervor strongly colored every object that intruded into the visual field of those who contemplated the prodigious heart of Sister Clara, and the ocular witnesses were not only the sisters.

After the miraculous findings were initially recognized, a whole assembly of personages, ecclesiastical authorities, theologians, physicians, magistrates, and other "persons of quality" stood bedazzled, lost in wonderment before the heart of the blessed Clara, which kept disclosing its astonishing vistas. One examiner sees here the lance that wounded the flank of the Savior; another one, the vinegar-soaked sponge that was approximated to his lips while in agony; and still others, the crown of thorns, the nails that pierced the sacred limbs, and so on. The impression produced by these prodigies was so vivid, that one of the spectators "upon touching the tip of the lance and of the three nails was pricked, as if they had been of real fire."[14]

What determined that the body should be looked at as an object interesting in itself, was curiosity. Nothing but curiosity pure and simple, an invincible human propensity against which St. Augustine, the great mystic, philosopher and theologian of Hippo (A.D. 354–430) issued stern warnings. The senses, he said, look for pleasure in the stimuli that impress them: hearing likes harmonious sounds; smell, fine fragrances; taste, sweet and savory morsels; and sight, delightful combinations of forms and colors. This is the normal tendency that we try to satisfy. But curiosity is a different thing. When moved by curiosity, sensations of the opposite sign may be looked for. Not for the sake of experiencing the disagreeable, but for a relish of investigation and discovery. "What pleasure can there be in the sight of a mangled corpse, covered with wounds and cut to pieces, which is a thing that affrights and horrifies? And yet, wherever there is such a sight to be seen, many come to watch, and having seen it they are saddened and frightened." (*Confessions*, Book X, ch. xxxv.)

Thus, in addition to bodily appetites, which are the motives and tools of concupiscence of the flesh, St. Augustine identified a much more dangerous species of temptation, one that uses the special senses for the satisfaction of vain curiosity—*curiositas*—"disguised with the pompous names of knowledge and science." And because the eyes are preeminent in obtaining knowledge of sensible things, it is the eyes that are the first to be blamed for intemperance. There is, then, a concupiscence of the eyes, *concupiscentia oculorum*. And it leads to pride; for those who spend their lives studying with infinite attention the objects of the world often become vain. They delude themselves, thinking that they are already in the heavens they watch so ardently. But the true philosophy, says the mystic-philosopher, is the love and study of wisdom, which can only come if we guard ourselves against a guilty curiosity, and concentrate on the love of God.

However, we are not mystics. Our desire to see the interior of the body arose strictly from curiosity: the impulse to see "for the sake of seeing," that is, to investigate what lies concealed. Some think that the study of the body's interior arose "naturally" out of a desire to discover ways to treat diseases. But this is highly unlikely. The options that physicians had in ancient times were extremely limited. What good was the detailed knowledge of anatomy, if there was no possibility of active intervention? To open the thorax or the abdomen, not to mention the cranium, was tantamount to killing the patient. Galen, for centuries the maximal medical authority, discoursed about "excessive" anatomical knowledge, as contrasted with that considered necessary.[15]

He thought physicians should be familiar with the anatomy of the extremities. They could apply their skills to alleviate injuries sustained in war, accidents, and athletic competitions. But to know, say, the shape and number of the valves of the heart, or the course and distribution of the nerves that issue from the brain, was, in his view, utterly futile. For over a thousand years the work of Galen represented the peak of the scientific study of the human body. Many clinical observations owed to him and his school still deserve respect. But it may also be said that his influence retarded the development of anatomical knowledge, and was one factor in the abandonment of the practice of anatomical dissection, which did not restart until the thirteenth century.

In the Renaissance, cadaveric dissections began to be performed in earnest. As St. Augustine predicted, to satisfy *curiositas*, the dissectors had to withstand the painful and horrifying propinquity of bodies dismembered, quartered, flayed, and decomposed. This experience they thought amply compensated by the sense of penetrating a theretofore forbidden zone: the intricate, marvelous constitution of what a dissector called "a second universe." Thus, they reasoned that they were looking at revolting sights only as a means to look into something else, something glorious, uplifting, and essentially beautiful.

It may be inherent in the human gaze to project a special significance upon every object that populates the visible world. No object is seen as "neutral" or devoid of meaning. Aristotle reflected on the justification that anatomists may have for exposing themselves to the distressing spectacle of bodies eviscerated and dismembered. In a famous paragraph of his book, *Parts of Animals* (645a), he conceded that no one can look at elements of the human frame—the blood, the intestines, the vessels, and so on—without a certain sense of revulsion. But the mind of the student of anatomy does not stop here. It goes beyond the bodily parts, and focuses on the relations that exist between each part and the whole. In like manner, the object of architecture is not the bricks, the mortar, or the timber, but the house; "and so the principal object of natural philosophy is not the material elements, but their composition, and the totality of the substance, independently of which they have no existence."

The "something else" on which the gaze of anatomists focused during, and for some time after, the Renaissance, was the religious sentiment that inspired the Counter Reformation. Human anatomy became a territory for both scientific exploration and devout meditation. At last one could look at the body with the culpable, curious gaze that St. Augustine condemned, without feeling remorse. For not only was the regard penetrating into the arcane secrets of man's structure, it was also receiving a moral lesson of the highest order. Wrote a devout dissector of those times:

> I have yet to hear or read any anatomist who, when discoursing of his art, would not break out in exclamations prompted by the clear evidence with which such art makes us discern that there is a God. Hear one of them, a famous one [Andrea Laurentius, physician to Henri IV, king of France], who expostulates: "Let you, atheist, come into this sacred palace . . . and see if you do not exclaim 'O, admirable architect!, 'O inimitable artificer!'" And this is the sentiment common to all the professors of that science, one of which [Francesco Redi] told me that he could not find by himself any other which would in equal degree lift him toward God. At least it seems to me indubitable that until now no illustrious man of the profession has ever been an atheist. For it is unavoidable that by the light of his researches he should discover, and then venerate, a bounteous, clear-sighted, supremely attentive Divine Providence, the marks of whose mastery he can see all too conspicuously stamped over the most minimal mechanism of the human body.[16]

The body is the biggest miracle, the most astonishing of all natural marvels. Anatomy, for Catholic intellectuals in the western world during the sixteenth and seventeenth centuries, is as much anthropological as it is theological. The stupefaction produced by the body's complex engineering, by the subtlety and intricacy of the human machine, naturally conduces to the impassioned admiration of the invisible designer and planner of those marvels, the Supreme Maker. Which is why the Church, at first suspicious of the activities of anatomists, ended up granting them the full protection of the ecclesiastical authorities.

Those were times of intense, high-strung raw feelings. The habitual exposure to public executions, at times of incredible barbarity, was now complemented by the scientific and pious study of dissected human bodies. The gaze that this era cast over human remains was a morbid gaze, tinted with an unmistakable sadistic hue. Art reflected this mentality, whose favorite theme was the martyrdom of the Saints. The collective voyeurism could regale itself with the variegated spectacle of St. Agatha's brutal mastectomy, St. Stephen's piercing with arrows, St. Bartholomew's flaying and beheading, St. Lawrence's grilling, and sundry other heinous executions represented with flair by the plastic arts. An artist's rendering of the torture of St. Elmo (also known as Telmo, or Erasmus) is of especial interest, because it strongly evokes the dissecting table and the technique most commonly followed by anatomists of that time for the evisceration. The painting, by the Flemish artist Dieric Bouts the Elder (*ca.* 1415–1475), shows the saint lying on his back on a board. A hole has been cut in his abdomen, and through it his sectioned intestine is being extracted. The torture is proceeding as follows: at its cut end, the intestine is tied and rolled on a winch. Two executioners, symmetrically placed on each side of the easel, hold the respective handles of the rotating mechanism, which they sedulously crank, thus rolling on it the saint's gut, while some standing spectators watch the scene impassively.

Christ himself was depicted as an anatomist. An extravagant seventeenth century preacher's metaphor placed Christ the Redeemer in the garb of the anatomical dissector approaching the mortal remains of a sinner. He is going to scrutinize the entire moral body, organ by organ, in order to detect the presence of ethical corruption, degeneracy, and dissoluteness. "Christ the pathologist" would be the term we would use today, since he is after diagnosis, albeit of spiritual maladies. Armed with a two-edged knife (*gladius utraque parte acutus*, is an expression used in Apocalypse I), he will start by the head, dissecting the eyes that gazed on lascivious scenes; the gluttonous throat that disregarded the holy fasts; the ears that welcomed slanders and base rumors, while closing themselves to prudent counsel and wise enjoinments to character emendation . . .

He shall lance that tongue that delivered so many lies, so many calumnies, so many obscenities . . . He shall divide those hands, in whose nails still remain traces of the illicit favors, the hidden thefts, the grasped looting . . . He shall disarticulate those feet, that took you to jump in the most licentious dances, and to go hear the most lascivious comedies . . . He shall lift the skin, and discover the flesh of all the hidden dishonesties . . . Shall cut the muscles, shall break the bones . . . He shall penetrate to the very marrow of the vital spirit . . .[17]

This language suggests that, for the men of the Baroque era, even the Redeemer of Mankind could appear represented in the guise of a bloodthirsty torturer and merciless dissector, ready to mete out the just deserts of the sinner, using the hooks, blades, lancets, needles, and sundry instruments employed in anatomical dissection.

Today, the gaze upon the body's interior is, on the whole, appreciably more sedate. We have grown blasé over our inner structure. Not on account of a closer acquaintance with it, sharper or keener than the harrowing familiarity which the Renaissance and the Baroque epochs experienced, but because our science and technology have largely expunged the hurtful aspects. We have, in a sense, made the difference between inner and outer bodies less trenchant. Modern imaging techniques, increasingly familiar to the non-medical public, erase the covers that conceal our inner organs; they make the body amazingly transparent.

It all began with the discovery of X rays. This made it possible for a person to view the skeletons of others, as well as his or her own skeleton, without being divested of the covering flesh. Clearly, this was much more than a feat of modern technology: it was a discovery that had something of the demoniac in it. For the skeleton is our graveyard form, the future shape that we shall adopt when we become the tenants of our own tomb. Never before had it been possible to view ourselves that way; such sight could come to us only in nightmares, or in terrifying visions as a premonition of death.

The genius of Thomas Mann was sensible to this aspect of our enlarged vision. In *The Magic Mountain*, which he wrote when the widespread clinical use of X rays was still relatively novel, he described the emotional turmoil of the protagonist, Hans Castorp, when he peers into his body's interior. At the clinic where he is being treated for a pulmonary disease, the radiologist allows patients to look into the fluoroscopic screen. Castorp looks, and sees what he expected to see, but he is shaken nonetheless: he contemplates what he never thought would be vouchsafed to him to contemplate: the picture of his own future dissolution. He looks at his hand in the screen, and sees it reduced to its most elementary expression, the skeleton. Roentgen rays have peeled off all the layers of flesh, "as if this flesh in which he walked disintegrated, annihilated, dissolved in vacant mist, and there within it was the finely turned skeleton of his own hand."[18]

On the other hand, the temper of the times has changed. The patients in the clinic of Thomas Mann's masterful novel walk about carrying their X-ray films; friends exchange them with each other for contemplation of their respective organic disintegration; they can chat about them, follow the progress of their diseases with a certain detachment (except when the films reveal a disease at an advanced, incurable stage); and lovers can say, as does Hans Castorp to the woman he loves: "I have seen your outer portrait, I would love now to see your inner portrait." She agrees, gives him the X-ray "portrait," and it becomes for him a token of the amorous relationship; a cherished talisman; an object fit to evoke her presence when she is temporarily away, like a lock of hair for nineteenth century lovers. The Roentgen image is her "luminous anatomy."

To look into the interior of the body will always be unsettling. The sight is a powerful reminder, gripping and implacable like no other, of our fragile and transient nature. But we have done much to attenuate the shock and disguise the violence of the message. We have plates, films, tracings, graphs, and other paraphernalia that purge the sight from the morbid references of yesteryear. The harrowing spectacle of the offensive, bloody, putrescible innards is now confined to very few areas, such as anatomy laboratories in medical schools or autopsy suites. Most people no longer see the interior of the body as the sinister place where death lies in wait. The painful sight has become a "derivative" image that can be contemplated with equanimity, or even lovingly pressed against one's heart, and kissed, as Thomas Mann's personage kisses the films of his beloved.

II. The Body, Glimpsed from Outside

In a recent scholarly work, Shigehisa Kuriyama[19] contrasts two different visions of the human body, by placing side by side two artistic representations of the same. One is a drawing by the Chinese artist Hua Shou (1341), of a male figure on which are represented the energy points and tracts used in acupuncture; the other one, a print by Vesalius from his famous *Fabrica* (1543), showing a "flayed man" in a baroque posture, and set in a fanciful landscape, the kind of anatomical illustration in vogue during the Renaissance to demonstrate the muscles of the body. The contrast between these two representations could not have been more dramatic. They are separated from each other by about two hundred years, but the gulf between the respective kind of vision, that is, the style of visual perception, is incommensurable.

The Chinese diagram shows us a man destitute of muscles—it is interesting to remark that muscularity is absent from ancient Chinese medical discourse—but on whose bodily surface the energy points of a theoretical medical system are conspicuously displayed. The Western print represents a man whose surface integument has been removed (evoking the martyrdom of Marsyas, which, it is not idle to recall, was utterly familiar to every artist of the Renaissance) and displays the fleshy, strap-like, bulging or flattened, imbricated or adjacent, masses of striated muscle: the *fabrica* brought up to view in all its complexity. One artist saw the system of pulleys and cords of the human machine, but failed to represent the energy of which it is undoubtedly possessed; the other perceived the ethereal centers, the unseen qualities, the generated energy, but stood blind to the most obvious gross features, so that Westerners, educated in the former vision, see it as absurd and fantastical.

Kuriyama reminds us that in ancient Greece, the warrior-heroes of epic poetry were described as "sinewy." Thus, long before people knew what muscles were (all soft parts indiscriminately referred to as "flesh"), character was already thought to be expressed in a body that is lean, sinewy, sculpted, chiseled, sharply defined. The embryo is largely amorphous, as still undifferentiated and incomplete. And so is Woman, who, in the misogynist interpretation propounded by Aristotle, is developmentally incomplete, that is, a male who did not quite make it. In Homeric times, the body of Woman, smooth, soft, and regular, was viewed as inchoate, since it lacked the sheer embossments and bold etchings of masculinity.

To this was later added a subtler philosophical idea, exploited by the learned in different ways for many centuries, that muscles are the instruments of the will. Galen and other precursors of scientific medicine first reflected upon the existence of two sorts of movements, voluntary and involuntary. Among the latter are the peristaltic contractions of the intestine or the pulsations of vessels and the heart. These facts, which we now take for granted, were major revelations. Thenceforward, to account for the "natural history" of an individual life, it was needful to trace all the actions that fell under the control of the will, which were executed by the muscles. Personhood and muscularity were inextricably joined. And since even apparent inactivity implies voluntary muscle control (were it not for the right amount of tension between extensors and flexors, the simplest posture could not be maintained), it became very important to ascertain what the various muscles do: how the interplay of different muscles results in the acts that we perform as free agents. The door lay open to a detailed study of the body-machine, the *fabrica* in Vesalius's rendering.

The Chinese mode of seeing was not informed by these ideas. Not surprisingly, the Eastern vision that resulted was radically different. Kuriyama believes that one of its characteristics was its focusing upon the superficial planes. Whereas the Westerner sees the surface and imagines the underlying planes, the ancient Chinese vision proceeded along the reverse pathway, depth-to-surface, seeing the projected fields of force of the internal organs upon the bodily exterior. Hence the identification of specific points of stimulation in acupuncture or in moxibustion, techniques in which highly selected sites of the bodily surface correlate with organs that reside inside the body's cavities. Hence the exquisite attention that traditional Chinese medicine paid to the pulse, peripheral manifestation of internal disorders.

The surface is all important, since it is compendium of the inner forces that control health, and reception site for the external influences that affect it. But traditional Chinese medicine allows for a system of thought that approaches diseases as "layered" conundrums. It envisages pathology as surface-to-depth derangements of increasing severity. This is illustrated by a medical apologue well known in Chinese lore.[20] It features the semi-legendary physician Bian Que, prototype of physicians and model of clinical acumen, who is said to have acquired X ray vision after drinking a magical elixir, much to the enhancement of his diagnostic powers.

Bian Que was passing through the state of Qi, where his fame had preceded him, when he received a dinner invitation from the ruler of the realm, Huan, Duke of Qi. Bian Que did no more than to look at him, and declared: "My Lord has a disease that lies at the pores. It must be treated straight away."

The Duke was incensed, and dismissed him. He said: "The nerve of these doctors! I am not sick, I am feeling fine. But there is always a quack to exploit the fears of people."

Five days later, Bian Que was received again. He said: "Duke Huan has a disease whose seat is in the blood vessels. If not treated immediately, it will sink deeper."

Huan was again upset. "I am not sick," he said, and dismissed the doctor as he had done before. But he was curious enough to send for Bian Que a few days thereafter.

At this point, Bian Que pronounced: "My Lord's disease is in the stomach and intestines. It must be treated, or it will sink deeper."

Duke Huan made no answer. He had felt somewhat out of sorts.

Bian Que was summoned again to his presence five days later. Gazing at the Duke from a distance, the doctor said nothing this time, but recoiled and hurriedly went away. The Duke sent his attendants to detain him and to make him explain this behavior. The famous medical man made his celebrated reply: "When the disease lies in the pores, it may be treated with poultices; when in the blood vessels, it may be treated with needles; when in the stomach and intestines, with medicaments. But if it lies in the bone marrow, the God of Life himself would be helpless to cure it. This is where Duke Huan's disease now lies, and therefore I have no more advice to give." And with these words, the famous physician absconded.

Days later the Duke fell gravely ill. When he sent for the physician, Bian Que was nowhere to be found, he had left the state. The Duke died shortly thereafter.

The oft-related anecdote illustrates the theory of disease as disturbance that progresses by planes of increasing depth. Not that diseases start at the surface and progressively sink in. The etiology may be internal, but whatever esoteric, unperceived changes the Chinese sages may have thought of, these were supposed to reside at different planes at different times. Curable by acupuncture at the superficial stage, the disturbance becomes responsive only to ingested medicines when it has sunk to a deeper plane, and in the end turns refractory to all therapies, once it is ensconced in the marrow of the bones.

Bian Que did no more than glance at his patient from a distance, and he knew forthwith the nature of the disease and the depth to which it had progressed. He may have benefited from his acquired ability to see through walls. His modern colleagues lack the magical elixir that gave Bian Que his visual potency, but amply make up for the lack with computerized tomography, magnetic resonance, isotopic scanning, and other technology. Yet, none of these techniques replaces the careful inspection of the outward surface by simple, unassisted eyesight. The gaze sweeps the patient's bodily surface and records colors, textures, movements, growths, displacements, symmetries; all of which, by their apparent integrity or deficiency, harmony or discordance, will signal the existence of disease, and its nature.

And the dead body? What is there for the gaze to pause at, once color has turned to livor, texture has changed to stone, motion is frozen in immobility, and all attributes, formerly harmonious even in derangement, are now sunk into irreversible decay? Here, too, the eye sees what the mind of the onlooker knows, and what his affect desires to see. But the obscure desires that actuate those who seek the spectacle of dead human bodies elude our comprehension.

In the course of my career as a hospital pathologist, it always struck me as astonishing that persons unconnected with the care and treatment of patients who had died, should request permission to come to the morgue to view the cadavers. With few exceptions, this permission had to be denied. A distraught mother wished to hold the corpse of her son in her arms, for a few minutes, before the body would be transported to her home, and thence to the funeral home. It seemed strange that she would not have done before what she now felt inclined to do. Yet, it would have been callous to deny her request, and it

was granted, despite the unspoken apprehension that the mother's sorrow was having unpredictable effects upon her behavior,
which the morgue employees feared they could not manage.

In some instances the request was to watch the performance of an autopsy, under implausible pretexts, ill-disguised
as professional reasons. A detective engaged in the investigation of a crime could probably come up with valid reasons to
watch the cadaver's dissection. But a security guard of the
building? Yet, more than once I was asked whether I thought
it would be all right if a member of the security office— secre-
taries included!—was present in the autopsy room while a
post-mortem examination was being conducted. The real reason behind the request, I found out later, had nothing to do
with the requesters' job.

As it turned out, the afternoon shift of the security service
comprised a merry and congenial group. They frequented each
other's homes, where they organized weekend parties. It seems
that in one of these, amidst much quaffing, bets were crossed as
to who would be brave enough to endure witnessing the spectacle of post-mortem evisceration. The requests to attend the
autopsy, which of course were denied, came from those who
had wagered, and were now trying to win.

In another case, the challenge consisted in demonstrating
that one person had enough mettle to go, alone, unassisted, and
during the night shift, into the morgue, there to open the large,
walk-in refrigerators in which the cadavers were kept, and
bring out evidence that the valorous feat had been accomplished. Childish mentality of grown-ups who engage in games?
Unbecoming attitudes, incongruous with the solemnity that
ought to surround those who have ceased to live? Yes. Those
incidents reflect this, and more: a morbid fascination, irrational
fears, appalling immaturity; all states of mind incompatible with
a balanced, equanimous view of our natural, ineluctable end.
Nevertheless, these and many more obscure, ill-defined psychologic motives impel a very large number of people to seek the

sight of human corpses. For the number of those who actually look for this sight is very large, indeed. Otherwise it would be difficult to explain why the morgues of major cities in the West used to be open to the public, and generally as well attended as are today's museums, botanical gardens, or art galleries.

The morgue of the city of Paris in the nineteenth century (built in 1864 and moved to its present location in 1921) may be a special case, because its administrative directors at one time had no qualms in admitting that it was a place for spectacle, much like a wax museum, only "better," because the exhibits were not artificial contrivances or simulacra, but real human beings: flesh-and-blood men, women, and children. Here, visitors were admitted in groups to a large hall of two hundred and ten meters square, where they could see, behind large, closed off glass windows, the marble slabs on which rested the cadavers of unidentified persons. Corpses were laid out naked, except for a piece of cloth decorously covering the external genital organs. Their clothing and belongings were hung on the wall behind the body. Those who had died in accidents in the streets; those who had succumbed to violence and crime; the suicides who had drowned in the Seine; all ended up here.

The morgue was no scruffy den where a few squalid deviants satisfied a dubious propensity: it was a place where, if a cadaver had been the subject of journalistic sensationalism, up to forty thousand Parisians visited in a single day. A million visitors a year (!), according to a newspaper (*L'Eclair*, issue of August 29, 1892). The morgue was listed in fashionable tourist guides, with a comment: "there is hardly a Parisian who has not made the pilgrimage." The renowned travel company, Thomas Cook, included a visit to that gruesome spectacle as part of its guided tours. Busloads of foreign tourists were disgorged in front of the morgue's doors every day; and long lines, it is said sometimes of over one thousand persons, stood in the street, waiting their turn to walk in. These curious facts, and the social phenomena that buttressed such an institution, have been the source of much scholarly enquiry from historians, sociologists, and other specialists.[21]

. These scholars point out that the original intent of displaying cadavers on open public view was to ensure that unidentified corpses would be claimed by their relatives and friends. This was a function of the State, since "the social order," as it was said, was at stake; government had a role in restoring bodies found in the public domain to their families, friends and acquaintances. Therefore, a bureaucratic tone prevailed at first. But there is no contending with the powerful emotions that the sight of the dead can elicit. Soon, visuality superseded bureaucracy. A million visitors a year is patent proof that the search for lost relatives or friends became secondary.

The chief motivation of these crowds was to see. The very word "morgue" is traced to the ancient French verb *morguer*, to stare with a fixed, questioning gaze. The administrators soon found a way to enhance the visual qualities of the place, and the exhibit was turned—in a way that today we find distasteful—into a show, an entertainment. Green curtains overlaid the glass windows, that could be drawn partly or completely over the "stage," thus enhancing the theatricality of the spectacle, with this advantage over regular theaters, that the playbill changed constantly and entrance was free. There were neither subscriptions, nor season passes, nor favored patrons, but anyone could come in any time—and, mind you, the call was heard: big crowds of Parisians and tourists, rich and poor, old and young, male and female, came daily, from morning till night.

In effect, what Parisian theater could top this one? Centrally placed, behind the cathedral of Notre Dame, on the ile de la Cité, at the Quai de l'Archevêché (the area that is now called Square Jean XXIII), its former emplacement now bears the *Mémorial à la Déportation*. A multitude of merchants' stands had sprouted in the area, selling candies, gingerbread, toys for the children, and fruits. The actors were the cadavers, but the public did not see them as inanimate human despoils.

One might say, at the risk of incurring a hackneyed paradox, they were perceived as "living" presences: immersed in the narratives of magazines and newspapers, which set into relief their life mystery, their passion or their tragedy. Thus, the day after the media had announced that the dismembered corpse of a woman had been fished out of the Seine, the crowds swelled. The guards were forced to prod the onlookers to circulate faster, amidst protests, jostling, and irate complaints: "They hardly give us time to see anything!"

Of the dead it is said that they are "gone," that they have "departed." Yet their absence, though in a sense absolute, paradoxically coexists with a presence that inspires fear, or revulsion: the cadaver. The dead shown at the Paris morgue in the nineteenth century embodied this metaphysical puzzle in a strangely moving way. They were gone to that "beyond" that is the beyond of beyonds, the "ultimate ulterior," as a metaphysician once called it, yet they were highly visible, conspicuous presences that came up to the center of the limelight. This was their place, center-stage, representing their part, either like big stars who drew huge crowds of followers, day after day, or like simple *figurants*, mere extras or supernumeraries.

There was also a *mise en scène*, a stage design. The cadavers of children were clothed in quaint robes and sat on chairs, not laid out on the marble slabs, that the public could view them better. When effects of decomposition appeared, cosmetics were used to dissimulate the damage. In a particularly terrifying case, the head of a woman, a victim of homicide, began to decompose, and a wax sculptor was engaged to copy it. The replica still attracted great crowds. Consider, furthermore, the green curtains, the guards, and the expectation that the criminal was likely to come back to watch the victim—a common belief fostered in many works of fiction—thereby creating a sense of adventure. The members of the audience felt they could participate in the drama. "Interactive" theater, it is called today; but few contemporary plays can boast the intensity of

public participation of the Parisian morgue at the turn of the
century.

And the public itself? The members of the public were
themselves a spectacle. The stage was on both sides of the glass
window. Artists came to sketch, or to study, this side or that:
both held equal fascination. One of the most engaging descriptions of the public attending the morgue is that of Emile Zola
in his novel *Thérèse Raquin*. In this powerful narrative, two
adulterous lovers murder the deceived husband by drowning
him in the river Seine, and try to make their crime look like an
accident. But, alas, the cadaver of their victim fails to float back
up to the surface. The killer, the disloyal wife's lover, tortured
by dread and anxiety, goes to the morgue every day, expecting
to spot his victim. There, he encounters the old habitués of the
place, true amateurs who come from far away, and also the idle
strollers, who wander in for lack of anything better to do.
When few cadavers are exhibited, the people mumble their dis-
content; when the slabs are "well garnished," as Zola puts it,
they applaud, joke, or whistle.

Workers drop in from the job, carrying the tools of their
trade, and their lunch bags, and do not feel in the least compelled to appear solemn or quiet. Among them are young
apprentice boys who make the others laugh by imitating the
grimaces of this or that cadaver. They nickname the corpses.
This one, who died in a fire, is dubbed "coal hawker;" and the
drowned, the hanged, the stabbed, elicit in their turn their salacious, merry remarks. Then, there are old pensioners who come
into the exhibit room. They have a lot of time on their hands,
and have thought of nothing better to do than to come to the
morgue. "They look at the corpses with dull eyes, and make the
gestures of peaceable, sensitive men." Women, observes Zola,
come in large numbers. Other writers also commented on this
phenomenon. Pink-faced young working women clad in their
white coats, who pace along rapidly, looking through the windows with large, attentive eyes, as if they were in a department

store; and fancy women, well dressed, dragging behind them the train of their long, silken dresses. Writes Zola:

> . . . One of these stood a few paces from the window, holding a fine kerchief to her nose. She was wearing an elegant skirt in gray silk and a mantle of black lace; a little veil hid her face; and her gloved hands seemed very small and very fine. Around her hung the aroma of violets. She gazed at a cadaver. On a stone slab, a few feet away, was the corpse of a big, brawny young man, a mason that had just fallen to his death from a high scaffold; his chest was squarish, his muscles thick and short, his skin very white and smooth; death had turned him into marble. The lady watched him and seemed to turn him around, and to weigh him with her gaze, utterly absorbed in contemplation. She lifted a corner of her little veil, gazed a little longer, and then left.

To this intimation of decadent sexuality, Zola adds the following vignette:

> At times there were bands of boys, from twelve to fifteen years of age, who ran along the glass windows, stopping only before the cadavers of women. They pressed their hands against the glass, and ran their bold glances along the naked bodies. They nudged each other with their elbows, made insensitive callous jokes, learned vice at the school of death. It was at the morgue that these young rascals met their first mistress.[22]

The Parisian morgue was closed to the public in 1907. What did the onlookers come to see, after all? Like all who exert the visual function, they saw what they wished to see, and represented to themselves what was already engraved in their minds: they saw what they willed, and what they knew. The fancy lady, redolent of violets, who derived vicarious erotic thrills watching the statuesque, inanimate body of a young man; the band of adolescents that pressed their noses to the glass to get a good look the mystery of the feminine body, perhaps for the first time, blending cadaveric lividities with morbid sensations; the old pensioners who watch the spectacle of death with a sense of imminent, growing propinquity; the idlers who came in for no good reason; all wish to see, to look, to gaze, not knowing exactly what or wherefore.

Perhaps they see themselves. This motley crowd, on this side of the glass window, where rich and poor, young and old, the weak and the strong, mingle with each other, is like the material embodiment of the Great Leveling that shall take place one day, when every one of its members undergo the final transformation. For everyone is thinking that they *could*, one day, rich or poor, strong or weak, find themselves on the other side of the glass, transformed into actors of the silent play that draws the big crowds. Transformed? The word is pitifully insufficient to denote what will happen on the other side of the glass window. In every transformation there is at least a thread of continuity: one changes from something into something else, against a background of identity that remains constant. But there will be, on that side, no identity, no personality: a radical interruption, and no recognizable continuity.

Even the wildest transformations recounted in legends and mythologies can be understood: Circe transforming men into swine makes some sense; we can construct in our minds some explanation, our interpretation of the possible symbolic meaning. But the last transformation does more than transform, it imparts no form at all: it is an awesome, abrupt leap from all to nothing; an inexpressible, incomprehensible transilience, wherein what was before has no rapport with what is now.

What continuity from being to annihilation? This puzzle, this enigma, is what urges the onlookers to press themselves against the window, where they joke, and hoot, and whistle . . . What else could they do? It is distinctive of human nature, say the philosophers, to know that we are going to die. But it is a fact of common observation, for which we need not refer to the sages, that this knowledge, which should anguish us all, troubles only the hypersensitive few. Because the final transformation is ineffable, incomprehensible, and beyond all possibility of description, the enormous majority of us go on believing that death is a biologic phenomenon that afflicts all, *except* ourselves. Yes, we "know" this is a fallacy, but this knowledge is the kind of cognition that fails to penetrate our innermost self. It is the species of knowledge that never reaches the deepest layers of the mind, the source of emotions. Hence, death does not really touch us. For the simple reason that we do not, and cannot, understand it.

Therefore, at some level we believe that levity in the morgue is irreverent, indecent, and unjustifiable, but perfectly explainable. For it is also human, although not the best among our features, to rejoice upon reflecting that an ill, to which we fancy ourselves immune, strikes others while it spares us.

Seeing is Believing, and Believing is Seeing

I. Images as the Source of Chaos, Disharmony, and Sin

FRA BARTOLOMEO WAS A FLORENTINE PAINTER OF THE ITALIAN Renaissance (1473–1517; his real name was Baccio della Porta, on account of having been born near the Porta San Piero Gattolini, Baccio being the Tuscan diminutive for Bartolomeo), of whose talent it is impossible to doubt. Posterity has honored his memory by displaying his paintings in the great galleries of the world. But it seems that, to him, religious zeal was more important than painting. His heart was inflamed by the impassioned speeches of that controversial friar, preacher, reformer, and martyr, Girolamo Savonarola (1452–1498), to the point of wishing to become a Dominican friar himself, which he did in 1510. He is often referred to simply as *il Frate* ("the Friar"). But those were explosive times, when zeal easily crossed the boundary into arrant fanaticism; the defenders of the faith were known to wield a crucifix in one hand and a truncheon, sometimes a dagger, in the other. Inimical factions, albeit all within the same Christian creed, not uncommonly hatched murderous intents against each other.

During the Lent of 1497, Savonarola's power being at its peak, he fostered a "burning of the vanities" during which many objects of luxury and pleasure (including books of pagan inspiration and works of art that depicted the undraped human figure) were thrown into the fire. This only increased the enmity of the contrary party, and unleashed a furious attack against Savonarola and his followers, among which Baccio della Porta, the future Fra Bartolomeo, was counted. When violence erupted, the painter and his confederates took refuge in the Convent of St. Mark. Della Porta was naturally timid and retracted: the sight of the carnage that took place filled him with horror. So frightened was he upon witnessing the killings that were taking place in the very patio of the convent, that he swore he would become a friar if he came out alive. His life was spared, and his promise kept. Thenceforward, he was named Fra Bartolomeo, and with that name he is known in art history.

Attentive to the salvation of his soul, he had no time to keep up his pictorial activities. During four years he painted nothing; his days passed between fasting, meditation, and prayer. This gave rise to the rumor that his talents were limited; that all he could paint were conventional figures of religious themes, which he had picked up in the shop of his teachers; and that now that he had exhausted those themes, nothing else could be expected of him. Clearly, for all his exercise in austerity and mortification, he had not been able to subdue his feelings of pride and vanity, because these comments bothered him intensely. He "was bitten the most times," as Vasari says in his celebrated *Lives of the Painters*, by the rumor that he could not paint nudes (. . . *era morso piu volte che non sapeva fare gli ignudi*). To spite his detractors he decided to paint a St. Sebastian, the soldier-saint (along with St. Maurice and St. Martin) of the Catholic religion.

Painters who wished to give wide scope to their representation of the sensuous in the male body loved to portray St. Sebastian. According to legend, Sebastian was a young and handsome Roman soldier who had been promoted to Commander of the Praetorian Guard under emperor Diocletian. However, later it became known that he was a Christian, and he was martyred for having dared to defy the imperial order to deny his faith. He was condemned to be shot by arrows, although a tradition says that he survived this torment, then braved the emperor a second time, and was stoned to death. His body was thrown into the biggest sewer in ancient Rome's sewage system, the *Cloaca Maxima,* but was recovered by the faithful and given a proper burial. In the Middle Ages, he was often represented in Roman garb, or clad in armor or coat of mail, but since the thirteenth century it became the fashion to show him naked, tied to a column or a tree trunk, or with the hands tied behind his back, thereby displaying all the tensed, harmonious forms of a young and strong male body. This is the pose in which St. Sebastian was painted by Mantegna, Pollaiuolo, Botticelli, and other great masters.

Fra Bartolomeo applied himself to produce his own rendering of the soldier-saint, and the result exceeded all expectations. He used the colors that best simulated the hues of human skin, and gave such semblance of corporeality to his image, that those who contemplated it were astounded by its realism and genuinely moved by the sufferings of the martyr. But, after this painting was finished and placed inside a church, the priests in charge of the services began voicing serious complaints. They said that many women who came to confession told them that when watching this figure they felt they were being corrupted, in Vasari's words, "by the charming and lascivious imitation of the living state" (". . . *per la leggiadra e lasciva imitazione del vivo*") achieved in the painting. In refuting the claims of his critics, Fra Bartolomeo had succeeded only too well. The painting had to be removed from the sight of the parishioners in the church's nave, and placed in the Capitular Hall. It did not last long there, because it was bought by a rich man, Giovan Battista della Palla, who offered it as a gift to the King of France.

It is interesting that, in this narrative, women should have been shown as troubled by the sight of Fra Bartolomeo's all too evocative image. Men are traditionally credited with being more sexually responsive following visual stimulation. But it is a characteristic of the human mind that it evinces an exquisite suggestibility to the productions of its own creation. A young man looks in a magazine at a photograph of a disrobed woman in a lascivious pose, or a lewd image among the innumerable such vistas that offer themselves publicly in the western world, and reacts with a strong sexual response. Nothing more trivial, or more predictable, than this. Yet, at the same time, nothing more remarkable than this. The image, a flat, two-dimensional artifice, is not the woman, . . . far from it! It does not matter: the mind of the viewer does the rest: the eyes fix themselves on the marks of color—but color is not necessary, spots of gray and black will do—and out of those blotches on a paper, arises, like an ectoplasmic presence, a female body of such alluring and seductive attributes, that the sexual response in the male viewer is practically the same as if her real body were there.

This is quite amazing, but there is more. Such is the reconstructive power of "the mind's eye," that not only the woman does not have to be there, but the image does not have to be there, either. Under appropriate circumstances, a memory, an evocation, a souvenir, will suffice to conjure the female presence. Her "virtual" presence, which is but paltry succedaneum to the real, is all there is. But the sexual response, "for practical purposes," will be identical. The "mind's eye" accomplishes what the eyes of the face commonly perform. Which justifies saying that a distinguishing characteristic of human beings, one that identifies them as fundamentally different from animals, is (apart from the capacity to laugh, and to know that they must die) the ability to make love with ghosts.

If spots and marks on a flat surface can do this, it is hardly surprising that the three-dimensional corporeality of sculpture should succeed in persuading the viewer of the flesh-and-blood reality of a statue. The narratives of antiquity contain many examples of this blurring of the borderline between real and unreal in the viewer's mind. Pliny the Elder (23–79 A.D.), in his *Natural History* (XXXVI, iv, 20–22), mentioned a famous statue of Venus, the work of the renowned Greek sculptor Praxiteles, that provoked this confusion. The sculptor had actually chiseled two versions of the statue; in one, Aphrodite appeared draped, in the other she was naked. The former was bought by the people of Cos, as the only one which could be exhibited without troubling the public order. The other one was acquired by the people of the town of Cnidus, in Caria (a district of Asia Minor, in its Southwestern corner), and, as may have been predicted, achieved a much greater reputation.

In Cnidus there were three temples to the goddess of love; the statue that the townsmen bought from Praxiteles was placed in the temple to Venus Euploea (one of the surnames of the goddess). It is said that people sailed from all over the Hellenic world to come and admire it. One of the visitors, the king of a neighboring nation and a very wealthy man, named Nicomedes, fell in love with the statue and offered to buy it for an exorbitant price, a sum of money that would have been sufficient to pay the debt of Cnidus. But its inhabitants refused the offer, thinking that the statue was the glory of the place, and presumably so powerful a tourist attraction that it could, by itself, generate enough money to offset the public debt.

In this, the Cnidians were right: the marble Venus made the glory of their city in the ancient world. As is said in today's vernacular, she put Cnidus on the map. But it seems that they underestimated the seducing powers of their chiseled lady. They kept her in an open shrine, where her lovely forms were displayed to good advantage, and from every angle. A young man came around, and was smitten forthwith. Not having enough money to attempt to purchase her, nor enough good sense to rid himself of the obsessive remembrance of her morbid body, his febrile mind concocted a daring plan. He introduced himself in the shrine late at night, waited until everyone had left, and then satisfied his lust. It is a common version among the ancient chroniclers that the young man copulated with the statue (a rather *hard* thing to do, to say the least, but youthful prowess in this department needs no reemphasis), and that the lustful act could be detected the next morning by a stain on the statue.

One is at pains to know which is more to be admired for its power, whether Praxiteles' tool, or that employed in boldly desecrating his masterpiece. The ancients might have said, as hard the *corpus ad faciendum,* as the *corpus ad recipiendum.*

Nor is this the only case of its type. Praxiteles sculpted also a naked Cupid, which stood at Parium, a city on the Propontis known in the ancient world as a place where Apollo and Eros were worshiped. That this time the morbid marmoreal shapes did not represent a woman was no deterrent. Taking into consideration the known sexual preferences of the ancient Greeks, it may have been an added appeal. Be that as it may, a man from Rhodes named Alcetas saw it, his love for it was ignited, and at the first opportunity he did with Cupid what the young man from Cnidus had done with the marble effigy of the goddess of love. Pliny adds that Alcetas "left upon it a similar mark of his love" (*simile amoris vestigium reliquit*).

From the reiteration of examples it is easy to conclude that incriminating marks, in the form of stains that betray an accomplished sexual act, are a very old form of inculpating evidence. A president of the United States may have given them recent notoriety, and may be deemed the instaurator—i.e., the restorer after some lapse—but he was certainly not the inaugurator, of this style of culpability.

Another ancient example of passionate love for a statue is recounted by the Roman writer Aelian (Claudius Aelianus, born A.D. 170), in his *Historical Miscellany* (9:37). He says a young man at Athens, from a distinguished family, fell for a marble likeness of the goddess of Fortune that stood at the *Prytaneum,* the administrative center of the city. He was so inflamed with passion, that he embraced the statue, kissed it, and sighed most piteously, unmindful of the looks of reproof, alarm, or astonishment that witnesses of his bizarre conduct directed at him. Disheveled and distraught, he pleaded in the Council that he wished to purchase the statue and take it home. When his petition was refused, as was proper, the young man could not bear it. He decorated the statue with garlands and rich offerings, prayed in front of it for a while, and then killed himself.

In ancient Iran, a man was inflamed with desire for a statue of a female cupbearer (who allegedly became the king's mistress) in a grotto near the village of Taq i Bustân, at the foot of the Zagros mountains. To prevent this embarrassing incident from happening again, the statue's nose was struck off.

Among the artists of antiquity, the painter Zeuxis of Heraclea (flourished 420-390 B.C.) is famous for his ability to give his rendering, the semblance of volume, as if they were sculpted. He is said to have invented the method of representing light and shade. Quintilian[23] says of Zeuxis that he emphasized the limbs of the human body, for he was especially successful at conferring upon them striking roundness and solidity through his use of light and shade. In today's colloquial parlance, we would say he was "a leg man."

Quintilian also says that Zeuxis tried to impart an imposing grandeur to his paintings of female subjects, and that he followed in this the example of Homer, who cast his female personages in the heroic mold. Therefore, we can assume that his renderings of nude and semi-nude goddesses must have created at least as much havoc among male viewers as the sculptures aforementioned. A much-repeated anecdote says that Zeuxis had painted a bunch of grapes (probably for a Bacchic festival) so realistically, that birds were deceived and came to peck at the painting.

Not only in antiquity, but in less remote times, the power of realistic renderings in paintings was said to inspire amorous sentiments. Among the crowned heads of Europe, who often contracted marriages of convenience, it was a frequent practice to send to the prospective spouses a likeness of the potential mate; not so much in the expectation that the picture would suddenly inflame the heart of the viewer, as to delicately begin a mutual acquaintance, and to rule out an invincible repugnance or some very strong opposition that could bring on unwanted political and diplomatic complications.

One of the best known episodes of this kind was the presentation of the portrait of the Florentine Princess, Marie de Medicis, to King Henri IV of France. The event acquired some celebrity thanks to the exuberant talent of Peter Paul Rubens, the Flemish artist who immortalized the scene in one of a series of twenty-one large paintings depicting the life of the Medicis Queen, now at the Louvre, which originally decorated the Luxembourg Palace that she built in Paris. The paintings are highly conventional, fully suffused of the cultural clichés of those times. In them, mythical personages, gods and goddesses, naiads, nymphs, cupids, and so on, alternate with the queen, her royal husband, and other potentates of the era.

In the mentioned painting, the tutelary gods of Love and Marriage, Eros and Hymen, sitting majestically on a throne amidst the clouds, direct some chubby *putti* to present to King Henri the portrait of his intended spouse. Gallia stands by the delighted monarch, who holds a cane or a scepter symbolizing his authority. The king looks at the painting with a keenly interested, dreamy, and presumably enamored gaze. But against this romantic depiction, what sordid reality! The truth is that the King was an incorrigible philanderer, a satyr-like man, who would make his wife miserable with countless infidelities. He opted to marry the Italian princess strictly for money, since she was the daughter of the Grand Duke of Tuscany, and had the means to provide support for Henri's wars against the power of Spain. At the very time when, in Rubens's exalted vision, the king looks at the painting of the Florentine princess and is rapturously swayed into an amorous reverie, Henri IV was carrying on a torrid affair with the mistress in turn, Henriette d'Entragues.

The anecdote is sometimes told by historians that when the French king, hiding incognito in the crowd, first saw his bride in person, he exclaimed, "I've been deceived! She is not as pretty as shown in the painting!" Considering his insatiable sexual appetite, and his rather lax standards when it came to feminine appreciation, it is very unlikely that he really might have said that. The Italian princess, although no great beauty, was certainly far from ugly, and was not without a certain Latin attractiveness. But the truth is that she was already disembarking on French soil, when her royal spouse (there had already been a ceremony of marriage by proxy) was still shamefully cavorting in public with his mistress, the demoiselle d'Entragues. This one had a shrewish temper and subjected her lover, at that time already graying and suffering the sequels of a life of intemperance, to all sorts of abuse. The story is told that, irate at the impending arrival of Marie de Medicis, she asked the king when he would receive in his palace "his fat banker". To which the king replied, no less violently: "When I shall have chased all the whores therefrom!"[24] To this lamentable pass had come all the whispered sweet nothings and all the cuddling of those two lovebirds!

There is no dearth of examples, in old and recent history, of men in a position of great power who risk all their privileges and social standing, sometimes even the security of their country, for the sake of satisfying their lust. But it is difficult to find, in old or recent history, a ruler to match Henri IV's irresponsibility. He had actually signed a document in which he promised Henriette d'Entragues that, in the event she gave him a son, he would marry her. It is highly doubtful that the king really intended to honor this pledge. But Henriette became pregnant. Naturally, she dreamed of becoming queen, and founding a new dynasty that would devolve to her son. It is no wonder that she protested angrily upon learning of the arrival of Marie de Medicis. She threatened to ignite a huge scandal, in which she would make public the document in her possession, and expose the king for the hypocrite that he undoubtedly was. The political consequences could be very serious, indeed. There were enemy factions that would have profited immensely from this royal blunder.

Backroom politics have deservedly enjoyed the respectful consideration of historians: it is a commonplace, but true nonetheless, that the destiny of nations is sometimes decided by what happens outside of the palace halls, the Council rooms, or other spaces of officialdom. In this regard, the persuasion used to send Henriette d'Entragues back home must be counted as one of the great diplomatic feats of all times. Here was a temperamental woman, inflamed to the point of paroxysm by jealousy and spite, willing to bring down the king and the royal house with her to utter destruction, if she did not get what she perceived as her just claim. She kept the royal letter, signed of the king's hand and appropriately sealed, and she clung to the monarch desperately, disporting herself with him most arrogantly at the very same city where the queen and her retinue were about to arrive in the midst of a lavish reception prepared by the King of France. What cajoling, arguments, blandishments, threats, and other persuasion were used, is not consigned in official history. But Henriette packed up and left to her domains, and Marie de Medicis had a reception ceremony with all due pomp and circumstance, later immortalized by Rubens.

The end of the story is such as might weaken our faith in divine justice. One might have expected the wrath of heaven to strike down the impious, apostate, duplicitous, lecherous, reprobate king. In fact, the clouds did part, and the heavenly thunderbolt did come down to strike . . . Henriette! She gave birth to a stillborn baby, a fact that immediately freed Henri IV from his commitment, and not long thereafter she passed away herself. The king was then free to carouse again (his married state seems to have mattered little), which is something he did not fail to do, until he was laid low by the knife of an assassin.

He is remembered by the French as *le bon Roi*, the good king, chiefly for his successes in foreign policy, and for his commendable tolerance in religious matters during a time of unremitting, bloody religious strife. As for marital loyalty and circumspection, history has already passed its verdict, that he was the complete opposite of a paragon.

II. Images and "Last Sights:" the Search for
Inner Peace, Piety, and Salvation

If the productions of human industry could inspire erotic passions and morally reprehensible actions, works of art were also capable of kindling pious sentiments in the hearts of the viewers. At least, this is what Italians most assuredly believed during the Renaissance; for it was then that countless master-pieces of religious theme were made. These images were designed for being placed inside the churches, there to impress upon the gazers the edifying lessons of the Christian Gospels. But if the sight of those works of art could be spiritually uplift-ing, might they not also provide gracious and favoring succor to those who suffered most acutely? Some thought so, for there were religious paintings conceived with an even more dramatic end in mind. They were intended to soothe the anguish of pris-oners about to be executed.

In effect, during the Renaissance, there existed in Rome a religious brotherhood with the striking name of "Confraternity of St. John Decapitated" (*San Giovanni Decollato*), whose chief function was the provision of spiritual consolation to prisoners awaiting execution.[25] A member of the confraternity was informed in writing by the Roman magistracy that the capital punishment was going to be administered to a prisoner the fol-lowing day. Several members of the brotherhood would then visit the intended victim in his cell. One of the brothers was a priest ready to hear confession and administer absolution. Another one was a scribe or a notary, who would take down the prisoner's last will and testament, or write a letter to the rel-atives or persons dear to the intended victim, in case this one could not write it himself.

The visitors brought with them a book of prayers fit for the occasion, and, especially noteworthy, a wooden tablet with a religious scene painted on its surface, most commonly depicting an episode of Christ's crucifixion. These tablets (*tavolette*) have generally earned limited attention from art critics, although it is likely that for the most part their esthetic quality was not negligible, if we remember the end to which they were created, and the fact that in Renaissance Italy even obscure craftsmen and nameless shop workers seemed capable of producing works of art of considerable merit.

Imagine the last moments of the pitiable convicted criminal. The brotherhood members have been trying to alleviate his dejection, speaking to him in lyrical, moving accents of another life, and another world, in which the repentant shall be enfolded in God's mercy and become eligible for eternal bliss. It is the break of day, only a faint horizontal streak begins to gleam on the horizon. Then, guards and officers of the law come into his cell: one of them is the executioner. They pass a noose around his neck, and all march toward the street, the members of the brotherhood chanting litanies, and one of them approaching the tablet to the prisoner's face.

The procession advances through the narrow streets, led by a sacristan who carries a big cross covered with a black cloth. Next come men carrying torches, and the prisoner follows behind, not on foot, but riding on a horse-drawn cart that advances slowly, and accompanied there by two comforters. Behind the cart, several gentlemen walk slowly. To judge by their clothing, they are persons of some social standing, but it is impossible to tell who they are, because their faces are veiled with black cloth.

The facial expression of the victim is also hidden from sight, for a different reason. Montaigne, who witnessed one of these executions during his travels in Italy, wrote that one of the comforters continually approached the painted tablet in front of the victim's face, so that it was impossible to see his features.

The procession swells in number on account of the curious who come to watch the proceedings. It arrives at a chapel that belongs to the confraternity. Here, the condemned man takes communion and receives absolution. This is his last chance to say his prayers, for the chapel is immediately adjacent to the place of execution, the bridge of Sant'Angelo. They come out of the chapel, and a few steps away the grim site looms large. The group has arrived.

The condemned man is led toward the scaffold walking backward. Surely, this is not done out of a merciful desire to spare him the sight of the fearsome instrument of his impending annihilation. This peculiar advancing by retrogression is done so that the man can keep his eyes continually fixed on the tablet that a member of the brotherhood keeps all the time in front of his eyes, and sometimes presses against his face, so that he can kiss it.

A drawing of the celebrated painter Annibale Carraci (1560–1609) kept at the Royal Library of Windsor Castle, shows the very last moments of the wretched victim. He is being dragged by the executioner up a ladder that rests against the gibbet. The poor man is still advancing backward. In other words, he is backing up the steps that lead to his death, while

Figure 2. *A Hanging*, redrawn from a print by Annibale Carracci (ca. 1599)

the solicitous comforter keeps thrusting the little painting in front of his eyes. Some tablets were provided with a long handle, that they could be brought forward into the visual field of the condemned, even as this one reached the top of the ladder.

The scene is most poignant: we can tell that the pitiable wretch, manacled and unable to see the steps on which he is climbing, totters and slips, and has trouble maintaining his equilibrium. But each false step, or each beginning tumble, is rudely corrected by a pull of the halter around his neck, for the executioner is a few steps ahead of him on the ladder, and is holding the rope with one hand, on which he tugs every time he has to straighten the unsteady prisoner in his awkward, stumbling climb.

All this is done in order to ensure that the scene of the passion of Christ represented on the tablet leaves not for one instant the visual field of the condemned man. Mark the importance of this gaze: the last sight is his ticket to the ineffable joys of heavenly existence. His mind must be inundated by this ultimate visual impression; his soul filled with the dramatic representation of the crucifixion, for only this way will he be fit to appear in the sovereign presence of his Maker, about to receive him in his glorious kingdom.

The hurtful, lubberly climb does not last long. There are only five or six steps he must ascend. Then, the executioner loops the rope around the gibbet's transverse beam, ties it very securely, and drops the man to his extinction. In a further show of compassion, the executioner pushes down hard on the hanged man's shoulders, while an officer, no less warm-hearted, pulls down on his legs, to expedite the victim's death.

This is how humane tenderness manifested itself in the treatment of the condemned prisoners during the sixteenth century. There was supposed to be an uplifting, pious last sight for the condemned, and for the crowd, an emotionally charged, spectacular ritual, with all sorts of rich visual effects. These included the long procession, the penitential trappings, the confession and absolution, the dramatic jump from the gibbet, the pulls on the legs to expedite the departure of the poor soul, and, in some cases, the awful, prolonged exposure of the remains of the hanged, for intimidation and deterrence of any potential criminal. All of which was bound to impress the sensitive as overly cruel and barbaric.

The truth is that scenes of incredible cruelty were made into public spectacles in those times. A sketch by Jacopo Rainieri in 1540 illustrates a notable event of this sort. The drawing shows a man named Piron da Bazzano being tortured with red-hot pincers as he is dragged into the platform at the center of the public plaza, where he is to be dismembered alive. And here the narrative reaches extremes of sadistic detail. "The said Piron was always watching when the executioner plunged the knife in his chest, and even till he saw his own chest all opened up, so that he saw his own heart and the other innards."[26] Can one imagine a more terrifying "last sight" than that of one's own moist, palpitating organs as they are destroyed by the hand of the executioner?

Upon the mollification of customs that accompanied the Enlightenment, a new form of execution was devised, which was supposed to be swift, efficient, and imbued of the philanthropic spirit of the new era. Hence, the guillotine was born.

It fell to a physician, as seems right and proper, to come up with the new device of surgical precision. His name was Joseph-Ignace Guillotin (1738–1814), personal physician to the Count of Provence, and later elected to represent his district in the National Assembly. On January 20 of the year 1790, he proposed to the Constituent Assembly that the capital punishment by decapitation, theretofore the exclusive prerogative of the nobility, should be applied to every condemned criminal, regardless of social status. This was, after all, the revolution that exalted Equality as one of the fundamental social conquests: why, indeed, should only aristocrats qualify to be beheaded? The common man had as valid an inalienable right as the noble to have his head lopped off!

Thus, under the guidance of Doctor Guillotin, a German piano maker named Tobias Schmidt constructed the first of the infamous engines of death that were to make illustrious and plebeian heads roll. So precisely did the worker follow the specifications of the good doctor, that in one week trials were already being made on cadavers of prisoners in the courtyard of the Bicêtre prison. These rehearsals were, so to speak, a resounding success. On the 25th of April 1792, the first real execution was performed on a Nicolas Pelletier, a man convicted of robbery and aggravated, violent assault.

Although at first the guillotine was promoted on the basis of its clean, swift powers of extermination, and presumably as a means of abolishing the cruel spectacle of a prolonged agony (oftentimes with preliminary torture of the condemned), yet the crowds still had a dramatic ritual to watch. There was rolling of drums, solemn lining up of uniformed guards, priests elevating their prayers, and often the boisterous effusions of the crowd, whose violent motions, and sometimes insults and aggressive guffaws, were the last sight of more than one victim. No pious pictorial images to console the executed aristocrats: only derision and hatred.

But was this their last sight, or only the penultimate? There were some who disputed the claims of doctor Guillotin. Death was perhaps not as instantaneous as he claimed. Since this was the era of the Enlightenment, there were men firmly bent upon carrying out field research on the matter. One cannot read without a shudder the gruesome experiments that were actually conducted in the town of Vienne, during the time of the Terror. The morbid narrative of the chronicler is as follows.[27]

Renowned physicians, who opposed the ideas of Guillotin, obtained permission to attend the decapitation of three poisoners, there to realize their so-called "experiments." The medical men positioned themselves on the very place of execution, and as soon as the heads were severed from the body, they were given to them. The first one was the head of a young man: the eyes were closed and the tongue protruded from the mouth. "Eight minutes after the decapitation, they pricked the tongue with a pin: the tongue was withdrawn [into the mouth] and the face made a grimace of pain." The second head was a woman's; her open eyes emitted a suppliant glance, and shed abundant tears. "Fourteen minutes after the execution, it turned the eyes on the side whence she was called." The third was the head of the worst criminal. When slapped, the severed head "opened its eyes, and an indescribable expression of anger and ferocity distorted its features; the gaze was of a perfect limpidity, and adopted an ineffable expression of pain when the sectioned surface of the neck was touched."

I am reminded that the search for charitable treatments has not relented. In the United States, during the nineteenth century, there was no sighting of *tavolette*, but American ingenuity came up with a formula of an ideal ratio rope-length/body-weight, intended to expedite the departure of the prisoners' souls. [28] Alas, the theory was found wanting, and the sight of several protracted asphyxiations was deemed too hurtful for the ministers of the law. As to the executed, their last sight was a gibbet, and a professional executioner who placed a bag over their heads. Ungracious and cruel proceedings. Which is why the officers of the law had recourse to ether anesthesia preliminary to hanging. But this, too, had unsightly complications, and was abandoned.

With the progress of technology came a hope to foster human kindness. Thus, none other than Thomas Edison advocated charring prisoners with alternating current (AC), although such advocacy has been thought to stem less from charitable concern for the treatment of those unfortunates, and more from a desire to discredit AC, the form of electricity championed by his rival inventor-cum-industrialist, George Westinghouse. As it turned out, Edison wished to associate the electric chair, with all the negative feeling it elicits in the public's mind, and AC, the type of electrical energy whose use he hoped to discourage.

As a life-suppressing technique, the chair, too, had its disadvantages. More than one witness of an execution—and there were plenty, since twenty-five states and the District of Columbia ended up putting AC to work in this manner—must have been distressed by the sight of a man requiring two or more convulsing, smoke-blowing shocks to leave this world.

Which is why in Nevada in 1924 executioners preferred gassing; and so did ten other states. But no method was considered sufficiently "humane," which is perhaps a way of saying a sight tolerable to those who witnessed it, to say nothing of the victim. Today, capital punishment in the United States is done by administering a barbiturate that puts the victim to sleep; a dose of pancuronium bromide, which paralyzes the muscles; and another of potassium chloride, which induces cardiac arrest.

Curious to tell, the dominant preoccupation has changed. It shifted from beauty and drama to expediency. Formerly, a religious scene painted by a devout and skillful Renaissance master was the last sight offered to those about to be executed. The least one can say is that they took with them a beautiful, if not consoling, visual impression. Today, the search is for a clean, hygienic, smooth, and inconspicuous passing away. A soothing sight. Not for the condemned, of course, but for the survivors who witness the departure. As to those about to embark for the beyond, what do they see? A line of impassive spectators made up of officers of the law, a priest, a journalist, and maybe one or more special "guests" of the penal administration. In this gray, bureaucratic line, how they must yearn for a warm, eloquent human gaze!

Those who face a violent death often look for a human gaze that might cross with their own. Operators of the Metra trains in Chicago know this well, for they are on board when suicides throw themselves on the tracks under a passing train. As of mid-June, nine of sixteen deaths occurring in the year 2004 were self-inflicted. A train conductor said of a suicide: "He looked up at me right when I hit him," and added: "I've heard

other engineers say people committing suicide look at you. I
don't know why they do it. I sure wish they wouldn't, because
the picture stays with you. You try to forget about it, but you
don't ever, really . . ." Another conductor recalled that, when
the train got within eyeshot of the suicide, this one put his
hands in the air and dropped his head, a gesture that the train
conductor interpreted as saying, "I'm sorry for dragging you
into this."[29]

What is the gaze of those about to die trying to say?
Perhaps nothing at all. Since death can never be understood or
explained, the only important thing that remains to be done at
the last second is to look: to see, to watch, to perceive the flow
of the world down to its last details. Competent physicians
have remarked that in the very late stage of agony, the eyes
open wide and acquire the appearance of concentrated attention. "The attentive gaze of those about to die," says Tolstoy,
keener observer of these phenomena than most clinicians.
Attentive to what? Certainly not to the objects around us, but
perhaps to the supreme mystery that lies, beckoning us all, in
the infinite distance.

More Power to the Gaze

I N ANCIENT MESOPOTAMIA, DURING THE LATE URUK PERIOD, IN
the town of Tell Brak, today Northeastern Syria, there was
a temple dedicated to the eye. This assertion is based on the
finding by archeologists of thousands of figurines or "idols"
that appear to be some kind of personification of the eyesight.[30]
They were found in the ruins of a construction, apparently a
shrine to a god or goddess that may have been considered a
protector of vision. The objects found are roughly cut, made of
alabaster, limestone, or black clay, and seem to have been hewn
to represent the human figure, but in a very rudimentary way.
Thus, the stone shape gives only a rough approximation to the
contour of a human trunk. Without arms or legs, this rough
semblance of torso is continued upward by a narrowed portion
that may be taken for a neck, itself topped by a wider segment
that—one may suppose—indicates the head. Only there is no
face, properly so called. Thus, there is no head to speak of. All
there is, is eyes: two large eyes in the absence of a nose, cheeks,
ears, forehead, or skull. Nothing but eyes: two large eyes that,
in their isolation, appear to stare fixedly at the beholder.

Mesopotamia is not alone in this solemn reverence to the
visual function. Throughout the ancient world, all cultures
marveled at the puissance of eyesight, and wondered at the ability of the eyes to concentrate the expressive force. The Theravada
Buddhists of Ceylon have a ceremony that they call *netra pinkama*
or "eye ceremony," which dramatically underlines their belief

in the eyes as focal points of concentration of energy. During this ritual, they make a complete statue of Buddha, but they leave the painting of the eyes to the last. When they accomplish this last step, it is as if they brought the statue to life. Moments before, the effigy was like any other: a lump of inert material made roughly in the shape of a human figure. But as soon as the last touches are given to the eyes, it begins to be treated most reverently. The eyes have hallowed it, transformed it into a mystical entity. For its worshipers, it seems, the divine might is nestled in the eyes.[31]

The West is no stranger to this imaginative interpretation. The Greeks left us more than one narrative that attests to their belief in the power of the eyes of effigies. Thus, according to Pausanias, a statue of Arthemis *Orthia* ("Upright") was found that rendered the two men who found it insane when they looked at its eyes. This statue was called *Lygodesma* ("willow bound") by the Spartans, on account of having been found in a thicket of willows.[32]

A terrible deity, Arthemis Lygodesma was. She caused quarreling among her worshipers, and often of such violence that many fell dead at her altar. To believe her oracle, this was because she demanded human blood as an offering. In past ages, this requirement of the goddess was satisfied with human sacrifices, but times changed and customs were mollified: Lycurgus, the famous statesman, suppressed this barbaric ritual and decreed that the ceremony should be changed to simple scourging of young men. This way, the goddess would be appeased, since her altar would continue to be spattered with blood, as she thought it right and proper for her service, and as everyone at the time deemed it in keeping with her dignity.

Pausanias adds the curious incident that, on one occasion, the scourger relented out of respect for the person of a young man, whom he was supposed most vigorously to whip. The lad was of a noble origin and comely presence, circumstances that inspired restraint on the executioner. Seeing which, the statue turned so heavy, that her priestess could no longer move her, as was required by the ceremony, and the scourging had to be restarted in earnest.

Plutarch contributes another example of the fearsome might residing in the eyes of a goddess' statue. In his *Life of Aratus*, the ancient writer recounts that after the capture of the town of Pelene, the victorious soldiers came upon a statue of Diana that no one dared to touch. It became necessary to move it, but everyone whose help was requested seemed eager to avoid the task. Those who could not refuse approached it trembling, and their faces turned, to avert their gazes from the statue. Their behavior was this fastidiously cautious because they were convinced that whoever chanced to look upon the effigy would immediately fall dead. So terrible and hurtful was her presence, that even the trees that chanced to contact her became barren and lost their fruit. The vanquished people, the Aeolians, divulged the version that they were defeated in battle because the baneful image had been held up directly in their faces. But this account the proud general Aratus, the conqueror, adamantly denied, for he thought his glory was dimmed by attributing his victory to a supernatural agency.

The ancients cogently argued that there had been one man to whom responsibility for all this effigy malfeasance could be traced. This was none other than Daedalus, son of the Athenian Menion, in turn son of Eupalmos ("ready handed," a nickname that his grandson certainly deserved). Daedalus was the mythical Greek representative of all handiwork. Legend has it that he was craftsman, engineer, artist, and inventor, to whom are owed the axe, the bevel, and the awl, among other tools of his devising. He was also a renowned architect who built the labyrinth at Gnosus, for the Minotaur. But the benefits of his artistic achievement were less straightforward. For he passes for being the first sculptor ever to endow statues with eyes, as well as arms and legs, which he fashioned in apparent motion; before him, the extremities were always represented as rigid, elongate structures held against the trunk; and the face was made eyeless.

The destructive power of the gaze is probably no better embodied than in the Greek myth of Semele. In this well known story, Semele was a beautiful girl. Her father was King Cadmus, the founder of Thebes, and her mother Harmonia, a woman of divine ancestry. Although not a goddess herself, Semele was sufficiently beautiful to attract the attention of Zeus, the father of the gods, whose sexual desire, as all acknowledge, was flammable in the extreme.

The wantonness of Zeus became proverbial: to desire a woman and to contrive a way to satisfy his lust, were in him one and the same thing. Nor did it seem to matter much whether the object of his desire was a goddess, or, like Semele, a hybrid being descending from human and divine forebears, or even a mere mortal, an outright flesh-and-blood, perishable female. To Zeus, this made no difference.

In his accustomed, irresponsible (because godly) manner, he comes down from Olympus, and seduces Semele. No wonder that St. Augustine, a hater of the pagan gods, asked with irony how come the gods could have sexual intercourse with mortal women any time they wanted, but men almost never found occasion to do the same with Olympian goddesses: this the renowned saint and former playboy deemed "a harsh and intolerable condition!" (*City of God*, XIII, 3).

Be that as it may, Zeus got his way with Semele. But, as it turned out, his union with her was no casual attachment. Contrary to what might have been expected, the relationship did not wither immediately, but began acquiring the looks of an affair with good prospects to become durable—for Zeus, a most atypical occurrence.

It was then that vanity and curiosity, those two characteristics that an unfair tradition annexes to femininity, started working their familiar havoc. What good was it to be a god's paramour, if no one, not even herself, fully realized the awesome fact? Semele was not content with knowing that she had won the undivided attention and perfervid sentiments of an Olympian god. She wanted *to see* him, and that everyone should see him, invested in the full dignity that was his; to see him as what he was, not a mere man who would lie with her in bed, but the father of the gods presiding over the whole lot of celestial divinities.

Semele importuned her lover constantly. She let him understand that she was unhappy with the way things were between them; that to know she was joined to an immortal god, but to have this one assume the guise of a run-of-the-mill human being was, to say the least, frustrating. It was humiliating. She really wanted the whole world to know that she, Semele, consorted with the top brass in celestial circles. It was not enough, for her personal contentment, to know that she was now pregnant; she wanted everyone to know that she harbored in her womb a child of Zeus. At bottom, it was vanity that prompted her insistence.

So stubbornly did she urge her lover to reveal himself as what he was, that at length he consented. One day, he yielded to the woman's pressure and showed himself in the full, terrifying, overwhelming splendor of his divine majesty. No human being could stand that sight; anyone who confronted it was instantly fulminated. Accordingly, Semele was consumed, annihilated, turned to ashes by the flaming luminosity of the very spectacle she had requested.

She was charred and vaporized, reduced to nothingness. But Zeus, of course, knew that his beloved was pregnant, and, before she was totally consumed, he managed to remove from her body the burgeoning life sheltered therein. Next, he devised an extraordinary surgical method of preserving the life of the developing being that he had sired. He practiced an incision on his own thigh, thus creating a sort of pouch (surgeons, in their jargon, call this a "marsupialization"), inside which he deposited the premature fetus that he had extracted from Semele's dissolving body.

See how even the great have humble beginnings. Zeus's son is the little Dionysos, the future god of madness and of wine, whom the Romans called Bacchus. But at this time he is only a premature fetus of about five or six months of gestation, who undoubtedly would have succumbed if left to fend for himself outside the maternal environment. As it is, thanks to his father's foresight, the little fetus can complete its development in the pouch, as if he were a marsupial. And the still more astonishing circumstance is that the pouch is paternal!

The exterminating power in the gaze of Zeus symbolizes the deeply-rooted belief that some persons can harm others by merely looking at them: the so-called "evil eye," of which tales and folklore exist in practically all cultures. Among the ancients, virtually everyone, not excepting the wise philosophers, believed in the existence of persons capable of conveying hurt through the eyes. Those facts, they warned, may seem portentous and elude logical explanation, but they ought to be examined meticulously, and not rejected merely on our inability to explain them. The reason for the existence of cases of the "evil eye" (whose authenticity it never occurred to them to question seriously) had to reside in the existence of some form of energy or effluence coming out of the eyes.

Indeed, early theories on the mechanism of vision proposed that a stream of invisible particles flowed out of the ocular globe toward the object viewed. This being the case, the particles ejected could be hurtful to others. The ocular effluence could, on occasion, produce pain to the viewed. A curious, seemingly confirmatory observation was enunciated by Lucretius,[33] and repeated by the likes of Plutarch and Pliny, namely, that lions could not look directly upon cocks, because the latter emit tiny particles or atoms through their eyes, of such a nature as were able to stab the lions' pupils, causing them unbearable pain. The proud king of the jungle was ignominiously put to rout by a little rooster. Due to the visually induced pain, the simple sight of the barnyard fowl could send a ferocious beast of the jungle in cowering retreat.

Why were not other animals similarly affected? Presumably, because the particles emitted from Chanticleer's eyes could fit into the minuscule pores believed to exist in the pupils of all animals, but did not fit in the lion's. Such particles ("atoms") did not hurt human eyes because they coursed through the pores and exited immediately, not staying long enough to cause any pain. The entire phenomenon was rationalized as a matter of good or bad "fit" between the particles ejected by the eye, and the pores in the eye of the recipient.

Of all ancient theorists, the so-called "atomists" were the most consistent: they extended the theory to the entire physiology of perception. Empedocles thought that as in vision the particles harmonized with the pores of the eye, so a perfect adaptation of pore and particle had to be the basis of all sense perceptions. The total agreement of ocular pore and particle explained, in his opinion, why colors are perceived by the eye only, not by the ear or the tongue: honey is sweet to the taste, but highly irritating to the eye. Pore-particle congruence: this is what made perception possible; conversely, its lack was the cause of pathology.

What could be the nature of the eyes' effluent? To the earliest theorists, it was a kind of fire. Alcmeon of Croton, a disciple of Pythagoras and a man keenly interested in medicine, allegedly the first to practice anatomical dissections for chiefly scientific purposes, excised eyes (of animals?, of humans? We do not know) for his studies, and maintained that there is fire inside the eye. To prove his point, he resorted to this quaint experimental demonstration: Let the human subject close his eyes (important step that ensured that no fire would escape to the outside of the ocular globe), then give him a slight blow straight to the eye. The subject invariably reports that he sees sparks and cinders. (This was the Greek expression corresponding to our "seeing stars.") Now, where would sparks and cinders be coming from, if not from fire? Fire, in some form, had to be present inside the eye, and when struck it flashed forth.

Where in the eye was the fire? In some eyes, at the center; in others, more peripherally. This is why some animals see better during daytime, and others enjoy night vision.

Some theorists believed that another important structural component of the eye was water. The need for perfect transparency in vision seemed to require the presence of water, not just fire, in the eye. During the visual process, they thought, things reflected themselves in the eye's water, like trees being mirrored in the surface of a lake. This notion gave rise to thoughtful theoretical schemes about the arrangement of these two components in the structure of the ocular globe. Pores for water alternated with those for fire. Bad eyesight could originate from too much fire or too much water, for the excess of one would occlude the pores meant for the other. The best eyesight was believed to result from a perfect balance between the two elements.

Various other thinkers introduced their favorite ideas into the ancient theories of visual physiology. Some thought that air, or earth, were important in the constitution of the eye. Another school of thought held that, for vision to occur, not only was it important that the eye send out rays from its inner "fire" toward the object, as the Pythagoreans proposed, but it was also necessary for the visible object to emit a brilliance, which was then answered by the luminosity of the ocular fire.

The thinkers of Abdera hypothesized that infinitesimally small parts detached themselves continually from the objects perceived. These became organized into images or simulacra, the *eidola* (same root in our words "idol" and "idea"), in essence thin films made of atoms that kept the general configuration of the objects whence they had come out.

This explanation was not without a certain charm: it proposed the existence of ectoplasmic presences, which however were not at all ethereal or phantasmagoric, but clearly material, since they were capable of impressing our senses. An *eidolon* (ειδωλου) had the same form of the object perceived, and emerged from it in continuous waves. Just as we perceive movement in a movie by the quickly juxtaposed visual impression of a continuous series of static pictures in the film frames, so it was thought that we perceive the real objects of the world by the impression that makes a series of constantly flowing *eidola*—a sort of persistent bombardment—upon our eyes. The images from our own persons, which we detect on a mirror, are caused by these *eidola* or simulacra that, after detaching from our own bodies, are reconstituted at the surface of the mirror and bounce back toward us.

Thus, scholars rank ancient theories of vision into three kinds: those that insisted on brilliance sent out by the eye toward the object; those that emphasized the presence of *eidola* or images from the object; and those that required a dual luminous projection; in other words, the brilliance of the object coming toward our eye, and conveying the simulacra, had to collide with the luminosity sent out by the eye: the purer the luminous exchange, the more perfect the vision.[34]

Nor were ancient physiologists at a loss for explanations of the "evil eye." The fundamental premise was that strong emotions could alter the functions of the body. For instance, love could regulate the inseminating potency: all other conditions remaining equal, a woman was likelier to become impregnated by a man in love with her, than by one not subject to this amorous passion. Vision, too, was modified under the sway of emotion. Anxiety, like love, it was believed, enhanced visual acuity ("A lover's eyes will gaze an eagle blind," wrote Shakespeare[35] centuries later). Wrath, in contrast, decreased it: the eyesight of those engaged in a fight was thought to become blurred to almost everything except the adversary, and ferocious beasts in the midst of a rabid paroxysm were utterly blinded. Little wonder, then, that those affected by envy or by jealousy, inwardly poisoned by the noxious effects of their own passion, could have a poisonous glance. Their disturbed physiology resulted in an ocular effluence of distinctly toxic or harmful nature.

It is especially significant that the ancients should have theorized that fire was found inside the eye. For fire occupied a very important place in their minds: not in vain did they regard it as central in the composition of the universe. In the collective mind, it was a thing extraordinary: an element so exalted that they worshiped it as a divinity, which the Romans personified as Vulcan. It was the energy that animated all living creatures; the ineffable force that made the plants grow; the light that shone high up in the stars; the brightness and heat of the sun; and the explosive power that lay dormant in the bowels of the earth, ready to burst out in volcanic eruptions.

Theophrastus stated that a major fire "destroys" a smaller, less abundant one; and since the eye's fire is the same as the sun's, this explains why one cannot look directly at the sun, or at a very brilliant object. This curious idea was rather starkly exemplified, and much sung by the poets, in the story of Marcus Atilius Regulus, a Roman consul made prisoner by the Carthaginians in the year 255 B.C.

The Roman remained a prisoner for five years, until the Carthaginians were seriously defeated (in B.C. 250). The humbled nation opted to send an embassy to Rome, and the striking decision was made to let Regulus accompany the ambassadors as chief envoy, on condition that he solemnly swear to come back: so high an appraisement had the Carthaginians made of Roman honor, and of the character of their prisoner. Moreover, they figured that the chances of accomplishing his mission, which was to plead for the exchange of prisoners, would be enhanced, since his freedom depended on the success of this task. And they further assumed that his hearers would be favorably disposed, seeing it was one of their most highly regarded countrymen who addressed them.

Things did not go quite as planned. As told by Roman historians, Regulus became a paragon of heroic Roman virtues. When he arrived, he refused to enter the city as a captive subject, an intolerable condition for a Roman; later, he declined to address the Senate, because, as a prisoner, he thought himself unworthy of appearing before that illustrious body. The senators allowed him to speak, and at their prompting he delivered an impassioned speech advocating a tough policy in the interest of Rome. This meant the prisoner exchange was off. Out of sympathy for the speaker, and knowing what was at stake for him, many senators wavered, and would have given their assent to the Carthaginian petition, but Regulus dissuaded them. He forcefully maintained that the higher interests of the fatherland resided in staying the course.

Many friends and senators tried to persuade him to stay under the protection of Rome. This he refused: he had given his word. He went back to his captors and to a certain death.

It is recounted that the Carthaginians, feeling themselves betrayed, spared no cruelty in the execution of Regulus. The story goes that before putting him to death under terrible tortures, they blinded him. This act of unspeakable inhumanity was carried out in the following way: they cut off his eyelids, then threw the prisoner into a dark dungeon for some time, and suddenly brought him out to the intense light of the African sun. The enormously large solar fire, if we are to believe this story, put out the tiny ocular fire.

The Romans, irate at the way the enemy had treated their illustrious compatriot, retaliated by releasing two prominent Carthaginian prisoners into the power of the Regulus family. We may be sure, given the callousness of those times (when the blinding of prisoners with hot iron was an extended practice, and the appalling barbarity of the Roman circus was a sort of standard family entertainment), that the bereaved relatives must have fallen short of a compassionate use of the prisoners delivered to their discretion. It has also been said that the story of the refined cruelty of Regulus' execution may have been a fabrication tending to justify the subsequent Roman treatment of their prisoners of war.

It is warranted to suppose that once a man had breathed his

last, the ancients would conclude that the fire of his eyes was extinguished. But perhaps this was not so. Fire, as a divine element, was deemed eternal. Interestingly, the fanciful idea has occurred to a contemporary Italian writer, Guido Ceronetti,[36] that the refulgence of the eye is indestructible; that when a man dies and is buried, the light (the flame?) of his eyes is not extinguished, but is multi-fragmented, shared among the many creatures that invariably come to devour his body (". . . for when a man is dead, he shall inherit creeping things, beasts, and worms," says *Ecclesiasticus* 10, 11).

Therefore, I imagine the fire of the eye broken out into a myriad minuscule flames, parceled out into ever tinier brilliant points that travel in the jaws of ants, within the digestive system of worms, or in the bodies of maggots. Fireflies, of course, concentrate it abundantly. And when these creatures die, their luminous burden turns into dust and scatters as motes that swirl and gleam in the sun. But Ceronetti muses: "If a man is cremated, where does the light of his eyes end up? . . . flies don't live in a crematory, there are no ants . . ." Theophrastus had an answer to this question: the light of the eye is fire, and cremation joins fire to fire. Or, as he would put it, a bigger fire "destroys," *i.e.*, engulfs or absorbs a smaller one.

That daylight is an outpouring from the sun of the same kind of fire residing in the eye, was also proposed by Plato. In *Timaeus* (45b-46a), he asserted that daylight vision implies the issuing forth of ocular fire to meet the identical element of solar origin, and when this happens the fire of the eye meets that of the sun, "like to like, and coalesces with it."[37]

The no less fanciful idea that sight is the product of minute particles or atoms impressing the eyes and/or flowing out of them, keeps a strange appeal in our day. For, in effect, this theory characterized visual perception as a form of touch: eyesight was palpation at a distance. And who among us has not "felt," at least once, that someone was looking at him, or her, without knowing exactly how this realization came about? It is as if ectoplasmic hands, emerging from the pupils of the viewer, actually contacted the objects seen. For the gaze is more than visual perception. Some thinkers, like Merleau-Ponty, have discoursed of the synesthetic quality of sense perceptions. Musical sounds make some of us see colors; others "feel" the sound on their skin. Neurophysiology is more of a unity than traditionally taught, and the gulf that sunders the specialized senses is largely a cultural construct. This idea imposes itself every time we reflect that Western biomedical science was built by cleaving, slicing, cutting, dissecting or "anatomizing," since we find it easier to understand a complex mechanism by disassembling it or breaking it up into its component parts. "Analysis," that pillar of the scientific method, means just that (from the Greek *analyein*, to loosen, to dissolve).

I. The Material Power of Sight

In contrast to sight, touch is by nature "intimate." Touch abrogates the distance between object and subject that is congenial to sight. But also touch, unlike contemplation, is instrumental: one touches *in order to do* something: to grasp, to push, to pull, to test, to probe, to reject, or simply to caress. Hence the feminine complaint of lascivious gazes that pry, of glances that undress, or of hostile looks that challenge or provoke, and eyes that can singe, pierce, and sometimes kill. The girl upset at the insistence with which her boyfriend gapes and stares at the passing beauties knows this intuitively. She needs not to read Merleau-Ponty in order to conclude that all the man's protestations that "there is no harm in looking" are, strictly speaking, pure sophistry.

Nothing is more powerful, nor potentially more noxious, as Plutarch acknowledged, than the gaze in the lovers' eyes. Apparently, the violent commotions that originate in the genital glands find no easier exit than through the orbits and the ocular globes. Jonathan Swift brought to bear whimsical biomedical concepts to explicate the relationship of vision and libido: ". . . the spinal marrow, being nothing else but a continuation of the brain, must needs create a very free communication between the superior faculties and those below: and thus *the thorn in the flesh* serves for a *spur* to the spirit."[38]

Leonardo da Vinci, as an artist, was passionately interested in observation; as a scientist, he was just as keenly interested in the function of the eye. He did not subscribe to the Platonic theory that proposed an emanation from inside the eyes. In keeping with concepts derived from Aristotle, he used the term "species" to refer to images of things. These, he thought, were projected in all directions and in straight lines by the light rays, whose course they followed. In the *Codex Atlanticus*, Leonardo wrote: "The senses, when they received the species of things, do not send forth from themselves any power, but the air between the object and the sense incorporates in itself the species of things and by contact with the sense presents them to it."[39] Interestingly, despite this explicit denial of any "power" flowing out of the eye, the genial artist made an exception for "the beguiling power of a maiden's eyes."

Mark that the power of the eye was not thought to be an exclusively human attribute. It was shared with some animals, at least those with shining, staring, wide eyes. Montaigne says in his essays that he witnessed an example of this animal strength. He was at home when ". . . a cat was seen gazing up on a bird on top of a tree. And having fixed their sight steadily one against the other for a certain span of time, the bird let himself fall down as if dead between the cat's paws, either intoxicated by its own imagination, or pulled down by some attractive force in the cat."[40]

A particularly marked effect was discerned in the wolf's eyes. Pliny originally reported, in his *Natural History,* that if a wolf fixed his sight upon a man, this one lost the ability to speak, even if he was not aware that he was being observed.[41] Everyone repeated this strange notion, which became a commonplace in antiquity, and down to the seventeenth century. It is found in Virgil's *Bucolics* (IX, verses 54-55): *vox quoque Moerim iam fugit ipsa: lupi Moerim videre priores.* ("Moeris lost his voice: the wolves had seen him first."). Most major authors of past times, if they speak of the wolf, refer to the wolf's ability to deprive men from all utterance, and each time they quote Pliny almost verbatim. Conrad Gesner (1516–1567), the great Swiss naturalist and noted physician, claimed that it is only the "rustics," the ignorant and uncultivated, who adhere to this notion: *Rustici dicunt hominem vocem perdere, si lupus eum prior viderit.* ("The uncultured say that men lose their voice, if the wolf sees them first.")[42] But the fact is, he gives so many learned citations, that instead of combating, he seems to be actually promoting belief in the silencing power of the wolf's glance.

It was not until well into the seventeenth century that some scholars ventured to speak dismissingly of the lupine gaze and its alleged power to reduce the viewed to mutism. Sir Thomas Browne (1605–1682) was one of the skeptics. In his *Pseudodoxia Epidemica* (a book whose unwieldy complete title reads "*or, Enquiries into Very many received Tenets and commonly presumed truths*") written in 1640, he comments about such "an opinion that everywhere, except in England," is acknowledged as false. Sir Thomas Browne felt that the mentioned superstitious belief arose from the surprise and the silence that travelers invariably exhibit when they discover a pack of wolves watching them. A plausible source, since fright commonly gags its victims, and, the writer points out, may deprive them of the use of the voice forever. But let us note that, for all of the modern skepticism of our learned writer, he, like so many of his contemporaries, firmly believed in the existence of the "basilisk," a mythical creature said to be born from the egg of a seven-year-old cock hatched by a serpent, and whose glance and breath were fatal.

The lion merited a special commentary among the naturalists of yore. Pliny, once again, divulged the notion that this big cat's strength is concentrated in the eyes. In his *Natural History* (book VIII, ch. xxi, 54) he remarked that a Gaetulian shepherd, during the principate of Claudius, was able to subdue a lion by a method so simple that it was "almost one to be ashamed of for an animal of this nature." It consisted simply of flinging a cloak to a charging lion, so as to cover its head. To believe Pliny (which is something that cannot be recommended unreservedly), the trick became common in the Roman circus. As soon as the face of the lion was covered, even with a light wrap, the feline's otherwise frightful ferocity immediately abated. It is perhaps no coincidence that many centuries later, Conrad Gesner remarked that the lion is the only animal that is born with his eyes wide open, and that he keeps them open even while deeply asleep. ("*Leo dormit apertis oculis.*"[43])

Whether it be the silencing power of the wolf's glance, or the fascination lodged in the cat's eyes, or the "beguiling power of a maiden's eyes," or the harm ensconced in the "evil eye," or the energy residing in the eyes of the serpent and the turtle, that were once believed to hatch their eggs by the sole power of their glance; regardless of what form the legend takes, it always reflects the deeply seated belief of the elementary imagination, that the eyes have a material power. Not a purely psychological, unperceived or ethereal strength, but a tangible force that can act in the world and change things in everyday reality.

It is not surprising, then, that many have fancied that they could harness the power of the eyes, and direct it according to their wishes. They constitute a long list of naive dreamers, misguided simpletons, artful swindlers, disingenuous simulators, and more or less successful tricksters. A controversial figure, Franz Anton Mesmer (1734–1815), is worthy of note on account or his emphasis on the eyesight. This German physician thought he could activate a form of energy residing in us, the so-called "animal magnetism," largely by the power of his own eyes. Thus, although he passed into history fully immersed in the fuliginous cloud of a dubious reputation, many consider him a precursor of hypnotism, a therapeutic technique for which there are legitimate medical applications in our day.

Mesmer's methods relied largely on visual activity. The physician, almost always male, and his patient, most commonly female, started by looking long and fixedly into each other's eyes. Alternatively, the subject was instructed to concentrate her eyesight on other things, such as a candle's flame, or an oscillating pendulum. After some time, which could vary between a few minutes to more than an hour, the subject would enter into a "trance" or "coma," during which all sense perception was suspended. She had sunk into a complete unawareness of her surroundings. There were times at which the session terminated with the patient experiencing convulsive seizures. However, the subject could respond if addressed by Mesmer. Thenceforward, those who practiced his methods were known as "mesmerizers." Presumably, the patient's "animal magnetism" had been activated, a state that was supposed to foster health and well being, since, according to Mesmer's ideas, the body's energy had been channeled in such a way as to overcome the "obstacle" represented by disease.

The erotic overtones of the procedure are evident. There was a long and soulful look into each other's eyes. Then, there followed a most strange state of communion between male therapist and female subject. Mental communication made the patient aware of the mesmerizer's thoughts; on the physical plane, she shared his sense perceptions, while hers remained in suspension: she would taste the food he introduced into his mouth, or feel the contacts he experienced, in the corresponding part of her body. Furthermore, during the trance she had completely surrendered to him. He would guide her across imaginary travels, or she would otherwise respond to his commands obediently, betraying her marked suggestibility.

All of this did not sit well with the official medical establishment of the countries where Mesmer attempted to make a career. Expelled from Austria under the accusation of fraud, he settled in Paris in 1778, and for about six years enjoyed great privilege and prestige. But French physicians, like their Viennese colleagues, deeply distrusted his methods and the theories on which he professed to ground them. They complained to the king, Louis XVI, who appointed a commission of enquiry; this group counted in its membership two illustrious men, the American scientist-diplomat Benjamin Franklin, and the genial chemist Jean-Antoine Lavoisier. The commission concluded that Mesmer could not sustain his exaggerated claims, and once again the colorful physician had to leave in a hurry, this time to end his days in his native Germany. His influence, however, lasted a long time. Mesmer's ideas and techniques were the cause of a veritable "mesmerizing mania" in England during the nineteenth century,[44] and it seems appropriate to consider him a forerunner of hypnotism.

The ineffable power that emanates through the pupils has intrigued not only the eccentric, the impostors, and all manner of reprobates; it has also caught the fancy of well credentialed scientists. One of the most highly respected medical journals, *The Lancet*, published in Great Britain, but renowned throughout the world, published in 1921 an article that purported to demonstrate scientifically the force or ray emerging from the human eye.[45] This research was prompted, the author tells us, by a number of everyday observations, such as the fact that "the direct gaze or vision from one person soon becomes intolerable to another person." When two persons look directly at each other "it is a fact that after a few seconds the vision of one or the other will have to be turned away." More convincing perhaps, but unbecoming to a British scientist, would have been to adduce in his favor Leonardo's observation of "the beguiling power of a maiden's eyes." At any rate, with scrupulous attention to the scientific method, our man set out to objectively demonstrate the existence of a force stemming from the human eye.

To this effect, he builds a metal box, inside which he suspends a delicate solenoid made of fine copper wire and wound upon a celluloid cylinder. This solenoid hangs from a fiber of unspun silk, attached to which there is also a magnetized needle-like piece of steel. The function of this magnet is to keep the

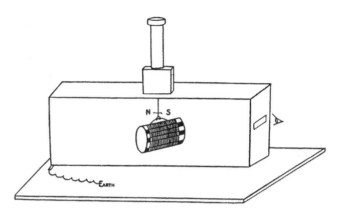

Figure 3. Instrument to detect the power of the eye to set objects in motion. The solenoid is suspended from a thread that comes down from the vertical tube. A magnetized needle oriented north-south (NS) presumably keeps the solenoid on a stable position. The observer's eye is indicated to the right.

suspended contraption at a fixed orientation, along the earth's meridian (since it will always be pointing in the direction of a compass's needle). The box is lined by aluminum sheet. The silk fiber is connected, through a conducting wire, to the aluminum of the box, which in turn is earthed. One end of the box is provided with an aluminum-screened window with a little slot for viewing. The results obtained are astounding:

If the human eye looks through the slot in the observing window and maintains a steady gaze at one end of the solenoid, the latter will be seen to start into motion, which is usually away from the observing eye. If the gaze be now transferred to the true center of the solenoid, the latter stops, and if the vision is now applied to the opposite end of the solenoid, the latter now moves in a reverse direction to that first induced. This maneuver may be repeated several times, each subsequent attempt being made only after the magnet has brought the solenoid to complete rest. Motion of the solenoid, though much reduced, was also obtained after interposing a column of water between the eye and the solenoid.

The researcher then describes a number of additional experiments in which variations and refinements of the described method are introduced, aiming to rule out spurious, non-visual factors that could account for the results. Did the solenoid move due to heat? Did static electricity have anything to do with the observations? What may be the effect of darkness? What possible role was played by electromagnetism? The author concludes that human vision "can distort the electrostatic state of an enclosed system." In other words, the "force" of the eye is real; it is not a figment of the poetical imagination. The nature of this force, however, remains enigmatic. The investigator remarks that there is electrical activity in the eye and surrounding structures: an electrical change in the retina accompanying vision; electrical changes also in the muscles intrinsic to the eye, such as the ciliary and the iris (for accommodation and pupillary contraction and dilatation), and in the extrinsic muscles that move the ocular globes. "Whether the fields from these sources are adequate to account for the effects cannot be answered at present."

Whatever one may think today of this research, it is still very rewarding to note the sagaciousness of design, the tireless pursuit of the answer, and the unflagging adherence to the strict scientific method. The question of the existence of a power in the eye is a question of fact, and therefore it is to be answered by science. Whether this is entirely answerable now is another matter. Today's scientists have other priorities, and many important things to elucidate before turning their attention to "the wounding power" in lovers' eyes.

Our enlightened times have ceased to believe in the evil eye, animal magnetism, and the multifarious expression of material ocular power. But, for all the advances in neurophysiology, our age still has to explain many reactions to the others' gaze. Not the least of these enigmas is why we feel uneasy when someone stares at us. The fixity of the eye upon us makes us apprehensive. It is as if a remote memory was stirring deep inside us; an atavistic remembrance of a danger sign that harks back to pre-history, when to be bracketed persistently into someone else's visual field meant that we were being watched by a predator; that some saber-toothed beast or some behemoth of a reptile was intently considering us for his lunch.

There must be a biologic explanation. What, if not a pro-found biologic mark, tells animals to beware of the staring eye? If there is imminent danger of being attacked by a dog, we are advised to remain immobile, and, above all, to avoid looking the animal in the eye. Expert primatologists observed that, to avert the terrible charge of a silverback, they had to cower to the ground, and especially to refrain from looking the gorilla directly in the eyes. For, more often than not, it is the sharp-eyed, undeviating, ocular focusing that is the premonition of deadly aggression.

It may be argued that there is no deep biologic reason at all; and that it is not the eye, but the whole countenance that makes us apprehensive. It is the knitted brows, the rigid facial folds, perhaps the whole bodily posture, which announce the poten-tial aggressor getting ready to attack. But if such were the case, we must explain why did natural evolution contrive to paint fake eyes on the body of some species, in order to deter preda-tors. For instance, the feathers of some birds, like the wings of some butterflies (brush-footed butterfly of Honduras, *Morpho* butterfly of Brazil and French Guiana) and moths (*Automeris*), display large, circular, eye-like spots, that appear to have no other purpose than to frighten away pursuers.

To the predator's voracious gaze, the prey somehow man-aged to oppose a contrary, mesmerizing, or intimidating gaze, as the lovers' eyes always manage to answer, to reply, and to engage each other in a mutual, highly nuanced, yet silent conversation.

In both, love and war, it is an eye for an eye.

That Perception is Tendentious

I N THE LOUVRE MUSEUM THERE IS A PAINTING ATTRIBUTED TO
Rembrandt that represents four human figures inside a par-
tially illuminated room. Three of these crowd together in
the better lighted area, thus enhancing the masterful treatment
of the light that is characteristic of that genial painter. Beamy
shafts of light irrupt into the place through the single open window; while away from it the shadows thicken, robbing the
objects in the room of all vivid coloration and sharp contours.

Of the three personages close to each other, one is a newborn
baby boy. His semi-naked body glistens, emplaced by the master
painter directly under the beam of light, and thus is made the
focal point of the composition. Next to him is his mother, who
bares her right breast and approximates it to the baby's mouth,
in readiness to nurse him. A dark-robed old woman (the grandmother?) is the third figure in this group. She approaches her face
to the infant and carefully removes a blanket from the child's visage, the better to lovingly contemplate his tender, innocent bliss.

Not far from this group, on the left, standing up and close
to the window, is the fourth personage. It is a man who appears
somewhat bent forward, as if performing some sort of manual
task, but we cannot tell exactly what, because his hands and
workbench lie hidden behind the trio formed by the baby and
the two adoring females. Although proximity to the window
imparts to the man's shirt a bright illumination, he remains a
subordinate figure, for he turns away from the viewer and

stands in a recessed plane with respect to the other personages. It is as if his function, apart from indicating by his presence that the limner meant to show us a complete family, were chiefly to reflect the light, using the back of his shirt as a reflecting screen.

It is especially interesting that this painting has been traditionally known by two names. Sometimes it is called *The Carpenter's Household*, and other times *The Holy Family*. In a brilliant essay, the contemporary writer Tzvetan Todorov[46] points out that our interpretation of this work of art will vary, depending on which title we know.

Figure 4. *The Holy Family*, also called *The Carpenter's Household*, by Rembrandt van Rijn.

If we take the first title as valid, we will see in this easel an example of the so-called genre painting, a representation of a scene of everyday life. This is the kind of painting that the Dutch brought to the forefront of artistic endeavor during the 17th century. Before that time, painters deigned to portray only the grandiose, the heroic, or the sublime: landscapes, the martyrdom of the saints, the legends of hagiography, and portraits of kings, sages, Church leaders, and wealthy aristocrats. Exalted subjects of this kind were considered worthy of the artist's brush. With the striking rise of the Netherlands to economic prosperity, scenes of the common life of the bourgeoisie acquired respectability. A girl in a poultry yard; a young woman playing the harpsichord in comfortable but not lavish surroundings; a village wedding; a rich bourgeois complacently sitting on the stoop of his house; a family at table, praying before a meal; all this, depicted realistically and not in a luxurious palatial setting, but in the lodgings of more or less well-off Dutch burghers, became the proper subjects of the most illustrious painters of the time. Genre painting had come into its own.

Thus, a viewer who looks at Rembrandt's easel and believes it is named *The Carpenter's Household*, will assume it is a painting of genre. The beholder's curiosity would be stoked in certain directions: he, or she, may wonder how a Dutch carpenter lived at that time, what his belonging to that trade meant to his family. A viewer knowledgeable in history might refer the painted figures to what he knows about the social stance of the trade guilds, the main political developments of the day, the artistic trends, and so on. The scene of domestic tranquility may seem to him to symbolize the virtues of work, industriousness, and profitable productivity.

However, if the viewer contemplates this painting under the impression that it is named *The Holy Family*, the evoked train of thoughts would be completely different. The image would be automatically linked to a set of Christian traditions. Instead of eliciting curiosity over the life of a carpenter or a member of any other guild, the interest would center on the manner in which the painter represented the divinity. For, in that case, the baby is not the offspring of a working man who hopes to see in him a continuator of his aspirations or the support of his old age, but is none other than the Son of God, the Redeemer of Mankind; and the beam of light is the radiance that descends upon his sacred person directly from the empyrean.

So it is that the painting will signify one thing when seen under a certain set of preconceptions, and another altogether when looked at under different assumptions. Now a genre painting, now a religious scene: the preponderant role of the mind in shaping our perceptions is evident.

A more vivid example of discrepant interpretations given to the same image comes to us from, of all places, the contemporary medical scene. It refers to a photograph taken in the operating room of Vanderbilt University Medical Center by a photojournalist who had been assigned to document a surgical operation for correction of *spina bifida* with *myelomeningocele*, a condition in which the spinal cord and its wrappings are exposed due to a defect of closure of the vertebral column. This is the commonest congenital anomaly of the central nervous system, and the cause of great suffering among the unfortunate children so affected and their families.

The circumstances surrounding this episode were noteworthy. The operation was to be performed in a fetus still within its mother's womb, at twenty-one weeks into the gestation. Although fetal surgery has been done for about three decades, the field is still sufficiently novel and controversial to deserve the attention of the media. Indeed, the question of whether to perform surgery on a healthy woman (the mother) poses a hefty ethical dilemma. Her body must be cut open; she will incur serious risks, and she will reap no benefit from the operation. The benefit is intended exclusively for the fetus in her womb, but even this is not certain. At the time, no child had been cured of the described anomaly, but the operating surgeons believed that the associated complications, often the cause of untold suffering and disability, were ameliorated in the majority of the patients. Still, the possibility remained of fetal death or prematurity.

Be that as it may, on the morning of August 19, 1999, a photojournalist for *USA Today* was admitted to the operating suite where Doctor Joseph Bruner and a team of neurosurgeons were attempting the delicate procedure. To gain access to the malformed bodily part, the surgeons must expose the maternal uterus, incise its wall, cut through the placental membranes, and in the process drain the amniotic fluid in which the fetus is normally immersed. The defect in the fetal body can then be treated. Next, everything must be sewn back and the fetus replaced in its original location, hoping that it will develop to the stage of fetal viability, as close to term as possible.

All this the surgeons proceeded to do, and the operation was successful. But, at a certain point in the surgical act, an incident occurred which was captured in a photograph that caused a worldwide sensation. A tiny hand, about the size of an adult's thumbnail, protruded through the incision in the uterine wall. This was, of course, an upper limb of the fetus being treated. The photographer immediately shot the picture with his camera. The fetal hand was palm down, its fingers slightly flexed, as is normal in a developing fetus. This allowed the chief surgeon to put one of his own fingers in the hollow of the fetal hand, which he raised once or twice, then gently tucked it back into the uterine cavity.

The incident is quickly told, and to the surgical team it was not unique, therefore not especially exciting. But to the photographer, who had never witnessed anything remotely resembling fetal surgery, and probably no other surgical operation, the sight of a little hand emerging from the open womb was most impressive. It was overpowering. In his words:

Samuel [this was to become the name of the baby] thrusts his tiny hand out of his mother's uterus. As the doctor lifts his hand, Samuel reacts to the touch and squeezes the doctor's finger. As if testing for strength, the doctor shakes the tiny fist. Samuel held firm. At that moment, I took this *Fetal Grasp* photo.

The effect that his photograph had on the large public was beyond description. Images of a child's small hand being held by the hand of a mature adult are endowed with a very strong suggestiveness: they call to mind the unceasing relay of generations, the passing along of life's burden of pains and joys from the senescent to the unfledged; they evoke the frailty of emerging life, and its need of sustenance and guidance by those further along on life's road. But the spectacle of the tiny hand of a fetus in juxtaposition to the surgeon's extended finger had an even greater power to stir people's emotions. This was partly due to the unaccustomed nature of the image: not many people are directly acquainted with the appearance of a human fetus, and therefore may have entertained vague or confused notions that were shattered by the unadorned reality of the photograph. For the truth is that at twenty-one weeks gestation the human form is already quite advanced, although some details are still rough-hewn: apart from its very small size, the proportions of bodily parts are still evolving, and the color of the skin is an eerie crimson red, due to the thinness of the epidermis, which allows the blood in the capillaries to be seen by translucency.

The dramatic photograph, which the editors suggestively called *Hand of Hope*, was reproduced in the media throughout the world. It was raised to the rank of those few, world-famous, emotion-laden images of unforgettable impact, such as: American infantry soldiers raising the flag in Iwo Jima; Spanish militiaman being mortally shot as he leaps into the air; naked Vietnamese girl running, mad with terror, from the incendiary devastation of napalm; or, more recently, aircraft crashing in a hellish ball of fire against the twin towers of New York City.

Needless to say, anti-abortion groups fully realized the power of this image, and promptly made it into a banner of their cause. Reportedly, the sight of the fetal hand emerging from its uterine shelter converted the photographer from pro-choice advocate to anti-abortion militant. His internet website[47] published a text in which the surgeon allegedly declared that when he felt the little hand grasping his finger "it was the most emotional moment of his life," an ineffable experience that left him momentarily "frozen, totally immobile." The mother, on her part, supposedly "wept for days" after seeing the picture.

A powerful image, we must allow, was one that could cause such a stir. It affected the photographer like an epiphany, not unlike the revelation of Saul on his way to Damascus; for he felt moved to date the crucial event at precisely the instant in which, in his own words (initially posted on his website), "the tiny hand reaches out of the womb to grab the finger of the surgeon . . . as if to say, 'thanks, doc, you did a wonderful job.'"

. But is it warranted to interpret the captured image this way? Can one really attribute intentionality ("reaches out to grab . . .") to the movements of a being who lacks a fully developed central nervous system? It seems highly unlikely that an inchoate human being, still secluded in the maternal environment and never having had a relational life, could express feelings of gratitude. But what if this was just a manner of speaking? What if we assumed that no well defined emotion was meant, but only some form of obscure reaction, a sort of ill defined human warmth, a primitive, sketchy response, the forerunner or antecedent of gratitude? Even this attribution to the fetus may be difficult to justify. The reason is that he was unconscious, and therefore insentient. As the surgeon declared when interviewed, the fetus and his mother were both anesthetized. This, of course, was necessary for the procedure. Neither could have felt anything at all.

The point is, what we see in the world depends on our desires, hopes, fixed attitudes, prejudices, and expectations. Even a photograph, which many suppose to be a "true and faithful" representation of objective reality—a snapshot that conveniently freezes for our inspection the perpetual flow of the world—is read differently by different onlookers. For some, like the nurses and physicians in the operating room, the fetal hand that protruded from the uterus has merely "flopped" outward, as fetal limbs not uncommonly do under the circumstances described. (Indeed, a comparable photograph, this one of a fetus at twenty-four weeks gestation, appeared in *Life* magazine.) For others, it is "reaching out" for help or to express gratitude. For some, the illustration graphically documents a brief moment, and a trivial one at that, in a technical step of a surgical procedure. For others, it symbolizes the helplessness of the unborn, and the heartlessness, nay, the moral depravity, of those who would decriminalize abortion.

Figure 5. Fetal arm and hand protruding through the incised uterus in the course of a surgical procedure on a fetal patient.

"A picture is worth a thousand words," declares a hackneyed saying. Mark, however, that the picture never *says* those thousand words. Words must come from outside the picture and sediment upon it: they are added to it by the men and women who comment on the image, and mantle it, so to speak, with discourse. Without the words, a photograph is an empty husk; a dumb sign that an event of some sort has taken place, or that something exists—or has existed—that looks like the image captured by the camera. Without its caption, a photograph means very little. It needs a context, if it is to signify anything. And the context is given by the words, which at the same time imprint a message on the image, and may thereby change its meaning wholly. "Strictly speaking," wrote Susan Sontag in her now classic work *On Photography*, "one never understands anything from a photograph." This is because real understanding is based on how a thing works, or at least what it does, not merely how it looks. Consequently: "Only that which narrates can make us understand."[48]

So much for the objectivity of vision and the impartiality of photographs!

But the mind can do much more than to induce diverging individual interpretations of the same object of visual perception. It can make us disregard the material things set in front of our eyes; and, conversely, it can make us accept as real what in fact is void and substanceless. In sum, our minds may blind us or delude us.

Hence, it may be thought that a vigilant attentiveness of mind suffices to dispel illusion; that, to chase away a mirage, it is enough to concentrate and to bring into sharp focus the things that impress the retina. But in this, as in all human activities, a just measure is essential. Apply too keen a viewing, devote excessive, protracted attention, and the result might be the opposite of that which was being looked for. This was the subject of one of Balzac's best known stories, "The Unfinished Masterpiece" (*Le Chef d'Oeuvre Inconnu*).

In this story, the action takes place in seventeenth-century Paris. Balzac chooses as protagonists two historical figures and one fictional. Of the former, the first is Franz Porbus (1570–1622), a court painter then at the peak of his celebrity, and whose fame as portraitist of royalty has come down to us. The second is Nicolas Poussin (1594–1665), depicted in the narrative as a fiery eighteen-year-old apprentice of the painter's art, ambitious and yearning for glory; in real life Poussin became arguably the greatest French painter of his time. The third personage is an entirely fictitious character, called master Frenhofer. He is a mysterious, semi-diabolical old man, the teacher of Franz Porbus, and presumably the possessor of precious technical secrets of his art, which he acquired in Germany as a disciple of Mabuse (1478–1503; original name Jan Gossaert). This Mabuse was a Flemish artist considered to be the first to introduce the style of the High Italian Renaissance into Germany and the Low Countries. He was a profligate drunkard who left no students. In Balzac's fiction, however, Frenhofer had formerly managed somehow to extract from him immensely valuable teachings: secrets on painting technique so precious, that by applying them faithfully he is able to elevate the pictorial art to unexcelled heights.

The writer recreates very effectively the atmosphere of seventeenth century Paris (although not without critics having pointed out some glaring anachronisms); at the same time, through the dialogues of his personages, Balzac makes an ostentatious display of his knowledge of painting and his esthetic preferences. His disdain of Rubens, for instance, is very much in evidence. Rubens's easels, says Frenhofer, are full of "mountains of Flemish meat, well powdered with vermillion, huge waves of red hair, and riotous dins of color." In contrast, Raphael (1483–1520), the Italian Renaissance master, inspires the old man (and Balzac as well, we may suppose) with a semi-religious reverence; at the mere mention of his name he removes his hat, and refers to him as "the king of art."

Poussin, the young apprentice, is very impressed by the
superior knowledge of draftsmanship that the mysterious
Frenhofer appears to have. All the more so upon seeing that his
friend Franz Porbus, a prestigious painter whom the young
Poussin greatly admires, seeks counsel from the old man,
alludes respectfully to his deep understanding of the philosophy
of painting, and suffers meekly the condescending, arrogant,
and even disparaging remarks that Frenhofer foists upon
Porbus's work.

One day, they visit together the old man's atelier. Poussin is
awestruck by the exquisite workmanship and superb skill evident in some paintings that are lying around, rather casually
thrown here and there. What seemed to him faultless master-
pieces Frenhofer discounts as mere sketches, careless slapdash,
or unfinished works still in need of much retouching. His truly
accomplished painting, Frenhofer now says, the easel that he
considers his most consummate opus, and on which he has
brought to bear all his long experience and the secret teachings
of the great Mabuse, is a female nude on which he has toiled
for a very long time. It has been seven years already since he
began putting his best efforts, and indefatigably perfecting this,
his most cherished work.

This sublime painting, this gem of meticulous technical execution and profound esthetic sensibility, is almost finished.
Alas, Frenhofer has been forced to stop the work, for lack of an
appropriate model. The woman he loved, and who initially had
posed for him, ceased to exist. By patient and tireless application over the years, the painter had actually composed an ideal
form, a figure of almost otherworldly beauty. Some details were
still missing, and although relatively trivial, Frenhofer was persuaded that a living model was needed to complete them.

Unfortunately, the master painter thought no woman sufficiently beauteous to pose as model; all who had been considered fell short of the standards that his mind, in its feverish and
protracted obsession, had set down, and which alone could

satisfy him. For years he had been patiently, lovingly, meticulously working on details; yet each time he concluded that a
model was absolutely indispensable. But such a model was
nowhere to be found. Therefore, the peerless masterpiece, having
been brought so very close to completion, remained unfinished.

Needless to say, Poussin burned of his desire to see the
painting. Vain hope: the old man allowed no one to see it.
Through the years, he had developed a sickly attachment to it,
a pathologic jealousy, as if instead of a painting it was a real
woman, his mistress, whom she kept concealed from other
men's glances. "She is mine. Mine only. I have given her so
much of my life! No one will ever part us." This is how
Frenhofer spoke of his painting. The very few times his two
friends were allowed to visit his shop, they found the painting
carefully secluded in a corner, and well guarded by a screen.
Young and impetuous, Poussin once managed to cast a brief,
surreptitious glance behind the screen, in the direction of the
easel, only to find it completely covered by a thick, dark cloth.

Poussin had, in his turn, a real, flesh-and-blood mistress of
semi-legendary beauty; her physical perfection was the talk of
all Paris. Would the master judge her worthy of posing for the
unfinished painting, that at last it be carried to full fruition?
Obsessed with the idea of being able to examine at his leisure
Frenhofer's supreme masterpiece, and in the process learning
the ineffable secrets of its execution, Poussin conceived a plan.
He would persuade his lover to pose for the old painter, who
then would be able successfully to complete the portrait on which
he had spent so many years of intense toil; and, in exchange,
Frenhofer would allow him, Poussin, to see it.

He introduces his mistress to the old painter, who is capti-
vated by her matchless physical beauty. The two artists soon
strike a deal. The young woman is to pose naked for Frenhofer.
The work of many years would thus be finished. The old
painter would enjoy the indescribable delight of watching the
loftiest production of his career become at last a reality. In pay-

ment of which, he would unveil the sublime composition to Poussin's avid and unhindered inspection.

Poussin's beautiful mistress is not easily persuaded to pose. She doubts the authenticity of a passion that so easily acquiesced to her exposing herself naked to the gaze of another man, albeit an old man and an artist. Her lover, however, represents to her that he is asking this for the sake of his future glory as a painter, and their common happiness. For he is sure that just to see the masterful work will deliver to him rare technical secrets that no one else in the world, besides Frenhofer, is privy to. Secrets of brushwork, toning, composition, and atmosphere that only the late Mabuse possessed, and that threatened to remain forever inaccessible to the world once his only pupil passed away.

The woman resists, but, while in the old man's atelier, she spots her lover watching spellbound one of the paintings found there, and realizes the intensity of his calling. "He never looked at me that way," she says. Poussin declares that if she is bothered that much by the idea of posing, he is quite willing to abandon his plan. This renunciation on his part softens the belle, who hints at the possibility of yielding to his wish. He then declares passionately that while she poses, he will be waiting by the door, a few steps away, dagger in hand. And that, if the old painter dared the slightest attempt against her honor, all she had to do was to scream for help: he would rush in, and stab the offender immediately, no questions asked. Upon these passionate expostulations, she consents to pose for the unfinished masterpiece.

They do as planned. She disrobes in front of Frenhofer. Poussin waits by the door, where he stands listening attentively, armed with a dagger and accompanied by Porbus, the two of them looking like a pair of conspirators about to carry out a political assassination. And the old master sets to work on the completion of the work that had cost him years of useless straining and frustration.

At last, the moment of revelation arrives. The masterpiece is finished. Porbus and Poussin are admitted to the old master's inner sanctum. They approach the much-vaunted easel, while Frenhofer keeps extolling the genial draftsmanship he displayed, and the felicitous solution he had found for the problems of composition and coloring that had vexed him for so long. Then, amidst great expectation and suspense, he approaches the canvas, removes, trembling, the thick cloth that covered it, and . . . surprise! To the utter perplexity of the witnesses, the masterpiece is nothing but a chaotic mass of colors.

Instead of drawing they see lines arrayed in incomprehensible scrawliness; instead of coloring, a disorderly mixture of spots of all tints; instead of design, an unintelligible assemblage of daubed, scumbled, and rubbed oil paints. The only element of portraiture is the depiction of a human foot in a corner of the canvas, presumably the last addition that the old artist had appended thereto.

Poussin and Porbus look at each other in consternation, and don't know what to say. At length they must voice their concern: "There is nothing!" And this statement seems to shake Frenhofer into the brutal realization of what was actually happening. He looks at his canvas and repeats with newly acquired clarity of vision the unforgiving assessment: "There is nothing! There is nothing here . . . Seven years I toiled day and night. All for nothing . . ." The two friends and the beautiful model leave the old painter's atelier. Frenhofer stays alone, sunk in despondency.

Then, in a melodramatic finale that must have been very much to the taste of his nineteenth-century readers, Balzac writes that the next day Parisians learned in horror that Frenhofer had committed suicide, having previously destroyed all his easels by setting fire to his house.

A superficial interpretation of this story may say it is a warning against excessive concentration. Obsessive attention to one subject to the exclusion of all else is counterproductive. What is viewed in this manner is not viewed well; for instead of enhancing the quality of our vision, too close and overly detailed a peering tends to blur the objects we see. Thus an immoderate will to see deforms our perception, and the distortion may be extreme.

In the realm of esthetics, however, a modern critic could argue that a painter is not restricted to copying the visible world; that the artist's role goes beyond mimesis; and that we expect artists to give us new insights, sometimes at the cost of disregarding traditions, rules, and the most cherished artistic canons. In this view, the "unknown masterpiece" described in Balzac's story may have been a true masterpiece, notwithstanding its having impressed two unprepared viewers as a hopeless jumble of colors. In a word, Frenhofer was ahead of his time: he had gone from figurative to abstract art. By long and obsessive concentration on his model, he could have conceived the theretofore unimaginable idea of representing the inside and the outside of her body, or her body and her soul, or her skin and her mucus membranes, or whatever other mightily clashing, unrepresentable elements his feverish artistic mind may have induced him to try to capture. The result of such clash, as Roland Barthes said when explicating the work of a contemporary abstract painter, may be "shrill noise." But it is no less respectable art.

However, the story takes place long before there was any talk of abstract art. The debate about figuration in art (a polemic much older than generally acknowledged) took then a different form and was particularly intense at the time when the action of the narrative supposedly unfolded. The central, hotly debated issue was whether the drawing or the coloring ought to reign supreme in pictorial representation. Ardent advocates of one or the other have existed ever since painting became a recognized art form. Drawing is the intellectual skeleton of the painting; it determines the subject, it establishes the plan or design of the work. Coloring is what imparts life, beauty, and atmosphere to what otherwise would be cold, lifeless forms.

Color is ornament, and without ornament art cannot soar, claimed some. But ornament, others replied, is supposed to enhance the beauty of form, not to dominate it. It was meant to show, not to be shown itself. Painters in the time of Poussin compared the wise use of color in their compositions with the use of cosmetics by women. Rightly used, cosmetics enhance the appeal of a woman's charms, but used excessively they hide her beauty and may transform her visage into a grotesque mask. As with colors, so with words: in poetry and rhetoric, an abuse of metaphors and literary conceits far from clarifying an idea render it obscure and confusing. Beauty, therefore, needs balance and harmony; break these, and that one shall vanish.

Feminine makeup is an apt simile: too much rouge on the cheeks conceals any attractiveness that may exist elsewhere; apply too strident a tinct on the lips, and all else recedes, wanes, and is bedimmed. It is the same with eyesight. Excessive focusing on a single object blurs its surroundings: the object of vision stands out while its context is obfuscated and blurred. This property of normal vision was the subject of a vignette owed to the ancient Chinese Taoist philosopher Lieh-tzu, who may have lived in the third or fourth century B.C., but of whose very existence, enshrouded in the mist of many centuries, some scholars have doubted.

In this anecdote, we are told of a man from the town of Tse, greedy for gold. This was all he could think of. One morning, he wakes up at dawn, dresses in a hurry, combs his hair, and goes to the market, wistfully anticipating that he could at least see the precious metal on the counter of merchants and changers. Once there, our man approaches the table of one such business man, and, without further ado, grabs the gold and runs away.

In the midst of a crowded market, there is not much chance of escaping by a 100-yard dash. The man is apprehended. The officer who arrested him is no little intrigued by the impudence of the thief. He cannot help asking him: "How did you decide to grab the gold in full view of so many people?" To which the man answers in all candor: "When I grabbed the gold, I could no longer see the people. All I saw was the gold."

As the mind can blur or distort reality, so can it preserve and reconstruct the objective world. The "mind's eye" has the power to retain unaltered what the eyes of the face once saw. However, this ability varies greatly from person to person. Who has not wondered at the retentive powers of visualization of some famous chess players? Some have been able to engage in seven or eight simultaneous games, and this while playing blindfolded. Some of the names were consigned to the records of past generations. Paul Murphy, an American, astounded the public with feats of this kind in the nineteenth century. Blackburne and Zukertort could play, blindfolded, up to twenty games, and win at least eighty percent of them. The "mind's eye" in these individuals was of unexcelled acuity and retentive strength. They were able to represent in their minds the chessboards, clearly and distinctly, to the point of recalling not just the position of the game pieces, but their detailed appearances: whether they were made of wood, stone, or other material, as well as their particular shape, carving, color, and sundry other features.

This faculty—the strength, so to speak, of visual memory—was made a subject of scientific study by Sir Francis Galton (1822–1911), a cousin of Charles Darwin, fervent advocate of the scientific method, and a convinced proponent of eugenics. In a pioneer monograph devoted to this question, he concludes that there is marked individual variability in the vividness with which objective reality can be called forth mentally, and that this ability is inheritable.[49]

Galton asked his subjects in the evening to think of their breakfast table as they sat down to it in the morning, and to consider the picture that arises in the mind. A very wide gamut of answers was elicited, ranging between the highly vivid and the piteously dim. Some persons could see all the objects on the table with great detail, as clearly and brightly as if they were actually in front of them. "I could draw [the objects evoked]" was the answer of some subjects belonging in this cohort. Their mental image appeared to correspond to reality in all details.

In other persons studied, this faculty attained only a mediocre degree. Their mental representation was clear in some aspects and fuzzy in others. The brightness of the evoked scenario fell short of the original, or the image appeared bright at first, but was bedimmed by focusing attention in some aspects of it. A typical answer of persons in this group was: "I can recall a single object, or a group of objects, but not the whole table at once."

Lastly, in another group of study subjects, the "mind's eye" was notoriously weak. Objects were obscure, indistinct, utterly blurred, and far from comparable to the reality. Although persons in this category might be able to give an accurate account of the breakfast fare, yet they were incapable of mentally shaping a pictorial representation of the same. A typical answer from an individual in this cohort was: "I am rarely able to recall any object with distinctness. I have a generalized idea of the object, but not an individual one." At the extreme, a subject in this group avowed: "My powers are zero. To my consciousness there is almost no association of memory with objective visual impressions. I recollect there was a table, but I cannot see it."

If we are to believe Galton, the mental ability that he studied is subject to improvement with adequate training. However, it turned out that, paradoxically, the faculty was least developed in the most highly educated; and conversely, it manifested unusual vigor in the least educated of his subjects. Presumably, the mental power of pictorial representation wanes among thinkers: those who exert themselves at handling abstract ideas and symbols, suffer of atrophy in respect to the capacity of "seeing" concrete things with the mind. Much book learning, Galton concluded, smothers the ability to produce vivid mental images. This faculty was at its lowest in scientists and philosophers, and keenest in children, unschooled adults, and individuals in preliterate societies.

The power of the mind's pictorial representation has been exploited in literature. The German writer Stefan Zweig (1881-1942) used his extraordinary powers of character depiction to describe a man in whom the mentioned faculty attains a supreme degree. This is the central theme of Zweig's beautiful short story entitled "The Invisible Collection."

In the story, an elderly collector of drawings and engravings from the European masters loses his eyesight and is reduced to poverty. He lives amidst hardships and privations, but clings tenaciously to his art collection. It is his most precious possession. All his hopes for a better future for his wife and daughter, the only two persons that accompany him in his old age, lies there. For sixty years he did away with luxuries; abstained himself from the least indulgence; renounced his little pleasures; shunned beer, tobacco, the theater; all for the sake of keeping his precious collection. But he is persuaded that the prolonged sacrifice was worth it. For he knows that when he finally passes away, the art collection will have a very high price, and will enable his loved ones to live a life of affluence. This is the considerable bequest that he plans to leave in the hands of the two women.

Meantime, he has become utterly blind. He lives in a small hamlet, hardly ever receiving visitors. Oftentimes, he draws out the container with the rare prints, drawings, and engravings that he cannot see any more, but reconstructs in his mind as his fingers lovingly caress the surface of the paper. He "sees" each one of them most vividly, although not with his extinct, useless eyes. And, since he knows exactly the order in which they lie, he can recreate himself and enliven his weariness by the evocation of every detail, while his fingers glide over the surface of the papers. From this activity he draws consolation and solace in his old age.

There is only one problem: the papers are blank. The collection does not exist any more. His wife and daughter were forced to sell the works of art, one by one, in order to survive through wars, famines, and periods of grievous scarcity. To spare him from despair, they replaced the sold items with blank papers and cardboards of the same size and consistency as those containing the artworks. But the old gentleman does not know this. He keeps "seeing" his beloved drawings and engravings as keenly and distinctly as when his eyesight was normal.

An old acquaintance, who is also an art collector, appears at the old man's home. The visitor is searching for a rare piece of artwork, and has reason to believe it may be in the old man's possession. He thinks he can probably buy it from him at a bargain price, since the old man, in his retiring and isolated existence, is likely to be ignorant of its worth in the current art market.

The two women of the household draw the visitor aside and tell him the truth: the piece he is looking for is no longer there, it was sold long ago. But the old man is delighted to have a fellow art connaisseur come to his domicile and share in the joy of inspecting his much-vaunted collection. He invites his caller to sit by him while he explains the particulars of each item.

In a most touching narrative, Stefan Zweig describes the profound emotion and bewilderment of the newcomer, who sees the old man draw the blank pieces of cardboard, caressing them lovingly as if they were so many living beings, carefully set them out, and then describe the nonexistent drawings and engravings, one by one. The blind old man's face is illuminated by an ineffable joy that lifts his spirits as he evokes the artistic renderings in prolix detail. And all the while the two women stand by his side, "like the female saints that one sees in old prints and woodcuts, ecstatic over the tomb of the resuscitated."

The visitor echoes the old man's comments. The more he professes to coincide in his assessments with the blind collector's praiseful observations, the more the withered old face of the latter relaxes and takes on an expression of jovial cordiality. He feels buoyant, energized, supremely happy to be able to share the delights of his love of art with someone who is, like himself, an informed appraiser and a genuine art lover. He seems rejuvenated by at least thirty years.

The visitor leaves profoundly moved. For a couple of hours he had "restored sight to a blind man, by knowingly lying and contributing to maintain a pious hoax." He had arrived with the uncharitable idea of acquiring, by means of shrewd negotiation, a rare artistic specimen at an unfairly low price. He did not get it, but in exchange he had acquired something truly inestimable: the realization that men can live with an undying veneration for art, and devote their entire lives to a spiritual ideal. He left the old man's home feeling "somewhat humiliated, without knowing precisely why."

In the usual, agitated tenor of our daily existence, we tend to forget this. But certain exceptional beings remind us, now and then, that when the eyes of the face are extinguished, and the outer world blacks out, the human mind activates its own, eyeless optical powers, ordinarily neglected or ignored. These resources include a magic lantern that, when successfully turned on, can project an inner spectacle for our private and consoling contemplation.

Specular Vision: Three Ways
of Looking at the Mirror

I. Through Distorting Glass Mirrors, Darkly

WE HAVE ALL FORGOTTEN HOW IT FELT WHEN, AS CHILDREN, we saw for the first time an image of ourselves reflected on a mirror. Some psychiatrists attribute much importance to this discovery; Lacan [50] has called it "the mirror stage" of the individual, and proposed for it a fundamental role in the formation of the ego. Presumably, this process takes place when the infant still lacks complete control of his bodily movements, between the ages of six months and eighteen months.

We were too young to recall that first experience. But to look at a mirror and receive a total representation of our physique, is something fundamentally intriguing and deeply troubling. For experience insistently told us, and biology later taught us, that we are unique; that each one of us is irreplaceable in his, or her, singularity; that there is not, there has not been, and there shall never be, another person quite like us. (The apparent exception of identical twins cannot shake our conviction: striking as their physical resemblance may be, parents or custodians soon learn to distinguish the marks of individuality.) But the mirror gives the lie to all the reiterations of experience, and confounds all the neat theories of biology. The mirror is implacable: it asserts once and again that we are not unique, that we actually have a "double" that is physically identical, in every respect and to every shade of detail, to ourselves.

Of course, this double does not live in quite the same plane of objective reality as ourselves. Our "double" exists in opposition to our real self, but it belongs in the world of shadows and insubstantial presences, the world of souls and ghosts. Like them, it first came into being in the reflecting surfaces of ponds, lakes, wells, or polished metals—the natural forerunners of that technological artifact that later became known as a "mirror." Nor is the ethereal quality of our reflection without importance. It gave rise to the notion, apparently common in primitive societies, that the reflection on the water is akin to, or identical with, the soul.

A widespread custom in southern Italy drapes all the mirrors in black cloth after a death has occurred in the household; or else the mirror is turned around, its reflecting surface against the wall. This may express a desire to solemnize the bereavement, and to mark with a note of gravity the loss of a dear person. For the mirror also has the metaphoric meaning of vanity. It is the tool commonly used to preen and compose one's physical self; and intuitively we feel that the tools of conceit or vainglory, like the desire to be attractive to others, should have no place in a household in mourning. But underlying these facile explanations is the negative value that the mirror has to the elementary imagination, as the trap that captures or enthralls the human soul about to take flight to the beyond.

A reflecting surface is a trap for the soul. Just so birds were ensnared by their own reflection in ancient times. According to Aelian,[51] basins full of oil used were arranged for jackdaws in flight to spot. These birds' friendly nature was the root cause of their destruction. Perching on the vessel's rim they saw their own image reflected on the oil, and mistook the reflection for a living member of their species. Given that jackdaws are eminently sociable, this feathered fellow they wished eagerly to join. This is why they went down flapping their wings, and in the process covered themselves with oil, so that they remained unable to fly up again, as if fettered, "though neither net nor trap had caught them."

A soul that tarried after death must have been suspected upon the passing away of Marguerite Yourcenar, contemporary French writer and a naturalized American. When she breathed her last in Bar Harbor, Maine, one of the persons present opened the window of the room where she lay awaiting her last hour. It is said that this was done to reproduce the gesture that Yourcenar had made upon the death of her companion, Grace Frick, and for the same avowed purpose: to let the newly freed spirit soar to heaven without hindrance.

The soul, like the shadow or the reflected image, is the *alter ego* that haunts the individual, "like a subtle and ever conjured away death" in the words of Jean Baudrillard.[52] Does this "ever conjured away" mean that death is chased away by some magic rite? Hardly. Baudrillard adds that "when the double materializes, when it becomes visible, it signifies an imminent death."

Baudrillard, a Parisian intellectual, speaks for the men he knows. His ominous interpretation seems to apply only to individuals in industrialized societies. A closer, more intimate relationship seems possible in so-called backward or underdeveloped communities. The "double" here is corporeal, and apt to enter into continuous symbolic interchanges with the "real" self. Italian anthropologists reported that among the Huave, a population of Mexico's Isthmus of Tehuantepec, the individual is said to have a double referred to as "*tono*." This may be the living, familiar figure of death. The relation of man and *tono* may be happy or sad, but in any case it is personal and concrete; real exchanges—of words, gestures, and rituals—take place. Such a rapport cannot be defined as a form of "alienation," and therefore differs radically from the idea of an individual's "double" in a highly industrialized society.[53]

How different are things in the so-called "developed" or "advanced" world! If a man constructs his *Doppelgänger* here, it has to be in the context of alienation and mental derangement: the individual's person splits only when the psyche has crumbled. "Civilized" and "primitive" doubles are both configured as specular realities, but the latter thrives in the realm of normal, everyday life, and the former originates from alienation and schizophrenia. This is why in highly developed societies only those writers concerned with the morbid, shadowy aspects of the psyche (themselves somewhat unbalanced, and perhaps able to find in their mental instability the source of their genius) have best exploited the theme of the double. One of these was Edgar Allan Poe, with a short story entitled "William Wilson" (1839). The other one was Feodor Mikhailovitch Dostoevsky, with a story appropriately called "The Double" (1842).

In Poe's narrative, William Wilson is a man haunted by a mysterious personage uncannily like him. He meets him first as a boy, while attending an English boarding school. Poe, born in America, and an orphan since very young age, was reared by a man who sent him to England (1815–1820), where he attended Manor House School at Stoke Newington. He may have used his childhood reminiscences in the school's depiction. Although his youthful environment was a far cry from the sumptuously luxurious ambiance that his prose so skillfully evokes, Poe's attention to detail is key to his successful renderings. His recreation of the boarding school's atmosphere is a remarkable example of this ability.

The story is narrated in the first person. A young boy strikingly similar to him in physiognomy, and also surnamed Wilson, registers at the school. Predictably, but much to the main protagonist's aggravation, boys at that learning establishment soon begin to take them for brothers. However, he feels an intuitive dislike for this youth, who seems constantly to oppose his plans and thwart his mischievous undertakings. For William Wilson is an impenitent, naughty, and knavish fellow. But his misdealing is consistently foiled, and his evil-doing stubbornly resisted by his namesake, who, strangely, appears to resemble him physically more and more as time passes.

Through perfidious scheming, William Wilson succeeds in getting rid of his opponent, who is expelled from the school. However, odd, fortuitous coincidences bring the two together at utterly unpredictable junctures. William Wilson seems doomed to meet his double over and over, and finds him invariably committed to counter his wishes.

The mischievous boy grows into adulthood steeped in vice; the passage of years turns him into a contemptible villain. One day, he is in a luscious casino, where he is about to win a fortune by causing the ruin of a gentleman in a game of cards. Our man has not balked at using all sorts of artful trickery to deceive his opponent and win the game. At the very acme of the game, when the duped victim has just waged and lost his entire fortune and gloomily confronts his ruin; when, choused as much by the swindler as by the rashness of his own actions, he despairs and contemplates suicide; at that very moment a mysterious personage appears in the premises. Who would that be, but Wilson's Nemesis, his persecutor and double.

In dramatic fashion, the baffling look-alike proceeds to publicly expose the cozening by which William Wilson had won the card game. Needless to say, the cheat is confounded: not only is he forced to restore his ill-gotten gain to the victim, but he is humiliatingly expelled from the casino. He is left angered, perplexed, frustrated, and reviled, while his denouncer disappears from the scene as mysteriously and unexpectedly as he had come.

Henceforward, in the heart of the shamed rogue burns a low flame of hatred for his untiring double. He cannot explain why his mirror-like replica follows him about, or how does he manage to materialize at critical moments, invariably to thwart his malfeasance and undo his every plan. But this he knows, that he cannot suffer the interferences any longer. When, on the occasion of a costume ball in Venice, the *Doppelgänger* appears before him once more, the slow fire of his hatred blazes into an all-consuming flame. In a fit of murderous fury, he provokes a fight, and fatally stabs his perpetual follower.

Just as his foe slumps in bloody agony, William Wilson is overcome by a new terror. He suddenly realizes the enormity of his crime. From that baneful day, he will live haunted by the memory of his victim, whose semblance is so much like his own, and which vividly rises before him at every moment, now a horrid specular image drenched in the blood of his wounds.

A facile interpretation, but one that surges naturally in the mind, is that William Wilson's double is nothing but a metaphoric representation of a man's conscience, that "inner double" that tenants the bottom reaches of our mind, there to take up the function of judge of our actions and motives. This "double" is the stern judge whose orders to conform to moral law we can disregard only to our great individual peril.

Such an interpretation cannot be applied to Dostoevsky's short story, "The Double." This work was first published in the Russian magazine *Fatherland Notes* on January 30, 1846, scarcely two weeks after another story of the same author, *Poor People*, had appeared in a different publication.

Not a symbolization of our moral faculty to discern right and wrong, but a clinical history of a mentally disturbed man, *The Double* courses amidst the impersonal, crushing machine of St. Petersburg's bureaucracy in the nineteenth century. Here, lost in the labyrinth of offices, chancery corridors, and reams of papers; waiting in ante-rooms, and walking in seemingly endless halls; forlorn in the midst of civil servants' intrigue; ground to insignificance by the ponderous, pitiless environment of the administration; we discover Yakov Petrovich Golyadkin.

Because there is precious little human warmth or authentic interpersonal fellowship in his environment, Golyadkin retreats gradually into ever greater isolation. In his solitude, he feels menaced from all sides; and this paranoiac feeling actually forces him to live in a cellar, like an animal burrowing into the ground. He says he would like to disappear, "to vanish from sight." In a way, he is Dostoevsky's first personage "from the Underground."

We are witnesses, first, to the effraction of his personality, then to the wasting away of its faculties, and then, perhaps as a bizarre defense mechanism, to the splitting into two of that injured, enfeebled personality. It is as if it were trying to regenerate by budding and reduplication, like a polyp or a hydra, or any of those biologic beings of low position in the evolutionary scale that reproduce by a simple "copy-and-paste" genetic process.

When, outside of his office, he comes across his superior, Andrey Filipovich, he becomes anguished. He deliberates whether to greet him or not; or whether it might be best "to pretend that I am not really me, that I am someone completely different, though strikingly like me . . ." Fleeing from the machinery that pulverizes his humanity, his mind resorts to the magical expedient of self-regeneration by *amitosis* or simple fission, like a bacterium. Indeed, the psychiatric interpretation given by some analysts to mental phenomena of this sort is that, by "duplicating" himself (or others), a patient displaces the inner disintegration to the Other. Thus, the patient feels himself at least partly freed from conflict.[54]

Unlike Poe's romantic-Gothic narrative, with its macabre and pathological elements cloaked in an elegant, sumptuous, and somewhat baroque prose, Dostoevsky's narrative is related to the psychological novel, a moving rendition of the genesis of madness. He is uniquely apt as the limner of mental illness, because he himself had first hand experience with this, or at least the approaches to this condition. Biographers tell us that during the writing of *The Double*, Dostoevsky seemed like a Golyadkin prototype. He evinced the same mood swings from self-contempt to exaggerated self-sufficiency; the same mistrustfulness bordering on paranoia; the same childish hypersensitivity. As sometimes happens with intensely creative artists, his identification with his personage was so complete, that the border between creature and creator was blurred: the two became indistinguishable from one another.

In 1846, the year of publication of *The Double*, Dostoevsky spoke of being tormented by anxiety and melancholy, which intensified after that story was ill received by the critics. The strain of intense concentration during the writing of two works, *The Double* and *Poor People*, was apparently too much for his health's integrity. It is recounted that his doctor encountered him on a cold St. Petersburg day on Senate Square, and was struck by his appearance: out in the Russian winter without a hat, his frock coat unbuttoned, his jacket threadbare, and being helped along by some office clerk. Upon seeing the physician, he screamed with all his might: "There is one who will save me!" It is reactions of this kind that led an authoritative biographer to write: "All of Dostoevsky's heroes are flesh of his flesh, and their respective fates aid us in unraveling the enigma of their author."[55]

Was the identification with his personage so great as to make one suspect that Dostoevsky actually *saw* his own double? We do not know for sure, but some creative artists presumably had this experience. Goethe and Maupassant reportedly did; the latter described vividly a hallucination episode in his story *Lui* (1884), and most ominously in *Le Horla*. It is not idle to recall that Maupassant suffered from syphilis, probably congenital, and that the recurrent theme of madness in his stories may reflect a preoccupation with his own deteriorating mental health. It is thought that perfectly normal persons, under the effect of severe anxiety, overwhelming fear, or toxic states (which, of course, may be accompanied by fear of impending death), may perceive their own double.

Other writers have used the theme of the double. Elias Canetti (1905–1994), winner of the Nobel Prize for Literature in 1981, described the *Doppelgänger* as a premonition of doom in his novel entitled *Auto-da-fé*. Prosper Mérimée, in *The Souls of Purgatory*, has Don Juan, the famous Spanish sinner, witness his own cadaver being led in a funeral procession in a memorable, eerie scene most effectively recounted. More recently, the great

Portuguese writer, José Saramago, winner of the 1998 Nobel Prize in Literature, published a novel entitled *The Duplicated Man* (*O Homem Duplicado*, in the original Portuguese).[56] This engrossing book reads like a mystery novel. A history professor accidentally discovers that there is another man, identical to him in every respect, down to birthmarks and scars, living in the same city. Although the idea is quite simple, the narrator intrudes with his cogitations and Kafkaesque asides (Kafka is, in fact, the author to which Saramago is most often compared). With light, cynical touches and characteristic bittersweet humor, the author succeeds in outlining the fundamental problems that relate to our personal identity: who are we; what defines the core of our persons; what would happen if our most distinctive features were reproduced in someone else; and what if we were actually interchanged with that "someone else."

Are these "duplicated" personages merely figments of the outlandish imagination of writers? By no means. It is perhaps a hackneyed commonplace, but it is no less true, that "reality exceeds or surpasses fantasy." Those who through personal misfortune or professional obligation must have intimate commerce with the mentally deranged, know that the haunting nightmare of the "double" is for some individuals a terrifying reality. They may actually see their own double, a distressing symptom that has been called "the Golyadkin phenomenon."[57] It is a striking example of the vulnerability of the human mind, and one of the ill understood "delusions of misidentification," in which the self and others are misidentified. Either the physical makeup or the psychologic identity are incorrectly identified. That form of delusion in which the afflicted see their own double has been called *autoscopy* or *heautoscopy* in the specialized terminology.[58, 59, 60] An example drawn from the psychiatric literature, one among many that have been reported, is as follows.

A middle-aged draughtsman from a working class background, unmarried, had been well until he was twenty-seven years old. Notwithstanding the pressures of an economically deprived family, he had done reasonably well in school, and was described by his acquaintances as generally pleasant and well liked, albeit a bit overconscientious. Then, following his mother's death, he began having bizarre ideas of bodily disintegration: he said he felt his nose was "continually dilating," and that his testicles were "frozen solid," threatening to break into pieces, and moving into his abdomen. He actually had somatic hallucinations, which led to a diagnosis of schizophrenia. Under appropriate drug therapy, the psychotic episode resolved after two months. However, he manifested difficulty sleeping, tardy arrival at work, and became progressively withdrawn.

He then suffered the death of his father, and this apparently triggered the first encounters with his double. This he described as "not unlike looking and being in the mirror at the same time." His double began accompanying him everywhere. "It" would enter in a room with him, but would sit on a different chair. They traveled by bus together, and commonly shared the same emotions; on occasion, both would have suicidal ideas. The patient could hear himself, *i.e.*, his double, talking. Strikingly, he saw himself, and *felt* himself in two places at the same time. Although he was perplexed by this experience, he talked about it in a flat tone. According to his treating physicians, he never had any true insight into the abnormal nature of the phenomenon. All the while he continued having bizarre ideas about his body, which he believed was "coming apart." He expressed fear that his testicles would fragment or "explode into many pieces," and a milky fluid would spill into the environment.

Remarkably, his double experienced a change in nature that the psychiatrists correlated to the effects of the therapy. Whereas before "it" had been perceived as real, solid, concrete, and tridimensional, it now became vaporous and transparent, "like a cloud." However, the patient continued to feel that this double followed him constantly. No longer was the *Doppelgänger* a simple companion; now, it was more like the man's shadow, immediately behind him and possibly attached to his back. He began to refer to this experience as "his ghost." He spoke of his fear that he might accidentally lose or misplace his ghost. That, he felt, would be like losing a part of himself. He was afraid that, if he suddenly changed places or rose abruptly from his chair, his ghost would be left behind. It was observed that he would go back to his original place, or sit again on the chair, avowedly for the purpose of picking up that part of his person that had lagged behind.

With treatment, the *Doppelgänger* gradually disappeared. But the belief in the existence of a double lasted longer than the actual hallucination. As put by the analysts, the cognitive outlasted the perceptual aspect of his illness. Commentators on the described case lay emphasis on the patient's feeling of being divided or torn asunder. That he experienced his self as not being a coherent whole, was thought to lead to a sense of duplication, but this may differ from actually perceiving—seeing—oneself outside of oneself. It is also of interest to note that the hallucination of a double has been defined as "a vision of [oneself] while retaining insight into the unreality of the phenomenon." In this sense, it differs from the delusion of misidentification, which goes beyond the purely hallucinatory aspects, and attains the intimate persuasion, characteristically defended with vehemence, that the self has been actually duplicated.

The perception of the double is not confined to one's own physical person. The delusion may refer to the double of others. In this case, the patient sees persons with whom he is familiar (usually, but not always, his close relatives or members of his own household), but is convinced that they are impostors. And the two delusions may coincide in one patient. Thus, a forty-three-year-old woman not only misidentified the members of her own family, but was convinced that she herself had been replaced by a double.[61] The turns that misidentification delusions may take are truly bizarre. For instance, in the *Fregoli syndrome* (named after an Italian actor that could assume many appearances on the stage), the patient believes that several persons, although having no resemblance with each other, are "in reality" a single individual, an evil person who constantly changes appearance, so that the patient cannot help encountering him in the most varied circumstances. And in the so-called syndrome of *intermetamorphosis*, the patient perceives changes while examining a face that transforms itself, so that it appears to resemble successively different persons.

Needless to say, these are manifestations of serious mental derangement. Often, they present in the context of a fully developed delirium of persecution, in which the perceived "doubles" have come to do harm. Although the classification remains controversial, delusions of misidentification are present in about five percent of patients admitted to a hospital because of mental disease, and about twenty-eight percent in cases of diagnosed schizophrenia.

A form of delusion that has received considerable attention in the psychiatric literature is that in which the patient believes that one or several familiar persons have been replaced by physically similar doubles. Strictly speaking, this is not a hallucination: the patient does not imagine the nonexistent. Rather, it is a vivid denial of the other person's authenticity, whose physiognomy is nonetheless recognized. Yet, recognition does not erase the firm belief that—regardless of the marked resemblance to the original person—this one has been replaced by an impostor, a look-alike. Can one conceive of a greater terror?

This delusion, the perception that others have been replaced by impersonators, is referred to as Capgras syndrome, in honor of the French psychiatrist who in 1923 described, together with a collaborator, Reboul-Lachaux, what they called the "illusion of doubles" (*illusion des sosies*). The French word *sosie*, a double or look-alike, makes reference to Sosia, a personage from Greco-Roman literature. Sosia (*Sosie*, in French) is the slave of Amphitryon, who is impersonated by the god Mercury in a comedy of Plautus (*Amphitruo*). Mercury and

Jupiter, allied roguish Olympian deities, steal the identities respectively of slave and master, with the perfidious end of taking advantage of Amphytrion's absence to seduce his wife.

Again, it may be said that the insight of writers anticipated the psychiatrists' observations. For Dostoevsky, once more, described something very like Capgras' syndrome in his novel *The Possessed* (also translated as *The Devils*). In this story, Marya Timofeyevna secretly marries Stavrogin. This one, an absurd anti-hero very much in the tortured Dostoevskyan mode, fails to acknowledge her in public, and tells her that she is not his wife. Later, when he goes to visit her, she, in her turn, refuses to recognize him as her husband, telling him: "You are like him, very like him, perhaps you are a relation—only mine is a bright falcon and a prince, and you are an owl and a shopman."

Another writer figures prominently in the history of misidentification delusion syndromes. Unfortunately, not as a literary explorer, or the retriever of new insights into the shady realms of the human mind, but as a piteous victim of its relentless deterioration. The man was Somerset Maugham (1874–1965), renowned English novelist, playwright and short story writer, famous for such well known books as *Of Human Bondage* (1915), *The Moon and Sixpence* (1919), *Cakes and Ale* (1930), and *The Razor's Edge* (1944), among many others. As a writer, he was enormously successful. His output was prolific and widely popular, thereby earning him financial security. He bought a villa in Cap Ferrat, in the South of France, where he lived a life of ease for nearly forty years. He named it Villa Mauresque, perhaps due to its decoration in the Moorish style, a fondness for which he acquired through his long-sustained interest in Spain, and Spanish art and history. But if his mature life was enviable for his superior achievement and well deserved, universal praise, his closing years could not have been more miserable and pitiful.

The ills of old age fell upon him most grievously. The stereotype image of the senile old man he seemed to incarnate with a vengeance: querulous, subject to unpredictable mood swings, his physical health continuously deteriorated. In his eighties he lost his hearing, and his vision was profoundly impaired due to bilateral cataracts. Then, he grew confused, experienced memory lapses, wandered off away from his luxurious villa, and more than once he was found on the road, disoriented, shoeless, and unkempt. One of his biographers wrote that he once defecated on the fine carpet of his living room.[62]

Handsome, he never was. But in old age his overly wide mouth, sunken upper lip, sparse hair, progressively depopulated eyebrows, and redundant, wrinkled, sallow skin, joined to watery dark eyes that retained a striking expressivity, imparted to him a gnome-like, malevolent air. Uncharitably, a member of his household said he looked "like a shriveled doll." This unappealing demeanor was made more somber by a cantankerous disposition increasingly difficult to bear. Periods of depression in which he complained of being abused and plaintively declared a wish to die, alternated with fits of anger that spared no one, then followed by effusions of exaggerated, maudlin affection.

His nephew, Robin Maugham, who also had pretensions of a writing career, and who familiarly called him "Willie," never reached a literary stature in any way comparable to that of his uncle, in spite of the somewhat condescending patronage that the latter granted him. Robin narrates the following anecdote in a book about his famous uncle.[63]

They were both having dinner in the villa one night, together with some members of the staff. The renowned novelist became nervous and apprehensive. His life companion (Somerset Maugham was a homosexual), Alan Searle, had gone out. The old man asked what time it was, and was told "about nine." He then asked where was Alan, and was informed he had gone out. Not five minutes had passed, when he asked again with a sense of urgency what time it was, and where was Alan. He was growing more and more apprehensive. Trembling, he asked the same questions over and over.

Then, red with anger, he addressed his nephew, telling him: "I know you are the stupidest member of your family, but perhaps you can answer a simple question: 'What time is it?'" Less than one-half hour had passed since he began asking that question.

Next, he addressed his nephew as if he were a complete stranger: "When will Mr. Searle be back?" This expression was indicative of his discomposure, for that manner of address, calling Alan "Mr. Searle," he had never used with Robin; only when talking to strangers.

Suddenly, he turned on Robin again. Wrathful, his face contorted by ill-restrained ire, he exploded: "Where do you live?" His intimidated nephew answered: "In Brighton." His uncle rejoined, menacingly: "Don't be wilfully stupid. I mean, where are you staying tonight?"

"Why," stammered out his contrite interlocutor, "here in your villa . . ."

"No, you're not! There's no room for you here." And, on these words, Somerset Maugham tottered out of the room, screaming irately at the servants, and asking them: "Where is this man going to sleep tonight?"

"Upstairs, sir," ventured one of them.

"But in what room?" rejoined the old man with a sense of urgency.

"Why, sir, in his bedroom . . ."

"Show it to me!"

All of them walk upstairs. On reaching Robin's room, Somerset Maugham turns off the light switch and tells his cowering nephew: "I am not going to pay any more electricity for you than that." And he goes out of the room screaming most harshly to the staff. Some of the maid servants are in tears.

That night, Robin writes in his diary: "I am sure that if Willie had a knife or a gun, he would have killed me. He is, I am now convinced, a maniac. It is his quality of malignancy that pierces me with fear."

Thus may end the most eximious glories of literature.

Three episodes of this nature in the life of W. Somerset Maugham were critically surveyed by a prominent psychiatrist who concluded that there was enough evidence to state that the novelist manifested the symptoms of Capgras syndrome in his old age.[64]

II. Through a Regular, Clear Mirror:
Its Uses and Abuses

The suggestiveness of the clear mirror is inexhaustible. Medieval scholars made much of the fact that its limpid surface replicates the entire universe. Smash it into pieces, and each of the shattered fragments can again accommodate the entire universe (No: only its image, Socrates wisely remarked); for wherever one turns it, each piece will offer a concentrated vision of any and all objects therein reflected. Moreover, visible objects will be captured wholly, in all their complex details, and down to their last imperfections. This awesome power of reproduction naturally excited the imagination. In the Middle Ages, Church Fathers, St. Vincent Ferrer among them, compared the Eucharist to a mirror, which broken still maintains the integral image in all its particularity. Thus, Hugh of St. Victor could proclaim: *Ubique est idem*, in every part [it remains] the same. All of which gave rise to the feeling that the mirror was potentially capable of making the chaos of the world more manageable and comprehensible. For the mirror is held not to distort things, but to reflect them truly. Not to hide truth, but to reproduce it, *i.e.*, to reflect it, and presumably, inferred the ancients, to clarify it.

No wonder, then, that the mirror was made into a symbol of supreme wisdom. The auspicious, positive value of the symbol was evident, which in the West soon passed into literary catchwords: "mirror of wisdom," "mirror of perfection," and so on. Magic mirrors are part of legend and lore worldwide.

On their reflecting surface one could see future events, secret facts, and even whole stories that were to become a reality later. "Catoptromancy" (from Gr. *katoptron*, mirror) was the term denoting the art of divination by looking into a mirror. Mixing superstition and orthodox religion, many believed that the reflections of the *paten*, the plate used to transport the bread in the Eucharistic service, and commonly made of a precious metal, had a specially high divinatory power.

In the Far East, the mirror was an amulet and a magical tool. In China and Japan, "magic mirrors" were used that, when exposed to the light, reflected a luminous image of the motifs embossed on the reverse face; in some cases the reverse had inscriptions meant to scare demons away. A Chinese mystic, Pao-p'u tzu, "the master who has embraced simplicity" (real name Kao Kung), stated that spirits "capable of adopting human form and deceiving the human eye with illusion, . . . cannot change their form in the mirror. That is why the Taoist masters in the past, when they went into retreat in the mountains, carried on their backs a mirror, big of nine *ts'un* in diameter, or even larger."[65] A Buddhist monk who was a famous pilgrim to Buddhist sites is so depicted.

In the celebrated painting by Jan van Eyck (1390?–1441) entitled "The Marriage of Giovanni Arnolfini" (1434; National Gallery, London) a circular mirror hangs on the back wall, between man and wife, the two principal figures in the painting. And all the exquisitely depicted objects in the room, brimful of a symbolism uniquely fit to exalt and hallow the couple's betrothal, are caught in that convex mirror. Interestingly, its all-inclusive surface is circumscribed by an ornate frame in which inset medallions represent scenes of Christ's passion. It is only on that central surface, and only there, that the scene can be reflected in its totality, not excluding the artist, who gestures as if to salute the spouses. Is the mirror, then, the all-seeing eye of God, as some have suggested, casting a benevolent, auspicious glance on the married couple? Or is the couple being placed under the invocation of the Holy Virgin, since one of her attributes is a mirror, especially a circular one?

The truth is, when it comes to the interpretation of symbols, innumerable are the avenues open before us. The mirror, in another tradition, is the Virgin Mary, since she is "immaculate," like a mirror (*speculum sine macula*), only one "that nothing can tarnish and is never dimmed." Being the Mother of God, her specular qualities are ideal and immaterial. Just as a concave mirror collects the solar energy, so a pregnant Mary received the divine Sun in her virginal womb, *intra uteri virginei*, in order that its light could be diffused throughout the whole world.

Or perhaps the famous Arnolfini portrait was meant merely as a statement of the presence of the artist, as indicated by that graffito-like, enigmatic inscription that the painter placed conspicuously on the panel: "*Johannes Eyck fuit hic*" ("Jan Eyck was here"). And the image of the artist appears in the reflection of the circular mirror. A public affirmation of his existence; a self-portrait of sorts, one might say.

The mirror is also the symbol of contemplation. In the *Divine Comedy*, Dante dreams of encountering two Biblical personages, Leah and Rachel, in Purgatory. Here, Leah, eldest daughter of Laban and first wife of Jacob, goes about a prairie gathering flowers: ". . . moving my fair hands to make me a garland. To please me, at the glass here I deck myself; but my sister Rachel never stirs from her mirror, and sits all day. She loves to behold her fair eyes; as I to adorn myself with my hands; her, contemplation; me, action, satisfies." (". . . *movendo intorno / le belle mani a farmi una guirlanda. / Per piacermi allo specchio qui m'adorno; / ma mia suora Rachel mai non si smaga / dal suo miraglio, e siede tutto giorno. / Ell' è de' suoi begli occhi veder vaga, / com' io dell'adornarmi con le mani; / lei lo vedere, e me l'oprare appaga.*") (Canto XXVII, 101-108).

The mirror that the sisters are watching is traditionally interpreted as the face of God. Leah signifies the active life; her sister Rachel, second wife of Jacob, the contemplative life. Both are indispensable to achieve spiritual perfection. This idea, which originated with St. Gregory (byname: Gregory the Great; 540–604 A.D.) and found theological justification in the treatises and allegories of medieval Church doctors, is encapsulated in verses 106-108 of the mentioned passage. Leah's hands are the instruments of her activity: she acts to perform good deeds, which form the garland on which she pleases herself; while her sister Rachel ceases not to look at her own beautiful eyes in the mirror. One acts, the other contemplates.

Rachel's fixed viewing of her own beautiful eyes in a mirror is not the conceited, self-centered gaze of female vanity. It represents its opposite, the self-abnegated spirit of mystical contemplation. The idea had been previously developed by Dante in *The Banquet* (*Il Convivio*: IV, ii, 18), where he speaks of philosophy falling "in love with herself," when the beauty of her eyes is revealed to her. Which "means . . . that the philosophizing soul not only contemplates truth in person, but also contemplates its own contemplating and [discovers] the beauty thereof, and falls in love with herself on account of the beauty of her first sight."

In the Renaissance, the mirror kept much of its positive symbolism. Cesare Ripa (?1560–1623) maintained that ideas, even the most abstract, can be visually and artistically represented. Thus, Time is symbolized by an old man carrying a sickle, because time shall mow down every living being without exception. A lion fittingly represents fierce power, since strength and ferociousness are this feline's universally recognized attributes. And so on. Virtues and vices, the emotions, scientific theories, the human races, the constellations in the heavens, etc.: all can be adequately and vividly expressed by appropriate images.

Ripa's codification of images was published in a book called *Iconology.*[66] (Today, it might be more properly called "Iconography," if one is to follow Panofsky's definition.[67]) There, he tells us that Prudence is represented by a "woman with two faces, like Janus, who looks at herself in a mirror, while a serpent is wound around her arm. The two faces mean that prudence is a true and certain knowledge, which orders what must be done, and arises from a consideration of things past and future together." In other words, the two faces of Prudence mean that a prudent person looks front and backward, *i.e.*, to the past for useful precedents, and to the future for an assessment of possible consequences, before making a decision.

Prudence reflects herself in a mirror in much the same way, for one looks at a mirror by directing the gaze toward the front, but the mirror allows us to see what is behind us. The mirror of Prudence, says Panofsky, belongs in the same class as other specifically medieval motifs, such as the eye-band of Cupid, the wheel of Fortune, or the heavenward stairs of Philosophy. These attributes differ from those used in classical antiquity, because they do not indicate a function, but rather "translate a metaphor into an image."

The symbolism of the mirror, however, goes much deeper than that. Its value as an instrument of wisdom or knowledge—*speculum sapientiae*—we have already noted. Sacred Scripture set forth the metaphoric analogy of understanding and mirror. In the *Wisdom of Solomon* (known in the Latin Vulgata simply as *Book of Wisdom*) we read that wisdom "is the brightness of the everlasting light, the unspotted mirror of the power of God, and the image of his goodness" (VII, 26).

Prudence's holdings were enriched by granting her one more possession: a stag. Sometimes she is shown actually riding this animal. Why a stag? A male adult deer passed for being a prudent animal. Endowed with strong legs, he is capable of running very fast, but he also happens to have large, branching antlers. Consequently, if he is not careful, he might easily become entangled in the underbrush. Therefore, the stag is of necessity prudent. Then, again, when he eats he ruminates. He eats slowly. And is not "rumination" commonly taken to signify slow, ponderous, prudent deliberation?

Figure 6. Iconography of *Prudence* according to Cesare Ripa, 1625. To her commonly depicted attributes, a mirror and a snake, Ripa adds a stag.

With respect to the meaning of the snake, its origin may be traced to a Biblical phrase. Matthew X, 16, admonishes: ". . . be wise as serpents and innocent as doves." Hence, the serpent is wise or prudent in the Gospel. Medieval men needed no higher authority to vouch for the reptilian character. Sometimes it winds itself around the arm of Prudence, sometimes it is twined in an arrow that she is holding. The arrow commonly stands for speed and unerring aim.

Figure 7. *Prudence* according to Hendrick Goltzius (1558–1617). The Janus-like two faced head has become a prominent feature. The serpent is now held directly in her hand.

As to the two faces of Prudence, the Church always regarded this feature with profound distrust. In effect, it is evident that the double-visage form had pagan roots. The "double" that a mirror sends back to those who look into its polished surface is likely to have inspired the creation of pagan idols of duplex bodies, or at least double-headed ones. Bicephalic deities exist in various pre-Christian civilizations. In Greece and Rome, Boreas, god of the wind, and sometimes Apollo and Hercules, were so represented. Such images were not uncommon. All over the Athenian landscape stood the so-called "herms" (also written "hermas"), quadrangular pillars or columns, about the height of an adult human being, surmounted by a duplex head of a god that appeared to be looking in opposite directions. The name "herm" or "herma" seems to allude to the god Hermes, who in remote times may have been depicted as bicephalic, but it is to be noted that no herm has ever been identified that shows Hermes in this fashion. Herms were used as milestones or boundary marks on roads and fields, or simply as decorative pillars in temples and public places. It made good sense that a two-headed deity, whose faces look in opposite directions, should be the god who stands on the road to propitiate the good fortune of wayfarers: those who are going, and those who are coming.

But possibly the best known bicephalic god linked to the latter function, was the tutelary god of doors, arches, and passageways, double-headed Janus (also written *Ianus*, from *ianua*, a door, in ancient Latin). As the doorman of heaven, Janus had to be the first name mentioned in liturgical invocations. The month of Janus, *mensis Jani* (hence our "January"), opened the year. His feast was celebrated on the first of the year, when revelers used to give each other gifts, known as *strenae* (hence the Sp. "estreno," and Fr. "étrenne," words which carry the connotation of first use, and of a gift offered to celebrate some inaugural event).

In the Middle Ages, the mirror was not just an adjunct of Prudence. Its symbolic meaning was broadened when it was given another singular use, namely: held by the delicate hands of young maidens, it was good to attract unicorns. In effect, various artworks show this imaginary beast coming close to a young lady who holds a mirror and approaches it to the animal's face. Especially notable among those works is the beauti-

Figure 8. *Sight* (detail), from the Lady and the Unicorn series of tapestries, executed between 1484 and 1500.

ful tapestry entitled *Sight*, part of a series that celebrates the senses, exhibited in the Cluny Museum of Paris. To understand this singular application, it is necessary first to refer to the significance of the unicorn in the popular mind.

No one knows who first conceived the idea of the unicorn. Its origin is lost in the mist of the remotest times. It probably originated in Asia, and paleontologists have ventured the hypothesis that in prehistoric times a powerful beast endowed with a single, massive horn may have existed there, although it is not clear that human beings lived then and were able to see it. At any rate, in the West, the first mention of the unicorn is that of Ctesias, a Greek physician of the early fourth century

B.C., who lived for some time in the Persian court, where he may have picked up the story from a Far Eastern source. In Ctesias' description, the unicorn was the size of a wild ass of India, and had a white body, but a red head provided with a single horn less than two feet long. Swift-footed and shy in the extreme, yet fiercely combative when cornered, the animal was very difficult to capture. Nay, it was impossible. One could only catch it by killing it. Those who used its horn to make a cup from which to drink, discovered that this rendered them immune to poisons and cured them of fevers and convulsions.

A medieval story gives a Christian slant to the curative property, in the following way:

There exists an animal called the unicorn. In the area where it lives, there is a very large pond, where all the animals of the forest gather to drink. However, before they come together, the serpent advances, and ejects its venom into the water. Therefore, the wild animals that perceive the poison do not dare to drink the contaminated water. They all wait for the unicorn to come. This one approaches, and, showing no fear, boldly gets into the pond. With its horn, it draws a cross in the water, and by this means removes all the harmful effects of the envenomed liquid, and drinks avidly. All the beasts of the forest then drink as well.

Aelian, in the early third century A.D., reported that unicorns existed in Scythia, and that their horns could hold water from the river Styx,—water that would cut through cups made of any other material.[68] One of these horns, he added, was presented as a gift to Alexander of Macedon, who in admiration left it as a votive offering at Apollo's temple at Delphi. In Aelian's version, the animal was smaller than a gazelle. But Strabo, in his *Geography* (XV, 1.56), concurred with other authors in saying that it was as big as a horse, that is, larger than an ass, and subscribed to the notion that it was a frightfully ferocious beast. The "eye" of imagination sees the unicorn variously.

A further elaboration of the myth of the unicorn is found in a fourth century Alexandrian text written in Greek, of obscure attribution, entitled the *Physiologus*. This work spread the quaint version that the unicorn was a small animal, like a kid or a goat, but of such enormous strength that it could not be caught alive by any known means. Neither the ruse of hunters, nor the combined force of large hunting parties, could hope to match the strength and the shrewdness of the elusive unicorn. Yet, there was one way of trapping it, and it is as follows.

A young maiden, an innocent virgin, is sent ahead of the hunters. Deep in the woods, she uncovers her breast. Immediately, the unicorn is attracted by the odor of the pure young body, and jumps at the girl, tamely resting his head on her bosom. She suckles the beast, who is so entranced by the experience, so overwhelmed by it, that he remains still, as if paralyzed. It is then that the hunters can come and seize the animal, and cage it in all tranquillity, for they can expect no resistance at all.

Medieval theologians were going to see the unicorn as a figure of Christ. In the Bible, one reads that the Lord God "raised up a horn of salvation for us" (Luke 1, 69), a "horn" being interpreted in Scripture as meaning effective strength (for instance, in Psalm 18, 1-3, God is again "the horn of my salvation"; or 75, 4: "I say to the boastful, 'Do not boast,' and to the wicked, 'Do not lift up your horn; do not lift up your horn on high, or speak with insolent neck.'"). The maiden became a symbol of, or an allusion to, the Virgin Mary. The unicorn coming to rest his head upon the maiden's lap was the Verb incarnate in Mary's womb.

Eventually, the religious connotation is effaced, and the unicorn adopts a more and more secular role. We then see him assuming a distinctly erotic significance. In the thirteenth century, Richard de Fournival (born 1204), canon of Amiens and Rouen, and author of texts in French and in Latin, equated the unicorn and the lover in his "Bestiary of Love." In this work, the narrator avows that he was "taken by scent, like the unicorn, who drowses off due to the sweet perfume of a virgin."[69]

Thus, no longer is the single-horned beast the quarry persecuted by armed men and dogs, in bloody scenes of hunting.

Now the unicorn appears in compositions of tender sentimentality. In the fifth tapestry of the Cloisters of the New York Metropolitan Museum of Art, it is not the hunters with their deadly accouterments, but a girl who subdues the mythological animal by the force of love. And, by extension, the unicorn comes to figure in scenes highly suggestive of carnal eroticism. On a painted Florentine coffer of the fifteenth century, a crouching young woman encircles the unicorn with her legs and combs its mane; male beast and human female look at each other with ecstatic delight, while in the background two women whisper to each other, one knows not whether in slander or in envy.[70] By the same token, a painting by Gustave Moreau (1826–1898), where three unicorns appear amidst women, of which some are sumptuously attired and others utterly naked, exudes an air of undisguised sensuality.

What, then, is a mirror doing in the "Sight" tapestry of the Parisian Cluny Museum? The woman tends it toward the animal's face, without even looking at it. And a unicorn, looking chic with a goat's beard, hoofs cloven in twain, a long, slender neck, and a long horn that shows spiral folds on its surface, looks at its reflected image on the mirror with fascination. As every aspect of the unicorn's mythology, this celebrated image has also been the subject of varied interpretations.

Some read in it the wiliness of deceitful women, intent on setting up a trap for the unwary. The unicorn, bamboozled by some mirror trickery, is being imprisoned. But some think this is a crass misreading. It fails to account for the look of melancholy, of strange longing, in the lady's eyes. She does not smile, nor is her expression one of dissembling. A medieval romantic story-teller puts an involved love story behind the scene depicted in the tapestry: the woman is saddened upon evoking her own future, where she is to face death on the presumption of her faithlessness. She tends the mirror to the beast because only the unicorn, by its submissive rapport with her, is the sole witness and guarantor of her purity and innocence.[71]

In still another reading, the *Sight* tapestry alludes to the fundamental deficiency that exists at the core of the lovers' yearning. Lovers wish for ideal harmony; a mutual accord of their personalities in every possible way; a meeting of bodies and souls into perfect unity. But this goal is unattainable. They would "fuse with each other," and "become one," but Nature has decreed that individualities should remain separate: they shall be forever two. The unicorn, which is a creature of the imagination, sees its own image reflected in the mirror: an unprecedented phenomenon for insubstantial and ethereal beings, who, in the world of myth and legend, never can project an image of themselves upon a mirror. And the beast seems content and fascinated, wholly absorbed in self-contemplation. It seems to find a true delight in its own individuality. In contrast, the woman's expression, while looking away from the mirror, is one of melancholy and reverie. The gazes of these two do not cross, do not meet one another: the woman looks—and how sadly!—at the unicorn; the unicorn looks at the mirror that she presents to his face.

These apparent incongruities bring forth, once again, the idea that the lovers' yearning is doomed to unfulfillment. For the gaze of those in love is often of specular nature: they see into each other's eyes only to search their own image reflected in the eyes of the lover, as in a mirror. The desperate search for the Other's soul turns out to be a groping in the dark for one's own individuality. And the deep, soulful look into the eyes of the beloved turns out to be the look of Narcissus gazing at himself.

This elaborate reading of the tapestry is a meditation on that curious human foible which is self-fascination, of which the unicorn is also a symbol. It is a sad pondering on the impossibility of encountering the Other. A sad reflection as well on the fact that love is often elicited in the love-object when this one is admired, and ceases when the other no longer admires, because, at bottom, "one only loves oneself."[72]

III. The Tool of Self-Inspection:
Uses and Abuse

Self-contemplation is, after all, what may be deemed the primary function of the mirror. It should not be surprising that the mirror entered human history chiefly as an article of feminine toilette. It is perhaps the hoariest symbol of female vanity. So close has been its historical association with women, that it came to symbolize femininity itself. In effect, some believe that the symbol that indicates female sex—a circle from whose lowest point emerges a long inverted cross—represents actually a portable mirror of the kind most commonly used in classical antiquity, made of polished silver, and having a long cross of small transverse bar as a handle. The symbol for masculinity, a circle from which arises an arrow pointing obliquely up and to the right, (presumably representing a shield and an arrow), alludes to the ideas of hunting and warfare. The mirror is the household article that most frequently appears represented in Greco-Roman vases, always in association with women. So often, indeed, that a scholar observed that the hand-held mirror seems almost like a natural extension of the woman's upper limb.

Woman's constant companion and confidant: such is the mirror. But this, alas, only while the face therein reflected is a thing of beauty. For when beauty fades, the mirror turns from dear friend and flatterer to abhorrent denouncer and betrayer. An epigram of the sixth century A.D. depicts a courtesan retiring from her profession and presenting her mirror as a votive offering to the goddess of love. The text says: "Laïs, whose resplendent beauty time has withered, can bear no proof of her age or her wrinkles; she has conceived a hatred for her mirror, cruel witness of her past splendor, and thus consecrates it to her sovereign: Receive from me, Cytheres, this disc that was the companion of my youth, since your beauty has nothing to fear from the passage of time."[73]

The courtesan alluded to was the famous Laïs, celebrated for her beauty, greed, and whimsical disposition. A native of Corinth, her name became proverbial. "Not everyone can afford to visit Laïs of Corinth" was said in censure of men who lived beyond their means. Corinth was noted throughout the ancient world for elegant and expensive women, just as the city of Thebes had a reputation of dullness. When Laïs died, a mausoleum was built to her, which shows the influence she had attained in her native city. It contained a sculptoric group showing a lioness devouring a ram. An allusion to her character? Possibly: courtesans, then and now, have had a reputation as predators of injudicious and reckless men.

Laïs seems to have had the wisdom and good sense of doing away with the tools of her vanity, when the ravages of age would have rendered grotesque their continued employment. The theme of a beautiful woman at her mirror has been used by numerous great masters of the pictorial art. From Memling to Picasso, and up to our day, the temptation of painters to try their hand at capturing the splendor of inviolate feminine beauty and its reflected image has been irresistible. In a majority of those paintings, the figuration symbolizes pride and vanity. But a few corrosive characters opted to become the limners of time's infringements and injuries upon physical beauty; they chose to censure Woman's stubborn attachment to the adjuncts of her spent glory.

Bernardo Strozzi (1581-1644), baroque painter from Genoa who was also a Capuchin monk (hence nicknamed *"il prete"* or *"il cappucino"*), was one of the keenest in this regard. He was only thirty-four years old, but had been ordained for at least a decade, when he painted his *Old Woman at the Mirror*. This easel is a cruel, merciless denunciation that gives us a startle or affects us with uneasiness and disrelish when we first see it. The subject is an old woman who sits in front of the mirror while she is arranged by two assistants with the makeup and adornments proper to a young girl.

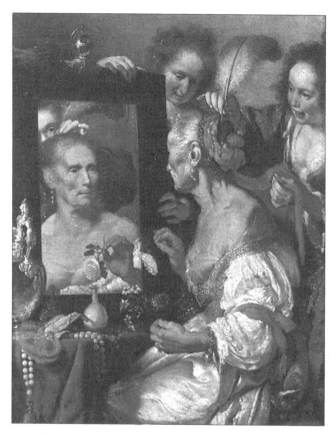

Figure 9. *Old Woman at the Mirror* by Bernardo Strozzi (1581–1644).

Strozzi's intent was undoubtedly to hold the crone up to ridicule. A monk's sour asceticism and intransigent misogynism must have guided his brush. By lavishing on her all the dainty fripperies and ornaments of a young woman, the sunken cheeks, the sagging flesh, and the wrinkled skin are rendered more apparent. She is not in extreme old age, but well past her prime and approaching senescence. Still, the incongruously low neckline in her dress exposes a dry, inelastic complexion and points to a sagging bosom wholly devoid of youthful turgidity. The marks of old age are accentuated by the blooming youth of the two rosy-cheeked adolescents that preen her. They have dressed her in white satin, and are now decking her with red ribbons and feathers. She holds a rose in her right hand, whose bony fingers portend the arthritic deformity of a superannuated skeleton. And she looks at her reflection with a wistful, semi-absent, probably senile, vacuous gaze. But behind this scene we seem to hear Strozzi's implacable, vitriolic chastisement that says: "These are the indignities and humiliations of contemptible old women, who would not resign themselves to the fading of the transient womanly beauty!"

Of course, much the same criticism could have been directed to many men. But in a patriarchal society, males usually came out with finer self-assessments. The use of the mirror by men, which, to be truthful, might have been linked just as often with vanity and pride, was said to be used for chiefly for didactic or edifying purposes.

Socrates, for instance, is said to have recommended the use of the mirror to his young students, who were, of course, all males. His idea was that the handsome ones would try to model their conduct after their looks, since bad actions would appear to them incongruous and out of place in their persons. As to the ugly ones, presumably the mirror would encourage them to try to hide their uncomeliness behind good actions, worthy achievements, and improvements in their education.[74]

Another Greek promoter of the use of mirror by men was Demosthenes (384–322 B.C.), greatest of Athenian orators. He ordered a large mirror made for his personal use, in which his whole body could be reflected. This, he declared, was a means to improve his oratorical performance. It is well known that since his early childhood, this man burned in the desire to become a great public speaker. Alas, never was a youth so unsuited to this avocation: for one thing, he was shy to distraction; for another, his voice was weak; and, to top it all, he stammered. What he did to overcome these difficulties is now part of his person's legend.

It is said that he shaved one half of his head, and secluded himself in an underground shelter, there to practice his exercises of diction and delivery, ashamed to come out with his preposterous tonsure. He would practice reciting verses and declaiming speeches after running long stretches or climbing steep inclines, in order to improve his breathing movements. The remedy he is said to have devised to overcome his stuttering—to practice speeches with his mouth full of pebbles—is simply incredible, and, common sense tells us, not to be recommended. But these stories certainly show how determined he was to achieve his end of becoming a great orator.

The problem was, after all these and other demanding practices, he still could not hold the attention of the public at the assembly. After studying the public speaking systems then in vogue, such as those of Isocrates, Isaeus, and other luminaries of oratory, he still could elicit practically no interest in his hearers. A failing all the more frustrating to him upon recollecting that drunken, ill informed, and illiterate fellows somehow managed to hold the public in suspense.

One day, he was going home feeling down, after one more shameful rejection at the assembly, when he was approached by a man curiously named Satyrus. He had been an actor, and managed to engage the dejected apprentice speaker in conversation. Hearing of his bitterness and disappointment, he offered a remedy, which his hearer was only too eager to accept. The former actor asked the would-be orator to recite some periods of the great playwrights of the time, Sophocles and Euripides. Next, Satyrus repeated the same passages, but this time in his own rendering, with all the gesturing, emphasis, and motions that his experience at the stage suggested to him. For Demosthenes this was a revelation: the speeches, flat and spiritless when he declaimed them, now seemed different, as if infused with a new life and full of zest and passion.

The lesson was not lost on Demosthenes. If he wanted to succeed with his public, it was not just the ear, but the eye, which he had to learn to captivate. The speech of a great speaker is as much heard as it is watched. The orator transforms his speech into a spectacle, and so ravishes his public with gestures, motions, and bodily expressions. Hence the helpfulness of the mirror. Frequent practice in front of it transformed Demosthenes from a boor into the greatest of public speakers. Cicero spoke of two elements in eloquence. One, that the Greeks called "ethic," is sweet, affable, and delights the audience with persuasive proofs and elegant statements. The other one, which they named "pathetic," is passionate, impetuous, and troubling. The former is pleasant and reasonable, but insufficient to remove the prejudices and received opinions that people harbor. The latter is irrational, troubling, and discomposed, but it breaks through the crust of stubbornness and preconception that insulates the hearers, and sways them any which way by stirring their passions.

However, there is danger in exaggeration. Too much self-contemplation in the mirror probably ended up turning Demosthenes into a narcissistic fop. He became excessively prim and proper: an affected orator-dandy. His contemporaries nicknamed him "pretty tunics," and Aiskhines, one of his enemies, accused him of being a pederast, and attributed to him "bodily impurity, even of the organs of speech."[75] However, we know that he did like women. In a famous anecdote, he secretly approached the famous courtesan Laïs of Corinth, and asked for her price. Having found what it was, and realizing that it was far beyond his means, he is reported to have said, "I will not buy regret for ten thousand drachmas." A witty repartee this was, albeit one prompted by the realization of the truth in the ancient Greek proverb that said the delights of Corinth are not for every man, or as Horace rephrased it, (although in a different context), "not every man may fare to Corinth town." (*Epistles* I, xvii, 36.)

In the Roman world, a renowned orator, Quintus Hortensius, followed the Demosthenes method with similarly undesirable social effects.[76] He spent many hours in front of the mirror, carefully arranging the folds of his toga, and practicing the gesturing to accompany his speeches. He turned out looking like another coxcombical individual, unbecomingly given to use exaggerated gestures with his hands when pleading. This made him the target of taunts like those hurled at Demosthenes. One of his enemies, named Torquatus, shouted at him in the presence of the audience that he was a posturer and a Dionysia, which was the name of a notorious dancing girl of the times. Quintus Hortensius retorted: "Yes, I'd much rather be a Dionysia, than like you, unknown to the Muses, to Venus, and to Dionysus." The latter triple invective was voiced in Greek, for greater effect among the cultivated, all of whom were fluent in this language and familiar with the saying, which was meant to depict his rival as completely insensitive and devoid of civilized graces. The implication was, under pain of being branded a churl, a man must show himself at least a little inclined to music, love, and wine.

Roman antiquity also had a man of very different temperament who made no pretense about the use of the mirror. He had plenty of money, with which he bought especially constructed mirrors with the sole purpose of enhancing the sexual pleasure he derived from his kinky proclivities. We encounter this singular personage in a book of the Stoic moralist, Lucius Annaeus Seneca (4 B.C.–65 A.D.). Curiously, it is a book devoted to questions of physics, his *Quaestiones Naturales* (I, xvi, 7). But, where we expect to find a discussion of technical aspects of light reflection and the mirror's optical effects, we are introduced to Mr. Hostius Quadra, the chap whose sexual depravity is denounced by the moralist with searing vehemence. So notorious was the man's deviancy, Seneca tells us, that his life was made into a theater play, although he does not inform us by whom or under what title.

Immensely rich and avaricious, he was one who would have easily afforded to "go to Corinth" as many times as he wished.

Instead, his desire took him to other, much more devious and quite a bit shadier, tortuous paths. Avidly bisexual, his millions allowed him to "maintain his every vice," and to realize his every fantasy. One of the latter included the construction of a series of mirrors, so shaped as to deform the images therein reflected. Some were artfully disposed, in a manner proper to magnify the size of objects viewed at a certain angle. The moving hand that displaced itself following a specific direction, would seem to possess fingers that lengthened and broadened to grotesque extremes.

Now, our man toured the public baths to recruit sexual partners of impressive measurements. But it was not enough that they should be well endowed: he still enlivened his appetite with the surfeit of illusion. "He soiled not just his mouth, but his eyes as well," writes Seneca, "with actions the likes of which, albeit secret and unnamed, weigh heavily upon the conscience, and whose commission even the guilty dare not avow to themselves." The moralist tells us that wickedness dislikes its own mien, and that even in those who are lost, depraved, and prostituted beyond all possibility of reform, "the shame of the eyes" remains, after they have lost all sensitivity to dishonor. Not so with Hostius Quadra, whose visual perception was precisely a vehicle of his sinful pleasure.

The man is actually defiant and exultant in his deviousness. Nature, he says, was stingy when it came to providing men with the instruments of pleasure. She was more generous toward certain animals. No matter: he is ready to remedy the deficiency by supplying with human art and clever industry what Nature denied. For he means to surround himself with artfully contrived mirrors, which will return images many times enlarged. And he adds: "If it were within my power, I would make the vain image turn into reality, but, since it isn't, I shall assuage myself with illusion." Which shows that this monster, as Seneca did label him, who "would deserve to be torn apart with his own teeth," is in reality profoundly human, inasmuch as his male sexuality appeared to be completely under the empire of the imagination.

Human industry he summoned to the service of his odd penchants; and ". . . not content with the spectacle of his own moral degradation, he still wished to see it multiplied in endless reflections." In other words, mirror optics at the service of his voyeurism. Nor was it only a matter of multiplication of images, which is perhaps the simplest trick that can be accomplished with mirrors. He still contrived to place the reflecting surfaces in such a way as to permit the clear vision of bodily parts and postures that normally fall outside of the field of vision. He would see what under normal conditions must remain hidden; he would fain visualize his own head even when it was, in Seneca's words, "sunk and lowered in the shameful parts of his companions in lasciviousness."

The moralist makes his scandalous pervert come up with a sort of manifesto of contumacious depravity: "A man and a woman I bear at the same time, and yet I can still play my role of male when I attack someone else with whichever part of my body remains free. All my limbs are used for rape; even the eyes participate in the feast, of which they are both witnesses and custom-house officers." It seems that, to carry out the contortions demanded by his strange sexual preferences, his "partners in lasciviousness" must have been forced to submit to attitudes and postures not much to their liking. This we are authorized to surmise when Seneca tells us that Hostius Quadra died assassinated by his servants. Emperor Augustus appeared so little troubled by this crime, that he did not prosecute the killers.

This ancient precursor of the Marquis de Sade also anticipated, as some scholars have ironically pointed out,[77] every optical apparatus that was invented afterward, from those applied to the magnification of images, or their multiplication, to "holography."

I am reminded of a first-hand experience when I had just arrived in the Chicago area and was looking for housing in preparation to settling there. The real estate agent accompanied my wife and me to visit a number of unoccupied, available

houses. In one of them, in the suburb of Skokie, the bedroom
had nothing to envy the most baroque designs out of Hostius
Quadra's brain. The floor was covered by a thick, shaggy, dark
gray, almost black carpet; the canopied bed was guarded by curtains of the same color in a heavy velvety fabric. This, together
with the ample drapes of identical color disposed over walls and
ceiling, whose redundant folds fell loosely on the floor, transformed the room into a dark, silent chamber. The agent activated
a light switch, and this revealed the source of light to be a pair
of chandelier-like fixtures, each with a central stem that was
clutched by the hand of respective life-size statues of nude black
women, standing at the two far corners of the room, like torch-
bearers. The whole arrangement gave an impression of irre-
deemable kitsch, but was nonetheless impressive for the considerable care and expense that had gone into its production.

With a move obviously calculated for effect, the agent activated other switches that automatically parted the curtains to
expose large mirrors that covered the walls, the closet's doors,
and the ceiling. The entire room appeared surrounded by mirrors, more lavishly deployed here than at the *Galerie des Glaces*
of Versailles. The images of the torch-bearing statues and the bed
were strikingly multiplied when mutually facing mirrors caught
their reflection. The salesperson announced with glee that this
property was referred to familiarly in the agency as "Hollywood
in Skokie." When she asked our impression of what we had just
seen, I did not know what to say. My wife answered that the
house was "interesting," but that the two of us needed to discuss
the matter in private before making any decision.

Later, in private, she plainly avowed that, had we struck the
deal, she never could have overcome the sensation of living in a
whorehouse. I could only think of Hostius Quadra's perver-
sions and Seneca's irate fulminations. I confirmed that there is
nothing new under the sun, and I am sure that Seneca himself
would have agreed; had he lived longer, he might have said so
himself: *Nihil novum sub sole.*

The Threatening Unseen, or Half-Seen: Blurred Eyesight in Renaissance French Literature

"AT DAWN, A SHUDDER TRAVERSES THE OBJECTS. DURING THE night, fused to the shade, they had lost their identities; now, not without hesitation, the light recreates them. I can already guess that the foundered barque, on whose mast there is a charred parrot that nods off, is the sofa with the lamp; that the slaughtered ox amidst bags of black sand is the desk; in a few minutes the table again will be called table . . ."[78]

With these striking images, the poetical genius of Octavio Paz vividly portrayed the transmogrifying risks that attend inferior vision. When eyesight is deficient, as in disease or in darkness, imagination is never tardy to supply the wants of an imperfect ocular function. However, once the imagination is let go, there is no telling what bizarre delusions it might incur: a lamp shade becomes a burnt parrot perched atop a ship's mast, and a desk turns into the cadaver of an ox whose throat has been slit. Hence the unbearable tension and enhanced terror of an object that is both deemed suspect and imperfectly visualized. Every detail in its outline threatens; a riotous fancy discovers a ghoulish menace in the blandest of its features.

This property of our minds is well exploited by creators of terror films and akin visual spectacles. Fright is potentiated when carefully dosed for optimal effect. The horrific image is not abruptly or suddenly exposed; instead, it is first suggested, hinted at, or approached gradually. All the senses are stimulated to a paroxysm, before visual perception delivers the final shock of revelation. The monstrous or loathsome figure seems to increase in ghastliness when it is first imagined, then heard, then perhaps faintly touched, and then seen under multiple covers that are slowly peeled off, one by one. The roughly outlined shape increases its hair-raising charge until all our senses are oppressed beyond endurance simply by its presence.

The effect is also known and exploited in suspenseful narratives. But these are not necessarily geared to excite awe or fear. A festive or comic effect benefits from coming after gradually increased tension. We are jarred out of growing apprehension by the sudden deflation of a happy ending. An interesting example of this kind is furnished by a sixteenth century French story-teller, Bonaventure des Périers (c.1510–c.1544).

This man deserves a brief preliminary note. Little known outside his native country, (and this chiefly by students of French literature), Bonaventure des Périers earned nonetheless some distinction in French letters. He was a mysterious and singular personage who became a secretary of Marguerite of Angoulême, Queen of Navarre (1492–1549), the remarkable writer-queen of the Renaissance, authoress of the *Heptameron*. Like her, he, too, wrote short stories that were usually amusing, often ribald, sometimes cruelly satirical, and never with a moralizing intent. He was skeptical of religion, and an acerbic, unforgiving critic of all creeds. This did not help his career, either at court or in the republic of letters. At the time, religions waged open war among themselves. Europe was steeped in doctrinal hatreds and bloody factionalism, and des Périers ended up being loathed with equal vehemence by Catholics and Protestants. His works were banned, and once he was a hair's breadth away from suffering a most severe physical punishment. He might have lost his life, but for the opportune intercession of Queen Margaret, who pleaded in his favor. The unfortunate des Périers escaped alive, but was not restored in the esteem of his contemporaries. Misunderstood, widely detested by his fellows, he committed suicide.

The story from his authorship that we wish to recount in abridged form here is a typical Renaissance narrative of amorous intrigue.

Two young men from Siena, Lucio and Alessio, are very close friends. There is nothing that each one would not do for the other, so strong is the bond of friendship that joins them. They travel to Spain, where Lucio conceives a passion for a young lady named Isabel. She is also attracted to him. Alas, sixteenth century Spain is prodigal in measures that enforce a fierce, unyielding separation of the sexes. Lucio and Isabel must content themselves with meaningful glances exchanged at rare occasions in a few places. No matter: as has always been the case, the expressivity of the eyes on such circumstances can convey messages more substantive, garrulous, and eloquent, than those printed in voluminous in-folios that fill whole library shelves.

To make matters still more complex, the lady happens to be married. Again, in the rigidly conservative Spain of those times, this was certainly no minor inconvenience: stains to a man's honor could be washed, according to the well-nigh universal persuasion, only in blood. But this does not deter those two, who promptly engage in the strategies known to illicit lovers since the world harbored concurrently men, women, and institutionalized monogamy. There follow the anxious spying for opportunities of encounter; the rapid whispering of words in the brief instants when no one is watching; and the involvement of an appropriate go-between. It is a risky affair, to bring in a third party to these machinations, but, in the lovers' estimation, safer than the drafting of potentially inculpatory billets-doux.

Isabel has a female servant, a pretty young girl who agrees to help in promoting the love affair. This girl, in her turn, experiences a tender inclination toward Alessio, Lucio's friend.

Alessio requites this feeling with youthful ardor. Thus, the symmetrical quartet is set in the typical and somewhat trite tradition of literary European Renaissance amorous intrigue: the dashing male protagonist enamors the lady, while his friend and accomplice woos her female servant. The latter, for the sake of symmetry, is also described as married, but the husband is conveniently away at one of the innumerable wars habitual in those tempestuous times.

At length, the opportunity arises for a more intimate encounter. Isabel sits at church, Lucio follows her there, kneels close by, and pretending a fervorous absorption in prayer, the crafty pair utters a profession of mutual everlasting affection, and concerts a soon-to-follow tryst. Isabel has a plan, the details of which she will disclose later. For the time being, she requests that Lucio and Alessio appear at her house on a specified evening.

Following Isabel's instructions, the two Sienese friends jump over the fence of her garden at night. Isabel ushers them into the house and reveals the plan she has devised. Her husband is in the house; he has just returned from the hunt. This sport is his passion, to which he devotes considerably more loving attention than to his wife (by now, the untoward effects of this miscalculation are only too apparent). She knows him for a heavy sleeper, especially after the strenuous exercise of a prolonged hunting expedition. What she proposes is the following: when her husband is in deep slumber, she will slide carefully out of the bed. Were she to remain away, there is a risk that her husband might wake up. But this will not happen, because Alessio will immediately occupy her place. Alessio, she trusts, will do this for the sake of the deep and inalterable friendship that joins him to Lucio.

The bedroom sunk in complete darkness, and the husband's known tendency to deep slumber, are the two conditions on which the plan is supposed to succeed. For, if the sleeping man should turn in his bed, he would feel a naked human presence, to which he was accustomed. Only this presence would be Alessio's, who would have to lie in bed totally undressed. Sometimes, Isabel's husband would entwine his leg with hers. This he would do unconsciously, in the depth of his sleep. Should he chance to do that on this occasion, he would encounter Alessio's leg, and, being sunk in the unconsciousness of a sound sleep after the hunt, he would not know the difference. This substitution was the only way that the two lovers, Lucio and Isabel, would be able to consummate their long postponed amorous union.

Alessio is shocked beyond words at the temerity and dangerousness of the plan. In vain it is represented to him that nothing could be seen inside the bedroom once the curtains were well drawn, and that he could safely hide there until the time of the substitution. He refuses to participate in such a risky venture. Lucio then pleads with him with all the eloquence that he can draw from his unassuaged passion. He appeals to their friendship, reminding him of their oath to endure any hardships in the name of their comradeship, and their often reiterated assurances that no worldly danger could diminish the brotherly affection they had for each other. But Alessio still refuses: the stratagem is much too dangerous.

It is then that a forceful persuasion is brought to bear on the hesitancy of the young man; namely, that after the deed was done, the guerdon for his courage and generosity would be the surrender of the woman he desired. Indeed, Isabel's young and pretty maid declared that, if Alessio were to show himself of such mettle as to lay his life on the line for the sake of friendship, then there was nothing she would deny him. No need to wonder what effect these words had: it suffices to recall that Alessio was young, hot-headed, and Italian: undecided when all the other arguments had been deployed, he yielded instantly when the last one was added.

The appointed hour arrives. Alessio is hiding, undressed, in the bedroom. In complete darkness, Isabel conducts him toward the bed, where he slides most carefully into decubitus position. There he remains quiet, motionless, mortally afraid of coughing or sneezing, not daring to move one inch, and serving as a substitute for the wily woman, so that, in case her husband should feel a leg or a shoulder next to him, he would be lulled into reassurance that his wife lies by his side. In reality, the disloyal wife is somewhere else in the house, with a young man that, this very minute, feels not the slightest inclination to doze off.

Meanwhile, Alessio is prey to extreme anxiety. His nervous apprehension surpasses all possible description: one minute he thinks the husband is about to wake up by himself; the next minute he trembles at the possibility of some unwanted noise that might bring him out of his slumber. Or else, he imagines that the wife is a perfidious woman who has plotted the destruction of the two friends, and plans to deliver him straight into the wolf's maw. He sees himself dead and blood-spattered, killed by an irate husband who defends his honor. The seconds feel to him like hours, and the hours like whole days.

Imagine his surprise when, at daybreak, Lucio and Isabel enter the bedroom making much noise. In the most carefree manner, they open the curtains, and ask him in all tranquility how he spent the night. Alessio is speechless, paralyzed by surprise and fear. Next, Isabel lifts the bed sheets, revealing her pretty young maid, who lies next to a perplexed Alessio, and who appears, the poor girl, not to have closed her eyes all night herself. Indeed, she, too, had been deceived into believing that she would substitute for her mistress.

This was too heavy a prank, no doubt, on Alessio and the young maid. But the pranksters later praised the two victims, according to Des Périers, each for a completely different reason: "Alessio for the danger in which he had put himself in order to advance his friend's romantic liaison, and his young lady for having behaved so modestly in spite of having been in bed with him all night."[79]

The raconteur ends his story by letting us know that these

two ladies upheld their profession of eternal devotion to their lovers, . . . eternal, of course, being a manner of speaking, which meant for the time that the respective husbands were away, serving the king in campaigns marked by combats of altogether different stamp from those in which their wives engaged, back at the manor.

Blurred, dim, indistinct, or ill-discerning vision is not used only as a vehicle of suspense in images and narratives. It may be directly approached as fit for comedy. The benighted, unobserving, or profoundly myopic personage who goes from blunder to blunder is a favorite of humorists. And it is telling of our uncharitable nature that the woes of imperfect eyesight are likelier to inspire laughter than commiseration. An example of this kind, one among myriads in this genre, may be drawn from the same author, Bonaventure des Périers. It is a ribald, earthy tale, which in its tone of gaiety, trickery, and licentiousness is indebted (like so many other narratives of its time), to Boccaccio's *Decameron*.

In the story, a wandering young man of delicate features is traveling through the countryside, and happens to catch sight, from a distance, of some nuns who worked in the orchards surrounding their monastery. He is impressed by the beauty of some of the novices and young nuns, and, in order to be able to approach them, he hits upon the extraordinary idea of disguising himself as a woman. Thus travestied, he can talk to them, and begins to frequent them. Growing familiarity increases his desire for still more intimate dealings with the attractive servants of the Lord.

As luck would have it, he meets the abbess of the convent, who is a profoundly myopic old woman. Hers is a highly suspicious nature, but her impulse to vigilance is amply countermanded by deficient eyesight. Moreover, the young man is of such delicacy of visage as would fool a keener, sharper-eyed observer. And to make matters worse (or better, from *his* point of view), he succeeds in winning the confidence of the abbess. For the boy is affable, serviceable, good-humored, and actuated by the desire to win the confidence of any one who might facilitate his access to the beauties he yearns for. In this undertaking, he roundly succeeds: the abbess begins by entrusting him with various errands, and, upon hearing that the young person is in dire economic necessity, she ends up offering him— always on the belief that "he" is a "she," for the crafty young man has taken the name of Thoinette—a nun's habit and modest lodgings within the walls of the convent.

The wolf is loose then, so to speak, amidst the flock of sheep. In the free, hale, and jolly style which is usual for this sort of ribald narratives, we are told that "Thoinette" goes from cell to cell, enjoying to surfeit the charms he had so ardently desired. But this paradisiacal stage cannot last. Rumors start growing in the hallowed corridors of the venerable place. There are noisy disputes among the young nuns, occasioned by the presence of the male who has, like the devil, sneaked into the holy bastion to disturb its peace. There are also invidious complaints of those who, less favored by Nature, would have liked their peace disturbed, but to their frustration could never attain what they longed for.

At length, the rumors reach the ears of the abbess. The sisters inform her that the cause of the disorder is the presence in their midst of a man disguised as a woman. She is scandalized. They say no more, not wishing to appear as invidious and mean-spirited informers, but also fearing that their denunciation might fall on deaf ears, for they are aware that the abbess has developed a great fondness and partiality for Thoinette. Should they mention this one by name, the abbess might become impervious to the most glaring evidence.

The head of the convent decides to adopt a drastic measure to clear the situation and reinstate order in the house. She is to inspect all the nuns in a state of undress, which is the most direct, immediate, and unambiguous way to discover the impostor and find out if there was any truth to the stories she has just heard. Therefore, she orders all the nuns to congregate in the convent's inner patio, and there she commands them to take all their clothes off.

Thoinette is in trouble. In great haste, and making use of all the shrewdness that procured him admission to the holy house, he comes up with a last-minute subterfuge to get out of his predicament. With a string of the nun's habit, he ties the organs that constitute the mark of his maleness, and manages to pull them back between the thighs, out of view of an inspector who would come to look at him from the front.

Incidentally, the same comic device was used in the ancient Greek comedy of Aristophanes entitled *Thesmophoriazusae* (sometimes translated as *The Poet and the Women*). A man, Cleisthenes, attends, disguised as a woman, a ceremony prohibited to men. Irate women suspect him, seize him, and he makes a great effort to keep up the pretense, to great comic effect. A woman lifts his robe from behind and catches a glimpse of male genitalia, but when another one comes to corroborate the finding, and lifts the robe in her turn, the organ of virility is no longer there: Cleisthenes has moved it anteriorly. The ensuing confusion is especially hilarious: "Where? I see nothing," says one. "It's back in front again!" says another. They run round to the front of the impostor. "No it isn't," they say. And from the back: "It's here again!" To which Cleisthenes says: "What is this, a shuttle service across the isthmus?"[80]

Thoinette, to continue our story, pulls on the string, and bends a little forward, thus making it possible for the anatomical badge of his manliness to disappear between his thighs, when viewed anteriorly. The abbess comes by, inspecting very minutely each one of the lined up nuns. Because of her profound myopia, she is wearing thick glasses. But it is clear that glasses produced at that time were very rudimentary, given the backward state of optical technology. Therefore, it is necessary for her to come very close to the object examined, in order to get a clear and distinct view of it.

And this is where des Périers ends his short story with a bang—of sorts. The abbess bends until her face is very close to Thoinette's pudendal area. But at this precise moment, Thoinette for the first time contemplates the spectacle of all the lined up nuns *au naturel*. And the view of so many coveted charms, formerly only dreamed of, and now all assembled together, so near to him, uncovered and fully exposed, proves too much for the young man. He reacts to the sexually stimulating sight as is physiologically normal for a hale and hearty young man; the string breaks; the tumescent organ suddenly swings in anterior direction; and the thick glasses of the abbess are sent flying to the other end of the patio.

The title of the short story is couched in the long descriptive sentences that were common in centuries past. It reads "Of how a young man, going through the town, and passing by the convent, contrived to usurp a female identity, and naming himself Thoinette [. . . etc., etc. . . .] managed to cast away the abbess' spectacles." Des Périers could have added: "And look at him: with no hands!"

The type of crass humor exemplified by these narratives seems to have been quite common in Italian and French Renaissance stories adverting to visual impairment. Why this was so, it is for experts to determine. (Defective vision, as in myopia, presbyopia, or astigmatism, is here alluded to. Blindness, the complete or almost total deprivation of eyesight, belongs in a different class: its tragic dimension cannot be consistently reduced to coarse-grained, indecorous hilarity.)

For decades, there has been a sustained interest in learned circles to investigate the "manner of seeing" of different cultures and epochs. Ponderous treatises have been written on the role of visuality in world literature. This almost cloying emphasis on the psychological and philosophical aspects of the visual function has been rightly called "oculocentrism." Whether to denigrate or to extol, there is little question that a concentrated attention on the eyesight and its multifarious significations has been a notable preoccupation of contemporary intellectuals. The pertinent literature that they have produced has now reached monumental proportions, and cannot be easily summarized.

What seems clear is that the process of what we term "looking," "seeing," or "gazing" was not always regarded in the same way. And whereas our own times scarcely pause to consider the psychological effects of diminished visual acuity (since at present this is reduced to a purely medical-ophthalmological problem, for the most part correctable with the use of glasses), or to exploit it as a literary theme, the European late Middle Ages and Renaissance took a perverse pleasure in satirizing it. When done with talent, memorable pages were contributed to this insensitive genre. But real talent being a rare and sparse commodity, a more frequent result was a ribald story couched in gaudy and meretricious prose.

A further idea of the tone of those narratives may be derived from the collection known as *Cent Nouvelles Nouvelles* ("One Hundred New Novels"). This literary work is of considerable historical interest, for it is thought to be the first collection of short stories to appear in French literature. It consists of one hundred tales, whose main protagonists were persons who really existed, some of them in highly distinguished posts, according to historians. For example, the personage referred to as "Monseigneur" in the book, presumably was Philippe le Bon, Duke of Burgundy; and likewise, other figures in the stories are thought to have been members of the Duke's court, or of his entourage, or other noteworthy contemporaries.

The *Cent Nouvelles Nouvelles* collection was written in 1462, most likely by a single author whose identity has been a matter of debate. Some have favored the writer Antoine de la Salle, but this opinion is not unanimous. The putative paternity of the work has also been linked with two other names: Philippe de Loan, Chamberlain of the Duke's Household, and Philippe Pot, celebrated Latinist and translator of the Italian Poggio. Whoever was the author, there is no doubt that he drew his inspiration from Giovanni Boccaccio (1313–1375) and his earthy *Decameron*. As in this work, a series of stories taken from oral tradition are presented, which are often ribald and anti-clerical, especially virulent in their anti-monk orientation.

Unfortunately, the parallel cannot be extended very far. The French imitation falls short of the work it pretended to emulate. Boccaccio's opus is justly renowned for its liveliness. The agility of the style and the irrepressible vitality that animates its pages (always earthy and sometimes outright indecent) are without peer; and so is the variety of inventiveness that the Italian author displays. In contrast, the French work gives the impression of monotony from a flat style and a reiterative thematic. Apart from its direct and concise language, which makes for emphatic expressiveness, especially in the dialogues, there is little here that would announce the vast, magnificent, glorious edifice that French language literature was going to become in succeeding centuries.

In several of the stories, the eyesight, hale or infirm, plays an important role, as detailed in what follows.

The Sixteenth Nouvelle tells of a one-eyed gentleman who goes to the war and leaves his wife behind in his castle. She is far from saddened by his absence. While he combats the Saracens, she engages in amorous combats with a young and handsome squire—the cheating, deceitful wife is a recurring motif in these stories—while monseigneur fasts and does penance, the lady carouses, frolics, and antics with the young squire.

The struggle against the Saracens turns out to be less protracted than anticipated. Seeing that his services are no longer needed, and taken by invincible nostalgia for his home and his familiar possessions, the one-eyed gentleman returns home in a great hurry. He rides ahead of his tired attendants; fully invested in his warrior appurtenances, booted, bedraggled, and mud-splattered from the campaign, he flies non-stop to his castle. There, his wife lies blissfully in bed in the company of her minion.

Our man must knock at the door vigorously and repeatedly before the wife, intentionally slow in order to make time for her lover to dress and hide in a wardrobe, comes down to open. To her husband's impatient remonstrances, she replies that she was in the middle of a dream, in which she vividly represented him coming back from the war, and having recovered the lost sight of his extinct eye. This dream seemed so real, so patently material and concrete, that she is absolutely persuaded that the celestial powers must have restored his blind eye to normal vision. "How can that be? This eye has been useless since long ago," says the husband. But his wife is so utterly persuaded that the bad eye is now healthy, and so excited at the prospect that a miraculous cure has indeed taken place, that the gentleman at length agrees to disabuse her and be tested.

To check his eyesight, the woman covers the seeing eye with one hand, while with the other she approaches a lighted candle to the blind eye. She repeats this motion once and again, asking him if he can see anything, to which he answers negatively every time. But this maneuver renders the gullible spouse completely unable to see, so that, while the "test" is being performed, the lover sneaks out from his concealment, greatly relieved at saving himself unscathed from his predicament. In the end, the lady declares herself undeceived, but happy: "The important thing is that you are back!" she exclaims rapturously. The husband is flattered by this touching expression of concern, embraces the lady, and all are happy.

In the fifty-third Nouvelle, the reader is introduced to the church of Saint Gudule, in the city of Brussels. The first mass is being celebrated that winter morning, and, as is customary, it takes place very early, between four and five o'clock. Among those attending the ceremony is a young couple of humble social status about to be married. Not far from them is a second couple, although the man and the woman are no longer young; however, it is a fact that their years are directly proportional to the wealth they had accumulated throughout their protracted lives. This pair is also expecting to be married that morning.

Now, the priest officiating is one-eyed, and his one and only functioning eye is more like the mole's than the lynx's. Being winter, the light in Brussels is pale; and with a flickering candle for all illumination the priest can hardly see. Which is why he gets a hold of the wrong partners, fits them with the marriage rings—at that time these were provided by the parish—and ends up joining in holy matrimony the old rich man with the young woman, and the poor young man with the rich elderly woman. An astonishing confusion, in which the men's inattention was more to blame than the women's, says the story-teller, because the former usually keep their heads straight and look up during the ceremony, whereas the latter "tend to keep their heads all the time bent toward the ground at holy Mass," and thus may not realize what is happening.

As soon as the ceremony is finished, the friends of the old bridegroom surround his brand-new wife, and carry her—literally—as was the custom, to her new home. Similarly, the old crone is transported to the humble house of the young man. The young bride was speechless with astonishment. She did not recognize the surroundings, or any of the guests. The richly furnished apartments of the luxurious mansion; the elegant tapestries on the walls; the exquisite taste of costly adornments that dress the rooms; the fastidious refinement with which wines, sweets, and viands were disposed on the table for the wedding banquet; all this had her lost in wonderment.

When her veil was removed, those present were as surprised as if they had seen a preternatural apparition. "What!" exclaimed the senile bridegroom. "Is this my new wife? She is *really* changed from yesterday. I take it she must have bathed in the Fountain of Youth. I am most pleased."

"We know for sure she is the one you have married," said the guests, "since we took her from the altar, and have not let go of her person for one instant until we brought her here."

When it became clear that the confusion stemmed from the imperfect vision of a priest, there was much laughter among the guests. "The Lord be praised for this change!" was the comment of the newly-minted old husband, who was quick to manifest his willingness to humbly abide by the wise designs of

Divine Providence. Not so the young bride. When she realized the mistake, she broke into sobs and plaintively pleaded to be taken to "the man to whom her father had given her."

The story then takes a surprising turn. The aged husband reassures her. He tries to reason with her. He lets her know that he is, thanks be to God, very well off; that she will lack nothing; that he can provide plenteously for all her family; that he earnestly pledges to be most considerate to her; and, now that the rites of the holy Church had irreversibly sealed their union, as good a support and as loyal a companion as it lies in his power. At length, the eloquence of the superannuated bridegroom succeeds in erasing her misgivings; she seems, if not rapturous or elated, at least calmly resigned. The two newlyweds end up taking their dinner, and retiring to bed as tradition enjoined, "where the old man did the best he could."

Meanwhile, the aged bride is up against the same shocking revelation. "What am I doing here?" she says when confronted with the squalor of the place, the meanness of the decoration, and the poverty of all the furnishings in her new home. The young man was no less surprised than his parents and the wedding guests, at the major mix-up. "You've been hoaxed, my son!" exclaimed the groom's father, "you got someone else's wife. It is all the fault of that priest, who can hardly see. And God played a trick on me as well, since at church I was so placed that I could not detect the confusion."

"So, what shall I do now?" asked the young man. And upon the father answering "I am no authority on these matters, but I think [under the circumstances] you may have another wife," the elderly bride loudly protested: "By Saint John! Little do I care to have a young gallant for a husband, who couldn't care less about me, who would squander all my money, and if I uttered the slightest protest might well smack me in the face. Away, away! Send for your wife and let me go where I ought to be!"

The father of the young woman, along with some friends, is deputized to go pick up his daughter and bring her to her originally intended husband. But when the delegation arrives at the rich man's house, they are met with a discouraging reception:

> You are too late. Let each one be content with his own lot. The lord of this manor is happy with the wife that God has given him. He is now married to her, and wants no other one. And don't you complain. You never were happier than today, when you have a daughter placed so high. All of you are going to be very rich.

The good father returned, and it cannot be truthfully said that he did so contrite or dejected. After he reported the result of his mission, the aged bride was furious: "What! Am I to be so vilely deceived? This is not going to stay like this, if I have to appeal to the courts of justice." The old woman was incensed, but no less than the young bridegroom, whose love had been cruelly frustrated. "He might have attenuated his pain," cynically observes the narrator, " if at least he could have fleeced the old woman of her riches. But there was no way: she made life so miserable, that she had to be let go back to her home."

The story is left unfinished. We are told that she was summoned to appear before a judge (presumably at the instigation of her young husband, whose greed may have been kindled upon fancying himself entitled to share in her wealth). She, in turn, initiated a legal suit against her quondam fiancé, now the aged husband of the young woman. The narrative concludes with the statement that a cumbrous and embroiled legal process was in course at the time of the writing. Since we know that the *One Hundred Nouvelles* were based on the lives of real people and on historically genuine facts, it is a sure bet that the issue of these miseries is consigned in old parchments somewhere, slowly decaying in some dusty, cobweb-laden judicial archive.

The literature of "oculocentrism" has given rise to innumerable disquisitions on the relationship between seeing and knowing, or between sight, knowledge, and power. The context of these relationships remits the reader to arduous philosophical problems that have concerned thinkers of all eras. But to see is a dynamic process that involves the seeing and the seen. The dynamics of this relationship may be forbiddingly entangled. Therefore, a number of psychoanalytic concepts, as well as historical and cultural analyses, may be brought to bear upon the interpretation of texts that refer to the gaze. (All this, which makes for rather dense reading material, is an attempt of learned critics to find new ways to interpret literary writings.) One or the other of these many aspects may be chosen to analyze a literary work, the so-called "reading strategy."

A modern critic of the *Cent Nouvelles Nouvelles* wrote that the author of the very brief narratives seems to be "extending a pact which is like one of those marriages celebrated in the twilight by a one-eyed priest, which couple an old man to a young girl, and an old crone to a young man, causing pleasure to the one, pain to the other, opening up onto infinite processes," as emblematized in the fifty-third Nouvelle.[81] Statements of this nature I find irredeemably obscure (just like a great deal of the exegetic, vision-related literature), but I take it to mean that the material is both painful and pleasurable to the reader, and open to numberless interpretations. We are amused by the jocular complications, the salacious merriment, and the Rabelaisian archness of the characters. We are repelled by the vulgar frivolity, the crass references, and the cynical, insensitive tone: the one-eyed always shall be duped or outright blinded. These tales have been rightly compared to stories told by men in the old "smoking room" of the men's clubs of yore.

A narrative of this kind, crass to the point of unseemliness, and therefore likely to give rise to abundant commentary among the literati, is the second Nouvelle of the collection. I summarize it in what follows.

The action is supposed to take place in the city of London, England. Here, a beautiful young girl passes for being a paragon of perfections. Not only is she beauteous beyond compare, but she is sweet of temperament, amiable of disposition, alert of mind, and pious of breeding. Alas, Fortune cannot suffer the concentration of her favors on a single person: having first lavishly dispensed her benefits on the girl, she now cruelly compensates by foisting on her a grievous ill. The maiden is afflicted with, in the words of the narrator, "a disgusting and dangerous malady that is commonly termed the *broches*" (ancient French word for a prosaic illness: piles, or hemorrhoids).

The poor girl does nothing but cry and sigh all day long, to the great distress of her parents. Her home, formerly a place of laughter, cheer, and good sentiments, is now transformed into a house of mourning. Nor is any measure fit to restore the suffering girl to her former good spirits. Household remedies are tried; the advice of savvy matrons is followed; diets, medicaments, regimes: all is to no avail. The most eminent physicians are consulted; they wish to see the pathology, but the patient's modesty cannot bear to make her private parts a spectacle to any man. At length, her parents, in despair, plead with her to submit to the medical inspection. They represent to her that the malady is a grave risk, that it may lead to death, and that to allow this is not a small sin.

On the strength of these theological reasons, she agrees to the examination. She is properly draped, and positioned so that only the affected part is exposed. A choice group of medicos gravely directs their collective gaze to the diseased part, and prescribe the apposite remedies. Woe is me! One more disappointment: the ill shows no signs of regression.

Months and months had gone by, and the girl, her parents, and her whole household sank in despair. An officious neighbor, feeling great compassion for the girl and her disconsolate parents, lets them know that a *cordelier*, that is to say, a monk of the Franciscan order (so called because of the small cord that Franciscan friars tie around their frock), is passing through town, and is reputed to have a remedy of proven effectiveness in the treatment of the cursed *broches*.

The monk is summoned without delay. He is—wouldn't you know it?—blind in one eye. He possesses a strong medicine against the piles: it comes in powdered form and must be sapiently applied to the diseased parts. In the extremity of their dispiritedness, the girl and her parents begin to see a ray of hope. They promptly agree to the treatment.

Once again, the girl is carefully made to lie prone, her behind exposed, all surrounding areas scrupulously draped, and the one-eyed monk approaches with his medicament in hand. He places the powder in a vessel, and after loading it unto a little tube, he sprays the medicine carefully on the afflicted site. To properly perform this procedure, he must come very close to the treated area. The friar's one eye must be brought into close proximity to "the eye of the arse"—("*el ojo del culo*": earthy term used by Francisco de Quevedo, the satiric genius of seventeenth century Spain, in one of his memorable, acid pieces).

The friar is keenly occupied in spreading the curative powder, when the girl turns her head and catches sight of his ministrations. The spectacle of this one-eyed healer, closely bent on her behind and straining his single, myopic eye in some sort of voyeuristic orgy, she finds funny in the extreme. The whole scene must have had much that moved to laughter: the clownish monk, the "eye-to-eye" confrontation, the position of the participants, and so on.

The girl makes a big effort to contain her laughter, and this effort results in her producing "a little sound" at the very site being treated. The accompanying rush of air blows off the powder, which is thus sprayed straight into the eye of the healer. The powder is corrosive, and the one-eyed friar is blinded.

The story finishes with the remark that the poor friar pressed the girl's parents for compensation and life-long indemnization, since once blinded he was reduced to beggary. At a time when respect for individual rights and tort civil actions were largely ignored, it is doubtful if he got any form of redress.

Let the savants and literary critics engage in farfetched, complex interpretations of this text. Let them argue whether the keen inspection of the girl's intestinal terminus represents, as a scholar wrote, "an indecent quest of interiority, of a bottom in *the bottom*, at which one may stop as if one had attained the exterior limit, 'the inside-out'."[82] Against these Byzantine, esoteric interpretations, which, I confess, for the most part exceed my comprehension, I feel that Renaissance narratives represent simply an instance of "letting off steam." I mean vital energetic excess, or, if I may put it thus, "spiritual tension." For such is the proper attitude of the new era, the Renaissance, the re-birth. There were stiff religious prohibitions during the Middle Ages, and these are now gone. There were taboos about the body, and the concept of the body is now radically re-evaluated. There were things that could not be said, and now the language is rich in words that shine like newly minted silver coins. Rabelais and Montaigne, the greatest contemporaries of the writers here quoted, unabashedly pile up synonyms, adjectives, hyperbolic terms, and diminutives and augmentatives. The age is young. The spirit of the age is drunk with the wine of vigorous, irrepressible youth.

Little wonder if, in the middle of this general inebriation, story tellers come up with the naughty, carnivalesque buffooneries that excited youths are known to indulge. Some are full of vulgarities and arrant obscenities. It is my humble opinion that it is wrong to read in them such profundities and obscure symbolisms as exhilarating stories of merry-making youths and jokes of revelers in a drinking party never had.

The Clinical Eye

I. Macroscopy and the Medical Gaze

"*Recordar es vivir*," is a common Spanish byword: "To remember is to live." Not to re-live, mind you, for the experience remembered is never quite the same as the one lived. Reminiscences surge to the light of consciousness always in an altered state: decayed or embellished, a recollection is ever changed in proportion to the length of its confinement. Thus, if we should descend to the lowermost depths of memory in search of whatever shreds of our past might still be lying in the murky bottom, we shall find them entwined with spurious fancies and all sorts of secondary accretions. In no other way the treasure chest discovered by sea-divers in a submerged wreck is seen encrusted with salt and entwined with streaming algae. It may be so with my present recollection: it is an evocation of things removed from my current horizon by the interposition of almost half a century.

I recall that, as a medical student in Mexico, as the decade of the nineteen-fifties was about to finish, I was taught the art of examining patients. This was done in a course with a high-sounding name, *Medical Propedeutics*. (from the Greek *pro*, before, and *paideuein*, to educate, therefore "to teach before," that is, the instruction preparatory to the acquisition of certain skills). Technology-mediated diagnostic methods were much less advanced than they now are, and the examiner had to rely largely on sense perception. To diagnose the disease it was necessary, first, to look at the patient, then to master the various techniques of interrogation, auscultation, percussion, and the sundry maneuvers designed to elicit specific responses.

Inspection was first and, in a sense, foremost among these approaches. There is scarcely a field of human endeavor in which the gaze has had as much importance as in clinical medicine. Perhaps only painting required comparable powers of observation. Merleau-Ponty wrote that the painter is alone in having "the right of the gaze over all things, without the duty of appreciation."[83] But the clinician shares the same right, in the sense that he starts by looking without any preconceived ideas, and, at least initially, approaches his subject invested with the unarmed purity of the naked eye.

The clinician's eyesight, we were told, should catch not only the obvious manifestations of pathology, such as scars, missing limbs, or the use of crutches or prostheses, but also the general appearance of the subject: facial expression, manner of dress and action, and the general bearing of the person. If at all possible, the physician must inspect the patient before this one sees him (or her); observe the patient while sitting, walking, talking; try to form an idea of the patient's personal habits, nutritional status, and so on. A medical textbook plainly declared that "the examiner should be trying to answer the question 'Who is this patient?' in all its ramifications."

But such a question is, of course, impossible to answer. Imagine: to try to ascertain character, temperament, or personality by merely looking! Yet, physiognomy—the judging of a person's physical, mental, and moral nature by his/her outward features—enjoyed no little prestige in former times. For a while, it became possessed of entitlements as weighty as those of physiology or anatomy. And the eyes, long regarded as "windows of the soul," figured prominently in that discipline.

A seventeenth-century treatise by Jean-Baptiste Porta (*circa* 1535–1615) devoted close to twenty-five percent of its total text to the eye.[84] It endorsed the ancient belief (already present in Aristotle) that the principal signs of disease, and those most certain, are to be found in the noblest and most remarkable parts of the body, which comprised the eyes and surrounding areas, and generally the face. In contrast, the chest and the shoulders occupy a secondary position as objects worthy of medical inspection; the limbs and the feet come next; and the abdominal region is last in importance in this regard: presumably, visible manifestations of disease were rarely made evident in the belly.

When he comes to the eyes, however, Porta expounds with boundless prolixity. No less than twenty-four chapters are devoted to descriptive, eye-related minutiae. Special sections are assigned to "the angle or corner of the eyes;" "the color of the eyes;" "the eyelids or drapes of the eyes;" "eyes that have circles of various colors;" "dark and light eyes." A part is entitled "of the movement of the eyes, and firstly of those fixed." There are learned discussions of "eyes that tremble;" "eyes that close;" "eyes that close and open frequently;" "eyes that do not blink;" "laughing eyes;" "sad eyes;" and "eyes that move upwards and downwards." It is impossible to make much sense out of this seemingly inexhaustible, eye-centered, physiognomic profuseness. We feel at a loss to interpret these baroque descriptions, because to fully understand them we would have to be acquainted with a whole mass of cultural references and idiomatic codes, familiar to clinicians of centuries past, but to which today we are complete strangers.

Be that as it may, keen visual observation remained paramount in medical practice. A rich lore among medical students in my day propagated the myth of "the clinical eye," a personal faculty of which a few gifted practitioners were allegedly possessed. Those so blessed succeeded in detecting the hidden clues, the slightest, tiniest marks of pathology. Where others had long strained their eyes, cogitated obsessively, and exhausted every conceivable laboratory test, the physician endowed with the "clinical eye," by the simple act of looking, succeeded in discovering the most arcane illnesses and established the most difficult diagnoses. It sufficed for him, or her, to enter into the room, to catch a glimpse of a faint skin rash, a barely perceptible tremor, or who knows what pathologic sign that the generality had overlooked, and presto!, the diagnostic puzzle was instantly solved. It could be said of such mythical diagnostician what someone said of a painter, that "his eyes had the gift of the visible, as the [divinely] inspired man has the gift of tongues."

No wonder that the young students, with characteristic levity, invented their own jocular stories about the training of the portentous "clinical eye." Some were of a distinctly unwholesome, vulgar, and morbid cast, as medical students' humor not uncommonly was; one of these, handed down from one class to the next, and, curiously, heard in student circles across continents, is as follows.

The rigorous medical training required, in the past, the systematic overcoming of feelings of disgust and revulsion. Since the physician had personally to examine the patient's excreta, and to contemplate undaunted the awful spectacle of pestilential sores, effusions of blood, pus, and other revolting sights, no person with a queasy stomach could be well advised to follow the medical calling. These considerations are keenly held in mind by the students who gather in the anatomy laboratory, around a a cadaver lying on a dissecting table. The instructor addresses to them a short speech in which it is question, again, of the necessity to master the natural responses of annoyance and rejection when one is faced by intolerable, disgusting sensations.

Next, the instructor says: "Watch me carefully." And without further ado, he introduces a finger of his gloved hand into the anal orifice of the cadaver. Then, continuing the very rapid motion, he withdraws it, and to the breathless astonishment of the group of students, who can scarcely believe the evidence of their own eyes, the instructor directs his hand toward his mouth . . . there to insert his finger, then hold it, and suck it in the mouth with apparent delight, as if it were a lollipop!

Amidst a gasp of undisguised revulsion of his audience, the instructor turns to one of the students, telling him: "Now let's see you try to do the same."

The interpellated student feels the ground beneath his feet sink, and his knees tremble. He cannot overcome the feeling of extreme repugnance, verily nauseating, that the witnessed act inspires in him. On the other hand, he is sincerely and ardently committed to a career in medicine, and is willing to subject himself to any sacrifice, no matter how harsh, if it will help him to become a doctor. Mustering all his courage, his teeth clenched and his brow covered with cold sweat, the poor student repeats the fulsome maneuver he had observed, all the while making strenuous efforts to suppress the overwhelming feeling of nausea that he experiences.

The instructor, unmoved, calmly says to the discomposed young student: "I am very impressed by your capacity for over-mastering the nauseous sensation. It shows your strong determination and cold blood. But when it comes to your powers of observation, I am sorry to say they are sadly deficient. You didn't notice that I inserted *this* finger, the fourth finger, but sucked this other one, the index finger. You really need to be more observant in the future if you wish to become a good practitioner."

Aside from this crass form of medical students' humor, inspection has been traditionally one of the mainstays of the physical examination of patients. Its importance in medicine cannot be minimized, and it is fitting that Michel Foucault (1926–1984), a towering figure of twentieth century philosophy, should have devoted an important part of his oeuvre to analyzing what he called "the medical gaze." Since then, all attempts to discuss medical visual perception would be incomplete without referring to his work, and particularly his book *The Birth of the Clinic.*

Foucault affirmed that exquisite attention to information gained visually is a feature of modernity. Before the eighteenth century, the physician conferred greater importance to theoretical knowledge. The best physician was thought to be the one who "knew" the most, and by this was meant the one who retained a vast farrago of medical hypotheses and intricate classificatory schemes, of which many, if not most, were airy notions inherited from antiquity, devoid of practical utility. "No disease ought to be treated before knowing to what species it belongs," was the profession's dogma: intricate classification and hypothetical speculation dominated a medical practitioner's every professional act. This was the physician so acidly and hilariously lampooned by Molière and other satirists: always ready to drop a Greek or Latin axiom, the more cryptic the better, with which to cover his ignorance and his powerlessness. In contrast, the modern era saw the rise of the experimental method, and, concurrently, the best physician ceased to be he who "knew the most" and became he who "had seen the most." Or perhaps it is more appropriate to say, as did the renowned thinker, that seeing and knowing became so inextricably intertwined as to be synonymous with each other.

Foucault's prose, heavily freighted with metaphors and unaccustomed symbolic tropes, and impelled by the winds of a seemingly overstrung, impatient temper, is no easy going for any reader. But those of us who gathered around a patient's hospital bed, avid to learn all we could about medicine, are especially sensitive to his affirmation that in the modern hospital setting there is no difference between seeing and knowing: "the act of recognition and the effort to know find fulfilment in a single movement." In the teaching hospital, Foucault wrote, there is no longer a division between those who know and those who do not. The clinical group is newly unified. The novel unity consists of "those who unmask and those before whom one unmasks. The statement is the same; the disease speaks the same language to both."[85]

But is this true? Far be it from me to pretend to contradict the eximious philosopher; still, the latter statements call for qualification. In the clinic, there may have been "a certain unity," since the spectacle is the same for all, but egalitarianism there was none. The teachers, "those who unmask," were not, and certainly are not, on a plan of perfect equality with those "before whom they unmask." The mere fact of doing the unmasking already points to the existing hierarchy; and the manner of doing it will determine what is learned. Nor is it true that the unmasked pathology "speaks the same language to all." It is perhaps a cliché, yet all too often forgotten (and for this reason deliberately reiterated with insistence in this book), that one sees only what one is prepared to see, or what one wishes to see. Clinical medicine is not exempt from this inherent bias. Wrote a distinguished clinician at a time when diagnosis was largely based upon the physician's sense perceptions:

> When a student has just read a treatise of medical pathology, it seems to him that he is already a physician, but, in the presence of a sick patient, he experiences the strangest embarrassment, and soon realizes that the ground is missing beneath his feet.
>
> I do not mean simply the embarrassment that comes from lack of habit; such a thing is easily understood; but I mean that the signs and symptoms will have much that is unusual and surprising to him. Even the commonest diseases, those that pass for being the easiest to diagnose, will present insurmountable difficulties. In the textbooks, the student has seen the general description, painted with large brush-strokes, of pulmonary tuberculosis. The author [. . .] may have stated that there are delicate nuances, and that there are many exceptions; but these nuances and these exceptions are what least impressed the young student, and they are precisely that which, from the inception as well as in the later stages of pulmonary tuberculosis, the true clinician finds most arresting . . .[86]

Clearly, experience and knowledge are chief determinants of what one observer sees and the other fails to see; and to optimally educate the "medical gaze" means to teach the eye to see selectively: the pupil admits or rejects incoming sights, as in a customs-house. To achieve the true "clinical eye" is a daunting undertaking that takes many years.

In my youthful naiveté, there was a time when I thought that the eyesight alone had to be educated; that clinical excellence stemmed, in large part, from sheer visual acuity; and that, therefore, medical training ought to include the learning of techniques to improve eyesight. I was, in this respect, like a personage of the ancient Chinese Taoist philosopher and storyteller Lieh-Tzu (*circa* 450–375 B. C.),[87] who painted, with a characteristic touch of humor, the tribulations of a young man who wished to achieve visual perfection.

In the story, a young man yearned to become the greatest archer in the land, and to this end asks the foremost master of this art how to perfect the eyesight. The techniques that the master recommends are quite original. First, the young man is to go home and lie on his back, on the ground, with his face directly under the pedal of his wife's loom. The wife will come to operate the loom, and he must practice to keep his eyes open, and remain without blinking even as the pedal plunges straight in the direction of his eyes. Once he is able to do this, he can move on to a more serious exercise. This consists in having expert swordsmen thrust their pointed weapons at his face, stopping a few millimeters short of his corneas. This technique must be maintained until the fearful approach of the sword's tip can be contemplated without blinking. Next, the young man is to suspend a tiny insect, a louse, from a hair. He is supposed to stare at the tiny louse for hours on end, every day, with his now blink-resistant eyes. If he does this, the master says, the tiny louse will seem to grow to the size of a silkworm, and eventually to the size of a pig, allowing the young man to see the slightest details of its outer anatomy. To arrive at this stage will have been no small accomplishment. Imagine, to visualize a louse the size of a pig!

In the story, the apprentice-archer realizes his dream. He became the greatest archer who ever lived. Proof of it is, says the narrator, that he could shoot an arrow, at the distance of over one hundred yards, straight through the heart of his hair-suspended louse. (How could it be ascertained that an arrow had been shot through the heart of a louse is a mystery that the subtle Oriental philosopher does not reveal to his readers. . . .)

Lieh-Tzu's humorous piece equates visual acuity with absence of blinking. But unlike the apprentice archer of his story, the modern clinician cannot aspire to perfect his diagnostic skills solely by enhancing visual power. Establishing a diagnosis is neither purely visual, nor the orderly piecing together of information that was taught to me in Medical Propedeutics. The skillful physician proceeds along irregular, disconcerting lines of thought. He, or she, forms an early hypothesis, tracks down a few clues, seeks "clusters" of data that strengthen his idea, quickly discards those he deems incompatible, and, in a manner that he himself is unaware of, and which usually he cannot conceptualize, zeroes in on the right answer. This mental process seems to advance by leaps and skips, and is of much interest to medical educators,[88] but not germane to our present concern.

All of this has not stymied the idea that eyesight-perfecting techniques might improve the diagnostic performance of some medical specialists, albeit those who rely heavily on vision for their work, such as radiologists and histopathologists, who are not thought of as "front-line" clinicians. How do these experts in visual search proceed in their daily work? Since they are trained to observe details, what role does perceptive experience play in their skills, and how can the latter be improved? These and other cognate questions were asked by two investigators, who took their cues from the "Nina Project," a program sponsored by the United States Department of Defense in 1976, to make pilots more proficient at detecting camouflage.

The name Nina was taken from the work of cartoonist Al Hirschfeld (1903–2003), well known for his drawings in *The*

New Yorker magazine. Nina is the name of his daughter. Since her birth, the artist used to disguise her name at least once in most of his caricatures and cartoons. Hirschfeld's fans strove to detect the concealed "Ninas" (a number inscribed to the right of the artist's signature indicated how many) amidst the tousled hairdos, clothes' folds, shadings, or other features in the drawings. Similarly, a contemporary cartoonist, Martin Handford, draws a personage called "Waldo," usually submerged in a crowd or somehow dissimulated in a motley background; and apparently this artist's followers also take delight in trying to spot the concealed "Waldos."

The aforementioned investigators monitored the eye movements of a group of radiologists who tried to detect Ninas.[89] They measured the number of times that the eyes paused to fixate here and there, and the duration of these pauses, trying to ascertain how many fixation pauses were necessary, and for how long, in order to spot Ninas. They also compared the performance of radiologists in this visual search, versus that of lay people. An aim of this research was to ascertain which is the best way in which an object, rendered unapparent by virtue of its position amidst a confusing background, may be more readily detected. The implications are of considerable importance to radiologic diagnosis. If there were optimal methods to visually scan radiologic films, or other images of medical technology, then the diagnosis of lesions difficult to detect may be facilitated. This topic, how images are scanned and how their visualization may be improved, has deserved some attention in the specialized literature.[90, 91, 92] Small masses, say incipient lung tumors, may be very difficult to diagnose, because they are obscured by a number of other structures that overlap them or submerge them.

The results of this study were striking. For one thing, the radiologists did no better than lay persons in spotting the concealed objects. Secondly, the number of pauses in the eyes' movement and their duration was greater when the objects were missed. As the investigators put it, "when a target was missed the viewer typically exhibited prolonged visual dwell fixating it." In plain words, the eyes saw, but the viewer did not see. The hackneyed truism is once again made apparent: it is perfectly possible to stare at something, and yet not see it.

Today, the medical gaze has been extended to an unimaginable degree. Aided by technology, it probes into the remotest, least accessible nooks and crannies of the body. We have X-rays, computerized tomography, magnetic resonance imaging, ultrasound, cardiotocography, positron emission tomography, and so on. By means of these techniques, the clinical eye peers into the *sanctum sanctorum* of the body's shrine. The "unveiling revolution" that began in 1816 with the invention of the stethoscope, has progressed to the point where any lesion that the eye can see is by definition ostensible to the medical gaze. Thus, it is possible to unveil a serious disease, to make its mortal signs open to the unaided eye, without experiencing any symptoms at all.

The medical gaze penetrates, surveys, peers, and canvasses every structural bodily detail. It scrutinizes the very foundation of corporeal individuality. Indeed, forensic experts know that, when there is need to identify a corpse, it is no longer necessary to have the individual's fingerprints, nor even the dental X rays. Computerized tomography (CT) reveals the shape of the frontal sinuses, and has demonstrated that "no two sinuses are alike," not even in the case of identical twins. CT is thus one more asset in the forensic expert's armamentarium.

Curious to remark, the extension of the medical gaze went on a par with the progress of psychoanalysis. As the body's deepest recesses were explored, the incorporeal aspects of the mind were being probed in parallel. It is no coincidence that, during the nineteenth century, the strongest advocates of perfecting the art of looking at patients were physicians interested in mental disorders and diseases of the nervous system. "In all the affections relevant to general medicine," wrote one of them, "the [visual] study of patients has a secondary place, compared to what it ought to be in mental patients." If mental derangements were illnesses of the soul, the countenance reflected its agitation. Hence the great impetus of scientific endeavors that, like criminal anthropology, sought to establish a connection between bodily morphology and disturbed mind, between the patient's appearance and madness, criminality, or the tempestuous discomposure of the psyche.

A foremost leader in this field was Jean-Martin Charcot (1825–1893), justly considered by many to have been, together with Guillaume Duchenne (1806–1875), the founder of modern neurology. Charcot was professor at the University of Paris. For thirty-three years he worked and taught at the Salpêtrière Hospital, eventually becoming its director. As a teacher, he was unexcelled. Students came from all parts of the world to attend his lectures and demonstrations. Among them were Alfred Binet (1857–1911) who abandoned a law career to follow studies in medical psychology, and later achieved fame in his own right by his contributions to the measurement of intelligence; Pierre Janet (1859–1947), who was instrumental in the delineation of important concepts of psychology, including phobias, anxiety, and behavioral disorders; and no less a renowned figure than Sigmund Freud (1856–1939), who avowed that his months of study at the Salpêtrière under Charcot were a turning point in his career: impressed by the master's use of hypnotism on some patients, Freud turned away from his initial avocation as a neurologist, and began directing his thoughts toward the unconscious. Here lies the earliest origin of psychoanalysis, according to some scholars.

Charcot's working style, and his studious emphasis on the visual inspection of the sick, became legendary. The reality of disease, he felt, was made evident to the examiner through the eyesight: seeing was tantamount to collecting scientific evidence, and this applied to psychological illnesses. Freud said of Charcot that he used to look again and again at the things he did not understand, until by dint of continual looking what seemed chaotic suddenly presented itself to the mind's eye as orderly and comprehensible. And he added: "Charcot was, as he said of himself, a *visuel*, a man who sees." As a scholar felicitously phrased it, "for Charcot all illness—mental and physical—had a somatic dimension."[93] Wrote one of his contemporaries in an unsigned note of the journal of the Salpêtrière Hospital:

> A great number of patients were examined using the simplest apparatus. The penetrating gaze of Charcot stopped at the slightest bodily anomaly: he took note, reflected, called another subject, compared him to the preceding one, called a third one, started all over the following day, and the next days, and of this minute observation—above all visual—there often resulted a precious discovery, sometimes even the revelation of a heretofore unknown disease. The artist, which in Charcot went hand in hand with the physician, was no stranger to these findings.[94]

This "simple apparatus" of Charcot's early career evolved to greater sophistication with the passage of time, as noted by a physician in later years:

> At the Salpêtrière, behind the vast constructions that house the elderly women, is an asylum for the insane. The hysteric women are consigned there. They are not disseminated in the various services, but put together in the same part of the hospital, where for many years they have been entrusted to the care of professor Charcot. This knowledgeable physician, desirous of applying to the study of nervous affections the accurate methods that are used in physiology, directed the construction, to one side of the patients' wards, of a laboratory where the most precise techniques may be applied to the study of diseases of the nervous system. To this laboratory is annexed a photography studio. It has been possible to reproduce with indisputable accuracy the principal phases

of the attacks of hysteria, epilepsy, and somnambulism. Thus, it has been possible to successfully describe psychologic phenomena so bizarre and fantastic, that scarcely two centuries ago they were attributed to the devil's breath and to all the demons of hell.[95]

At a time when photography was still of recent invention, we can understand the enthusiasm of the physician who salutes this striking technologic innovation as a means to capture, with unprecedented accuracy, the real appearance of disease. In a letter to Sigmund Freud dated November 23, 1891, Charcot complained that the transcription of his famous Tuesday lectures to the public (the lay public could attend, and the talks, that he delivered with unsurpassed sense of theatricality, were generally directed to the educated middle class) could not do justice to the complexity of the subjects studied, for "the stenographer is not the photographer."[96] Apparently he opined that only the photographer could succeed in this formidable task. The very essence of various pathologies might be revealed, he must have thought, in those astounding, quasi-miraculous photographic plates.

But, at more than a hundred years distance, how sobering it is to reconsider the initial excitement! For one thing, who were those poor women, the "hysterics" locked up inside a forbidding construction at the back of the Salpêtrière? The diagnosis of "hysteria" that dominated the psychiatric literature for many decades, so that about eighty percent of the articles published in the first part of the twentieth century were connected with this entity; this diagnosis is no more. It does not exist. Patients who formerly would have been so labeled are now classified under other, more current and presumably better grounded classificatory schemes.

And those "new diseases" that the keen, penetrating gaze of Charcot and his votaries brought forth from the inchoate state in which they existed, where are they now? For his superb clinical descriptions, and his thoughtful studies correlating symptoms and anatomical lesions, Charcot has deservedly won a place of distinction in the history of medicine. But together with those masterful insights, how many fanciful, erratic notions and ill-directed, yet pompously vaunted researches!

I open at random a few dusty volumes of Charcot's house journal (it was published from 1888 to 1918), and glance through their pages. The journal was appropriately named "Iconography." Here and there I encounter images of women kneeling, with arms outstretched, as if in prayer. Others are disheveled, discomposed, contorting themselves in painful spasms. Still others, shown in facial close-ups, stare vacuously ahead with a glazed, fixed, troubling gaze, too pathetic for words. They are the "hysterics" that vegetated, sometimes for life, behind closed doors, inside the gloomy ward at the back of the Salpêtrière. They adopt bizarre postures that were captured in the photographic laboratory of that famous institution. The investigators of the day believed these attitudes to be revealing physical signs of the diseases they described—pathologic entities that fitted nicely in the admirable, elaborate nosology which they themselves had assiduously constructed. Alas, their sedulous efforts did not amount to much, in the end. Today, the prevailing professional opinion is that those poor women, bearers of an abnormally high suggestibility, learned to complacently reproduce the postures and the gesturing that the investigators expected.

Suddenly, I come across a report signed by two disciples of Charcot that strongly draws my attention. It is the description of a peculiar malady characterized by "the impossibility to sit down." Of course, it comes couched in appropriate, high-sounding medical terminology: it is the *"psychasthenic syndrome of akathysis."* The authors modestly state that neither the term nor the syndrome are original: a previous author, a Doctor Haskowec, had formerly described, in the *Revue de Neurologie*, issue of November 30, 1901, page 1107, another patient afflicted by the same disease, for which he proposed the term akathysis (in French, *"akathisie"*), Greek for inability to sit down.

The patient was a mature man in his early forties, and had been a jeweler, but was now unemployed. His family history was a gripping recitation of misery: both parents were alcoholic; an epileptic sister died during a convulsive seizure, and there was a living brother who was deaf. This depressing family history ended, according to the insensitive statement of the authors of the report, in "the poor devil here presented" (*le pauvre diable que voici*)—a language inconceivable in today's medical literature, but evidently not at all uncommon in the halcyon days of the Salpêtrière.

The singular disease is plainly evident. The man cannot bear the idea of sitting down. At first, everything seems normal: he is invited to sit down and does so without difficulty. It is neither a physical incapacity, nor forgetfulness, but rather a phobia; for some time later, about ten minutes if he is being observed, he fidgets, then his body stiffens, especially on the left side; he sweats, he pants, and his whole expression appears markedly distorted by anxiety. If he resumes the standing position, he will be all right: his breathing becomes normal, regular, and his countenance expresses great tranquillity again. However, if forced to remain immobile, the symptoms and signs reproduce themselves. "The man is only happy when he is walking," we are told.

The learned doctors amply speculate in the discussion section of the report. The disease is placed within the broad concept of hysteria (as were, in fact, the majority of psychiatric conditions at the time), and deemed to be akin to "*astasis*," the hysteric incapacity to stand up (from the Gr., meaning "instability," derived from "stasis"). "As the harmony of innervation that actuates the gait may be altered by various causes, just so the harmony of innervation that produces the normal act of sitting down may be altered by the same causes."[97] The man, they conclude, has a phobia of the chair. As a jeweler by trade, this was most hurtful to his *modus vivendi*: the sitting position is the prototypical posture of jewelers. But it is not uncommon for patients to develop phobias associated with their working conditions or

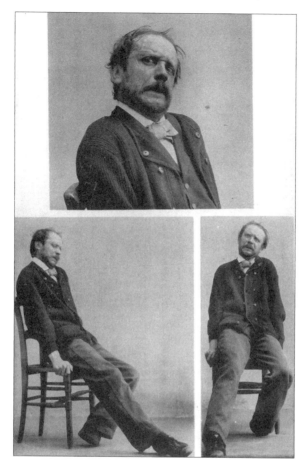

Figure 10. Mental patient, adjudged to suffer from "impossibility to sit down," as reported in 1902 in the journal of the Salpêtrière hospital of Paris, work site of the celebrated doctor Jean-Martin Charcot, founder of modern neurology.

with tools of their trades: phobia against razors in a barber; against scissors in a tailor; against a telegraphic machine in an employee of the telecommunications company.

What arrested my view was the photographic "iconography" of this patient. It has captured a face of acute suffering; the face of a mind violently assaulted by madness; a visage that succeeds in expressing an inconceivable mixture of pain, anger, and terror. The eyes are widely open, as if about to pop out of the orbits. The brow is covered by sweat and girded by disordered locks of hair. The eyebrows are lowered, and a transverse skin fold that joins their inner tips bespeaks an invincible, uncanny anxiety. Anguish and panic have altered the head and contorted the body; that one is held back, as one who seeks to avoid a blow; this one is stiffened, the legs held apart and extended; and, to enhance the pathetic air of the unfortunate sufferer, the left foot is missing: a stump is all that remains after an amputation rendered necessary by complications of intractable and painful muscular contractures.

This man, so utterly shaken by the furious gales of his psyche, is seen desperately to grab the edges of his chair with this hands; he clutches them with all his might, until his knuckles turn white, as a drowning man might seize a floating object. This is the picture of a man who feels that he is being ejected from existence, as from a roller-coaster in free fall; the image of a man in the midst of existential vertigo, whirling down headlong on a precipitous course that—he knows—is not far removed from death. No one can tell what awful storms, what Apocalyptic disasters were unfolding in the depth of that man's pitiable brain. But for the clinicians at the Salpêtrière, his disease is simply "an inability to sit down"! Can there be any doubt that the world is dark or rosy depending on the *color of the glasses* through which we look at it?

II. Microscopy, With Some Personal Reminiscences

I don't know why in my youth, so prodigal of strength and enthusiasm, I decided to retreat from the stress of clinical practice into the quiet environment of the laboratory. It could be that the daily spectacle of miseries greater than I could bear had me baffled, despondent, and weary. Or perhaps my idea of the doctor-patient relationship was too lofty and idealistic, and the frequency with which it was vitiated by the prevailing reality proved too much for an immature sensibility. Or then, again, parodying a great statesman who allegedly claimed that he loved France but detested individual Frenchmen, I might say that I loved the study of disease in the abstract, but could not stand individual sick patients in the concrete. These and other reasons are sometimes confessed by honest students of medicine—and full fledged clinicians— as personal motives to choose to specialize in those disciplines that allow the theoretical study of disease, and still permit the moral satisfaction of contributing to alleviate the suffering of the sick, while being only "cousins once removed" of the clinic—removed as well from front-line, hands-on clinical practice, and hence from the stress and perturbation of direct patient care.

What the reasons are for choosing one course of life over another, is usually a mystery, most of all for the chooser. To speculate on past decisions is as idle as to launch guesses on what is to come: in either case our thought runs its head against the closed door of destiny. Longfellow put it in pretty rhyme: ". . . destiny remains untold; / For, like Alcestes' shaft of old, / The swift thought kindles as it flies, / And burns to ashes in the skies."

Still, if I were forced to name a single determinant of my choice of specialty, I believe I would use one word: Microscopy. It is much to be regretted that growing up erodes the capacity to marvel at the views revealed by an optical microscope. Perhaps our stunning technological progress, offering so many—and so spectacular— causes for wonder, has made us jaded. In a world of satellites, superconductors, and images beamed to earth from the ground of Mars or the rings of Saturn, what response, if not tedium, will provoke a eulogy and glorification of an invention that goes back over three centuries?

On the other hand, it may be that a world in which photographs are transmitted across interplanetary distances is a world inherently more susceptible to the appeal of microscopy.

Pascal exhorted us to contemplate the whole of Nature in all its vastness and majesty.[98] This comprehensive view will make us realize, he pointed out, that our visible world is but a tiny dot, an almost imperceptible speck in the limitless universe. In vain we stretch our imagination to the limit, we always fall short of reality. By the side of all this, man will feel as if lost, and will "estimate at its just price this little dungeon in which he is lodged, I mean the earth, the cities, the kingdoms and he himself . . ." But then, to come up with another, equally astonishing portent, the philosopher prompts us to consider what we know of the littlest objects; ponder on the fact that a mite presents, in the smallness of its body, parts incomparably smaller still: legs with joints, minuscule channels or veins, blood within the veins, particles within this blood . . .

The immensity that Nature deploys in every tiny thing is mind boggling. Within the smallness of things, wrote Pascal, there exists "an infinity of universes, each one with its firmaments, its plants, its earth, in the same proportion as the visible world . . ." It is warranted to suppose that there are animals in this sub-world, and these will have mites, that in turn will offer as great complexities as those we had appreciated first. In other words, the views delivered to us by the unaided eye ranged between the mite and the elephant. Suddenly, the microscope reveals to us an unimaginable dominion populated by living forms for which the mite is elephant.

For Pascal, our body, which considered in the bosom of the universe was a minute, scarcely perceptible thing, now becomes a "colossus." Man was virtually reduced to nothingness when conceived in the midst of the infinitely vast universe. He is "the whole" when compared with the "infinity of universes" that lie in the smallest things. Thus, we are suspended between two abysses, that of infinity and that of nothingness. "Whosoever reflects on these marvels is prone to change his curiosity into mute admiration." And so, I believe that a world that has both, a Hubble telescope surveying interstellar space, and electron-microscopes scrutinizing the infra-universe of molecules, ought to be a world, as Pascal would say, "prone to change its curiosity into mute admiration."

Of course, these high-flown philosophical reflections never occurred to me as a youth. But it was the microscope that made me alive to the realization that "there are infinities everywhere." The first peek through the ocular piece is akin to an epiphany. Children fortunate enough to be initiated in microscopy by a sensitive tutor will never forget the experience, regardless of which career they happen to follow afterward. I was lucky to have such instructors: humble, ill-paid high-school teachers who prepared drops of muddy puddles, wings of flies, grubs, and parts of roaches for our visual delectation. Their quiet, patient ministrations showed us, better than any learned discourse, that every realm of Nature is marvelous, and that it was childish to recoil with aversion from the study of those things.

An ancient tale says of Heraclitus that, when foreign visitors came to see him, they found him warming himself up near the furnace in the kitchen, and hesitated to go in. Upon which Heraclitus reputedly told them: "Come in, come in, for there are gods everywhere, even in the kitchen." Aristotle draws a moral from this vignette, when he says that "just so we should venture on the study of all kinds of creatures without distaste; for each and all will reveal something natural and something beautiful"[99]

Although my youthful fascination with microscopy was strong, it may not have sufficed, by itself, to turn me away from the clinic as a *modus vivendi*. The trained "medical gaze" can spot, by the bedside, views as interesting as any that a microscope might unfold. At its best, the medical encounter with a patient can be an extraordinary experience; an enterprise that engages the physician's powers of observation, imagination, inference, and empathy, in addition to technical knowledge. It is an act that goes beyond the purely cognitive realm, and whose fundamental nature one is at pains to describe with words, although one feels the need for such terms as "profundity" and "spiritual engagement." That the so-called doctor-patient relationship very often falls short of realizing this exalted potential, is the fault of external constraints, and the shortcomings of individual physicians, but certainly not of failings inherent to medicine as a human endeavor.

Thus, I might have stayed in the clinic, charmed by the revelatory powers of the "medical gaze." I was dissuaded from this by new mentors that rekindled my earlier fervor for the microscopic views. As luck would have it, most of these guides were displaced Spaniards; and this fortuitous circumstance in my life can be traced to the tempestuous history of Spain.

While the ships of state of the great world powers cruised along the sea of history with billowing sails and on a steady course, it was the ill fortune of the Spanish navy often to run into choppy seas, where it advanced with horrific lurches from side to side, creaking and rolling, always on the verge of going down, and each time scaring the wits out of the poor Spanish people. The last violent tipping to one side was the Spanish Civil war, and it had for effect the throwing overboard of many of the passengers: I mean the diaspora of Spaniards that were forced to flee the cruel persecutions and merciless savagery that characterized that conflict.

Spain's loss was Mexico's gain, because among the refugees were many prominent intellectuals who sought asylum in Mexico, a country with a shared culture, and favorable to the political persuasion of the exiles. Among the latter were medical professionals who eventually joined the faculty of the medical school where I was a student. By this odd concatenation of circumstances, I came under the influence of brilliant microscopists who had been disciples, directly or indirectly, of Santiago Ramón y Cajal (1852–1934), one of the greatest histologists of all times, winner of the Nobel Prize in Physiology or Medicine in 1908 for studies that established the neuron as the fundamental unit of the nervous system. "Cajal single-handedly mapped the totality of the nervous system," I once heard an American neuropathologist declare. And if this encomium seems a bit hyperbolic, it is still true that Cajal developed techniques for sectioning and staining tissues, and performed microscopic studies of such exquisite descriptive accuracy as to form the foundation of most of what is presently known about neuroanatomy.

I heard it said, by those who knew him personally, that Cajal had in his late years the appearance of a venerable sage: a reposed mien, whose dark eyes and soft, intelligent gaze conveyed an impression not of keen intensity, or of troubling penetration, but of settled attentiveness, tranquillity and peace, which turned to restlessness only when conscious of being observed. There was as much of the artist as of the scientist in that patrician head. His fondness for the plastic arts was well known; and the ink drawings that illustrate some of his scientific works, copies of his own hand of microscopic fields, bespeak an uncommon facility with pencil and pen. At the university of Zaragoza were kept large plates with oil paintings of anatomical preparations, faithful artistic renderings by Cajal. These plates were lovingly preserved by a curator who had them bound, and were proudly displayed on a stand specially constructed to facilitate their handling.

Those peaceful-looking eyes registered numberless microscopic patterns and immediately filed them in a prodigious memory. It could be said with greater propriety of Cajal what was once said of Charcot, that he was "a visual man." There are many recorded examples of his astounding visual memory. Someone would raise a question about a rare, seemingly unprecedented detail of microscopic structure, and Cajal would say: "I remember having seen that before in the brain of a developing cat embryo. Come with me and I will show you." The questioner would follow Cajal to his office, where the renowned scientist would open a drawer containing hundreds, perhaps thousands of histologic preparations, all lying in complete disorder. Some were dust-covered, for they had not been examined in years. This was the most heterogeneous collection, for it comprised tissues from human beings and from animals of the most varied species, normal and pathologic, and in various stages of development. But, to the amazement of all who watched, Cajal would promptly come up with precisely the preparation he was looking for, and unfailingly identified the features he wished to demonstrate.

I was convinced that the ink drawings that illustrate his scientific treatises were somewhat idealized copies of microscopic fields, many hand-drawn by the master himself before microphotography was perfected, and probably "retouched" to enhance their didactic value. After I became familiar with histology, I learned that small imperfections, such as folds in the tissue, tears, or staining flaws, are almost universal in the material observed. When, on one occasion, I was privileged to look at microscopic preparations from Cajal's original work, I was stunned: their appearance was identical to the ink drawings; better, perhaps, than the latter, in the sense that the real model is always superior to the best pictorial rendering. The impeccable detail with which the nerve cells' bodies and their delicate cytoplasmic prolongations were outlined; the neat tree-like branchings of the dendrites, the intricacy of the neural foliage; to the minutest detail, all was displayed with exquisite clarity. I felt that I was gazing at marvelous arabesques, or at a beautiful tracery that somehow managed to be as informative of the brain tissue structure as it was pleasurable to contemplate.

Much of the work of Cajal and his disciples was done with techniques that used silver nitrate, or gold salts, to stain the tissue sections. Despite their usefulness, these techniques were notoriously difficult to reproduce. The capriciousness of the results was the chief cause of their eventual abandonment, but not without a rich body of anecdotes first growing around the inconsistencies of the results, the lack of standardization of the techniques, and the uncanny ability of a few investigators, mostly Cajal's students and collaborators, to produce satisfactory preparations. A story told by one of his students underscores these problems.

A group of foreign visitors arrived, who were desirous to learn, during a short stay in Spain, the staining methods that had made so much elegant work possible. In defective French (at the time the preferred language of communication among the learned), they conveyed to the great scientist their frustration at not being able to stain the Golgi apparatus, a cellular structure admirably portrayed in Cajal's monographs. "How can that be possible, when my technique is so precise and so constant?" mumbled this one, and added: "The secret of success lies in the correct preparation of the fixative and its proper use. Come with me, let me show you."

The visitors followed the master to the laboratory, where in a very matter-of-fact way he said: "Look, we start with ten percent formalin . . . ," and while saying this he seized a not so clean flask lying close by, in which he poured water directly from the faucet (!), added a jet of formalin, then smelled the bottle (as if gauging its composition by olfaction were a valid substitute of carefully measured volumes), and said: ". . . then you add from two to three grams of uranyl nitrate . . ." And this new utterance was accompanied by his taking a container of the said reagent, emptying a small amount of this powder on the palm of his hand, and making up and down balancing movements, as if his hand had been a plate in an old fashioned analytical scale. He then dropped the reagent into the bottle with the formalin, and triumphantly concluded: "There you are! All that needs to be done now is to leave the tissues in this solution for about . . . Oh, some eight to twelve hours, after which they must be transferred to the silver nitrate solution."

The visitors were dumbfounded. One of them was bold enough to ask: "And how would we know when the staining is well done?" Cajal rejoined: "Just look at the tissue slices. The color they adopt will show you when they are ready to be sectioned for microscopic study."

Upon which, another member of the group of visitors handed him a flask with the formalin-fixed specimens that they had unsuccessfully tried to stain in their home country, and put forth one more question: "Can you tell if these samples have been processed adequately for staining of the Golgi apparatus?"

Cajal took the container, gently shook it to agitate the fluid in which floated some tissue blocks, held it against the light, looked at it squinting a little, and rejoined with a very expressive gesture:

"I can truly tell you that these specimens are no good. You can be sure that the staining will not work on these slices, which you might as well discard right away without the least compunction. I don't know how you processed them, but they are useless." And with this, he left to go back to his work.

The truth is, those visitors had processed their tissues adhering meticulously to every step of the technique that Cajal himself had reported in the scientific literature.

These wild, unsystematic goings-on were difficult to reconcile with the excellent results obtained, and gave rise to plenty of ironical commentary among those who were familiar with the work of the Spanish histologists.[100] I heard it said that perhaps the impurities in the water, or in the reagents, had something to do with the marvelous results achieved in the face of a lack of adequate quality control. This explained, ironized some, that first-rate laboratories in the most advanced nations, which used chemically pure reagents and de-ionized, distilled water, could not match the work done first in the budget-constrained science institutes of Spain, and later in the impoverished laboratories of the Latin American nations where the disciples of Cajal settled after the Spanish Civil War.

Professor Isaac Costero Tudanca (1903–1979) was a second-generation disciple of the great man, and one of the Spanish émigrés in Mexico. His sharp sense of humor joined to an astonishing erudition earned him innumerable students and admirers in his long, productive career. He communicated his great love for the silver impregnation staining techniques to his closest collaborators. Among them, a few cultivated those methods with equal fervor, and continued to use them in their daily investigations; many others, discouraged by the fastidious, time-consuming steps required, looked upon them with distrust, and scoffed at the inconstancy of the results. "When the professor says to stir the solution," one of the unconverted said to me in derision, "you must move the stirrer counter-clockwise. If you stir clockwise, the stain will not work." "And the recipient in which you stir the solution cannot be just any recipient: it must be one into which you have blown cigarette smoke previously," said another scoffer. "But not just any cigarettes," added a third one, "they have to be of the Belmont brand."

Except for very few laboratories in the world, the staining methods of Cajal and his votaries generally fell into disuse. They have been replaced by others more reliable, more informative, and easier to reproduce (though not, perhaps, as esthetically pleasing). Certain methods, currently of widespread application, employ silver salts to stain tissues, and technicians complain that they are difficult to perform. The difficulty lies chiefly in the fact that tissues take up the reagent in unpredictable ways: some fast, some slow, so that close individual supervision is required to ascertain when the reactivity is optimal. Such methods tie up the technicians' time, and do not lend themselves to automation, which is presently the favored tendency in most laboratories.

I believe that there was an element of the artistic in the old-fashioned techniques. I like to think that some deep-rooted esthetic impulse, alien to conscious awareness, moved the Spanish scientists to turn toward using silver and gold to stain cells and tissues. Regardless of their primary purpose, the microscopic preparations were, to some extent, things of beauty that had to be worked through with loving attention. They were pieces of handicraft; objects of the investigators' own creation, and as such not to be left in the hands of a technician. This personal attention must have been, in no small part, the secret of their success.

Indeed, the idea of microscopic preparations being made by a machine, as is now the standard practice, was utterly repugnant to traditionalists. Doctor Isaac Costero, heir in direct line of the old school, insisted that his collaborators perform the various technical steps with their own hands. Routine chores could be left for technicians to do, but a silver stain that outlined brain cells was closer to a work of art, and therefore could be entrusted to no one. Was not the microscopic image, after all, a portrait of the anatomical substratum of the mind? Those spidery cells so elegantly revealed, were they not, strictly speaking, the warp and woof of the psyche, the very core of our being? Doctor Costero, irritated against neuro-pathologists who remained aloof from the tissue laboratory, waiting for uninterested technicians to bring to them the preparations they produced, had this quaint rhetorical outburst:

"God Himself fashioned man by hand, out of a piece of lowly clay! Only thus could He have made us, such as we are, in His image and semblance. Had he entrusted this task to angels and seraphim, I am afraid we would have turned out not much better than gesticulating monkeys!"[101]

Many years of my professional life were devoted to looking at microscopic preparations: loose cells or tissue sections appropriately stained and mounted on glass slides. The visual study of such objects often allows us to diagnose a disease. This activity was a very large part of my *modus vivendi*. Accordingly, the question of whether the "slides" were pretty to look at, or no, had a special relevance from my vantage point. And there is no doubt that there are visual as well as intellectual rewards from this activity.

Take, for instance, the humble "Pap" smear (common colloquial abbreviation in America for the test devised by Doctor

George Papanicolaou in the early 1920s, although it did not become generalized until the 1940s): cells collected under direct vision from the cervix and vagina of a patient are fixed onto a glass slide, and stained for microscopic study. That cancer cells can be identified in these preparations was an important discovery, described by Doctor Papanicolaou as "one of the most thrilling experiences" of his entire life. Since these cells may be obtained very easily, and at minimal expense, it became possible to study cancerous changes from their earliest beginning. Early detection allowed opportune intervention, and thus therapy for the first time achieved cures against a formerly irreversible, dreadful disease. Here, it is not idle to remark that while billions of dollars were being spent to curb cancer; and whole teams made of the best minds were actively pursuing sophisticated research in forefront anti-cancer institutes; the first real progress of world-wide impact was achieved by the industry and genius of a single individual indefatigably peeking through his microscope and disposing of a rather meager budget.

The pathologist finds intellectual satisfaction in arriving at a diagnosis. But the artistic sense, if it may be so called, is equally rewarded. For apart from its medically informative value, the microscopic preparation may be beautiful to look at. The traditional stains used for the "Pap" smear (Orange G, eosin Y, light green, and hematoxylin) produce a number of combinations of hues and multicolored figures that are pleasant to see. Some look like abstract paintings. Now and then, the microscopist comes across fields that, suitably framed, would compare advantageously with the displays of any museum of contemporary art.

The question is whether esthetic enjoyment, granting medical microscopy has any to offer, is relevant to the chief goal pursued, which is to make a diagnosis. How does the pathologist go about to attaining this end? The received opinion is that he, or she, gazes intently at many microscopic fields, carefully records each observation, then confronts this observation with a hefty catalogue of images and non-visual concepts that are stored in his brain, and by putting all this together, a diagnosis is arrived at. The method seems to follow the injunction contained in an old German poem:

> This is why God gave you the steelier eye of the spirit
> That it may serve you to perfect the eye of the flesh.
>   When you look with the one, appeal also to the other,
>   With the two you shall see well, if one does not suffice . . .[102]

In sum, the generally accepted version is that the microscopic diagnosis is a strictly cognitive process in which artistic emotion plays no part.

Elaborating on this opinion, Dutch investigators used a device that traces the displacements of the gaze using infrared light reflections from the eye.[103] Pathologists were fitted with this device attached to a helmet, and instructed to analyze microscopic preparations trying to make a diagnosis, as they normally would in their practice. Computer analysis and the use of a display monitor permitted to ascertain the eye orientation at various time points, and to know where exactly the pupil was directed. In other words, it was shown how the different experts looked at the slides; how they aimed their gaze; what did they look at first, what last, and for how long. This study paralleled the previously mentioned investigations on how radiologists look at medical images of their specialty field.

A major conclusion was that individual pathologists varied markedly in the way they scanned the slides. Some focused on many points, but only for a short time. Others searched selectively, stopping the gaze at specific points, and detaining it there for relatively long periods. Purportedly, eye-tracking devices and the studies they render possible may become important in training histopathologists on the optimal ways to look at slides. Although the authors were reserved in this regard, an implication was that experienced pathologists, those who are good at diagnosing, know how to scan a slide: they know where to look first, and where to go from there.

Thus, this study reinforces the common notion that the histologic diagnosis is a matter of "knowing" how to look, not of "liking" what one looks at. But this proposition harks back to an old, old philosophical question, which may be summarized by asking which is first, to know or to like. What comes first, the head, or the heart? When a new object intrudes into our horizon, do we know it first, and then we like it, or do we like it first, and then we know it? Common sense tells us that we need to know it first; for how could we possibly like or dislike something *before* we even know it? That would be like putting the cart before the horse. On the other hand, history shows that Mr. Common Sense is a straitlaced character whose admonitions we do well to question; for nothing grand would ever be attempted if we always followed blindly his advice.

Max Scheler (1874–1928) was among the few who disregarded common sense. He proposed that liking is first, and knowing second. Everything we do is ultimately traceable to the passions of love and hate. At the bottom of all the acts of our will, from the simplest to the most complex; at the bottom of every one of our choices; of everything we perform or accomplish; there shall we find the stirrings of the heart. Affect, the interplay of likes and dislikes, *i.e.*, of love and hate, forms the subsoil of the psyche: it is the nourishing turf out of which grows all knowledge. For knowledge arises from interest or preference, which are movements of the heart assimilable to love. And because love incites us to know and to act, it is undeniably the progenitor of both cognition and will. Thus, in the order of things of the spirit, love is first.

Love is first. This is the "*ordo amoris*" of which Max Scheler spoke. Love comes before knowledge and even before acts of the will. Or, as he put it, unable to resist the adoption of a donnish air—German professor that he was— "Before man is an *ens cogitans*, or an *ens volens*, he is an *ens amans*."[104]

We find ourselves in the world as "affected" beings, not as

neutral entities. Everything we perceive attracts us or repulses us. To some things we would submit; of others we would become the masters. A system of preferences and rejections, of likes and dislikes, underlies even our most trivial acts. The gaze is not excluded. I look at a blank wall, and this is seemingly an "indifferent" act; or I gaze at a white sheet of paper, and I am not conscious of being affected by any emotion at all. But, while I gaze at the wall, my eyes focus on a little fissure, or a brick's border, or some other detail. By the same token, while I look at the sheet of paper, my pupils stop their scanning movement upon a slight fold, or a shadowed area. Thus, my ocular movements are not entirely random. There are features that awaken my interest. I am affected positively by these details: love, in its broadest definition, is at play. However unconscious, the system of elementary likes and dislikes guides my eyesight, according to the rules of the order of love and hate, Scheler's "*ordo amoris.*"

Why would the archetypal diagnostic microscopist be exempted from the universal rule? The investigators that follow his eye movements with a fancy, computerized, gaze-tracking machine, may be able to map the gliding movements of his eyes across the microscopic field. But if his gaze stopped here or there, on a cellular nucleus, or on a surface epithelium, or elsewhere, the interpretation of the stoppage remains open to question. The investigators will say that knowledge comes first; that the eyes were arrested at a specific area, because the examiner *knew* that area to be relevant to his diagnostic idea.

On the face of it, I find it just as possible to argue that the eyes of the microscopist were actuated by the *ordo amoris.* They stopped the scanning precisely there *because they liked it there.* For no reason, or as Pascal—another man who had no fear of disregarding common sense—phrased it, "the heart has its reasons, which reason itself does not know." Once the eyes paused, interpretation and reasoning took place, knowledge made its entrance, and a diagnosis was established. In that order: the heart first, the head second.

Notes

1. See Jules Michelet's *Histoire de la Révolution Française* (in 2 vols.) Vol. 1. Gallimard, Paris. 1952 p. 698.

2. For a study of Nicolas Venette's work, see: Roy Porter: "Spreading carnal knowledge or selling dirt cheap? Nicolas Venette's *Tableau de l'Amour Conjugal* in 18th century England." *Journal of European Studies*. Vol. 14, 1984. Pages 233-255.

3. For an extensive, scholarly comment and illustrated description of Miss Sprinkle's show, see "Retooling the Speculum: Annie Sprinkle's 'Public Cervix Announcement'", chapter five in Terri Kapsalis' book, *Public Privates*, Durham, N.C., Duke University Press, 1991.

4. Some newspaper reports of such voyeuristic activity are: Sue Carlton: "Tampa Video Voyeur Gets Probation," *St. Petersburg Times*, March 30, 1999; Lisa Sink and Linda Spice: "Man Accused of Videotaping Under Skirts," *Milwaukee Journal Sentinel*, July 11, 1998; Patricia Davis: "Video Peeping Toms Seeing More Trouble," *Washington Post*, June 7, 1998.

5. The historical information quoted here on the court of Henri IV of France and his times, was obtained from the monumental collection of memoirs edited by Claude Bernard Petitot and L.J.N. Monmerqué: *Collection complète des mémoires relatifs à l'histoire de France depuis le règne de Philippe Auguste jusqu'à la paix de Paris conclue en 1763, avec des notices sur chaque ouvrage*. Series I in 52 vols., and Series II in 78 vols. Paris, 1820–1829.

6. The memoirs of Madame Campan have been reprinted several times. I consulted: Jeanne-Louis Genêt, Mme. Campan: *Mémoires sur la vie de Marie-Antoinette, Reine de France et de Navarre, par Madame Campan*. Nelson, Paris, 1823.

7. The personal memoirs of a lady of the court are: Jin Yi: *Mémoires d'une dame de cour dans la cité interdite*. French translation from the Chinese by Dong Qiang. Philippe Picquier, Marseille 1993, reprinted in 1996. See also: Juliet Bredon: *Peking: A Historical and Intimate*

Description. Kelly & Walsh, Shanghai, 1922; and Mary Holdsworth: *The Forbidden City*. Oxford University Press: Hong Kong, 1998.

8. An accessible discussion, in the English language, of trial by congress, is the book of the French historian Pierre Darmon: *Damning the Innocent. A History of the Persecution of the Impotent in Pre-Revolutionary France*. Viking, New York, 1986.

9. My source of this celebrated affair is the seventeenth century chronicler and story-teller Tallémant des Réaux. His work has been published contemporaneously as *Historiettes* (in 2 vols.), Gallimard (collection Pléiade), Paris, 1970. The story of Madame de Langey is in volume 2, p. 887.

10. Committee on the Judiciary—Masur Statement. *http://www.house.gov/judiciary/10147* (As posted on May 21, 2000.)

11. For a fine survey and bibliography of the controversies surrounding the role of the media and the privacy of individuals, see: Clay Calvert: *Voyeur Nation: Media, Privacy and Peeping in Modern Culture*. Westview Press, Boulder, Co., 2000.

12. See the section etitled "The Arts of the Diviner" in: A. Leo Oppenheim: *Ancient Mesopotamia: Portrait of a Dead Civilization*. 2nd Edition. The University of Chicago Press, 1977, pages 206–227.

13. L. Oppenheim: *loc. cit.*

14. Quoted in: Piero Camporesi: *La Chair Impassible*. Flammarion, Paris, 1986, page 7, cf. (French translation of the Italian, *La Carne Impassibile*. Il Saggiatore, 1983)

15. *Galen on Anatomical Procedures*. Translated by C. Singer. London, Oxford University Press, 1956, p.34.

16. Giovanni Ciampoli: *Del corpo humano. Discorso primo*. Venice, 1676. Quoted by Piero Camporesi in: *Le Officine dei Sensi*. Garzanti, 1985, p. 121 (author's translation).

17. Father Romolo Marchelli: *Prediche Quaresmali*. Venice, Gasparo Storti, 1683, pp. 55–56. Quoted by Piero Camporesi in: *Le Officine dei Sensi*, Garzanti, pp. 138–139 (author's translation).

18. Thomas Mann: *The Magic Mountain*. Translated from the German by H. T. Low Porter. The Franklin Library, undated, page 223.

19. Shigehisa Kuriyama: *The Expressiveness of the Body, and the Divergence of Greek and Chinese Medicine*. Zone Books, New York, 1999.

20. The story is told in Sima Qian's (also spelled Ssu-ma Ch'ien) celebrated *Historical Records*. Sima Qian (145 B.C.–85 B.C.) is to the Chinese world what Herodotus or Thucydides are to the West, one of the most famous historians of ancient times. His *Historical Records*, a monumental work in one hundred and thirty chapters, attempted to summarize all of the known history of China from its beginnings to the author's times. The work was organized, and prob-

ably partly written, by his father, Ssu-ma T'an, who was astronomer and Grand Historian at the court of Emperor Wu, of the Han dynasty. Sima Qian followed his father in these posts and, displaying the filial duty that the Chinese value so much, carried the paternal writing plans to term. For an English translation, see: *Records of the Grand Historian*, by Sima Qian. Translated by Burton Watson. Columbia University Press, New York, 1993.

21. For a rich bibliography see Vanessa R. Schwartz's: *Spectacular Realities: Early Mass Culture in Fin-de-Siècle Paris*. University of California Press, Berkeley, 1998. See chapter two, "Public visits to the morgue. Flânerie in the service of the state," pages 45–88. A master's thesis that took the Paris morgue as its subject is: Bruno Bertherat: *La morgue et la visite de la morgue à Paris au XIX siècle, 1804–1907*. (Master's thesis, Université de Paris, 1990)

22. Emile Zola: *Thérèse Raquin*. With a preface by Robert Abirached. Gallimard, Paris, 1979, page 128. Author's translation.

23. *Institutio Oratoria*: XII, x, 4-7.

24. Duc de Castries: *Henri IV. Roi de Coeur, Roi de France*. Librairie Larousse, Paris, 1970, page 187.

25. A good source of primary references on the brotherhood of San Giovanni Decollato may be found in: Andrea Carlino: *Books of the Body: Anatomical Ritual and Renaissance Learning*. Translated by John Tedeschi and Ann Tedeschi. University of Chicago Press, 1959.

26. Jacopo Rainieri: *Diario Bolognese*, edited by O. Guerrini and C. Ricci. Regia Tipografia. Bologna, 1887, page 50

27. Recounted in: Jules Janin: *La Révolution Française*. Ch. Lahure, Paris, 1862, page 98.

28. Facts on the history of the manner of executions in the United States were taken from a *New York Times* article by Mark Essing: "Continuing the search for kinder executions," October 21, 2003.

29. John Hilkevitch: "When Death Rides the Rails: Lifting the veil on a silent public safety crisis: Metra's grim toll of roadbed fatalities." (Photos by Jose M. Osorio) *Chicago Tribune Magazine*. July 4, 2004.

30. Jeremy Black and Anthony Green: *Gods, Demons and Symbols of Ancient Mesopotamia: An Illustrated Dictionary*. The British Museum Press, London, 1992, pages 79–80.

31. Richard F. Gombrich: The consecration of a Buddhist image. *Journal of Asian Studies*, Vol. 26, 1966–67, pages 23–26.

32. Pausanias: *Description of Greece*. Book III, xvi (Laconia), 7–11. Translated by W.H.S. Jones and H.A. Ormerod, Loeb Classical Library, Harvard University Press, Cambridge. Reprinted in 1993. Pages 101–103.

33. *The Nature of Things* IV, 12 ff.

34. W. K. C. Guthrie: *A History of Greek Philosophy*. Vol. II: *The Presocratic Tradition from Parmenides to Democritus*. Cambridge University Press, Cambridge, 1965 (reprinted 1990), pages 235–6.

35. William Shakespeare: *Love's Labour Lost*, Act IV, iii, 330.

36. Guido Ceronetti: *L'Occhiale Malinconico*. Adelphi, Milan, 1988, pages 58–9.

37. Francis MacDonald Cornford: *Plato's Cosmology: The Timaeus of Plato translated with a running commentary*. The Liberal Arts Press, New York, 1957.

38. Jonathan Swift: "A Discourse Concerning the Mechanical Operation of the Spirit, &c." In: *The Writings of Jonathan Swift. Authoritative Texts, Backgrounds, Criticism*. W. W. Norton, New York, 1973, page 413.

39. Quoted by K. D. Keele, in: "Leonardo da Vinci on Vision." *Proceedings of the Royal Society of Medicine UK*: Vol. 48, 1955, pages 384–390.

40. Montaigne: *Essais*. Book I, ch.21, in: *Oeuvres Complètes*. Seuil, Paris, 1967, page 57.

41. Pliny: *Natural History*. Book VIII, ch.xxxiv. 2nd ed. Translated by H. Rackham. Loeb Classical Library, Harvard University Press, Cambridge, 1983, page 59.

42. Conrad Gesner: *Historiae animalium liber primus. De quadrupedibus viviparis* [. . .] 2nd. Edition. Frankfurt [*Francoforti in bibliopolio Camberiano*] 1603, in-fol, page 641. (1st edition: 1551).

43. Conrad Gesner: *Loc. cit.*, page 578.

44. For an exhaustive, scholarly study of "mesmerization" in Victorian England, see: Alison Wintler: *Mesmerized. Powers of Mind in Victorian Britain*. The University of Chicago Press, Chicago, 1998.

45. Charles Russ: "An instrument which is set in motion by vision or by the proximity of the human body." *The Lancet*, Vol. 2, July 30, 1921, pages 222–224.

46. Tzvetan Todorov: *Eloge du Quotidien. Essai sur la peinture hollandaise du XVIIe siècle*. Seuil, Paris, 1993 (reprinted 1997).

47. The photographer's name is Michael Clancy. See: http://www .michaelclancy.com

48. Susan Sontag: *On Photography*. Delta Books, 1977, page 23. Reprinted from Farrar, Straus & Giroux, New York, 1973.

49. Francis Galton, F.R.S.: *Inquiries into Human Faculty and its Development*. London, Macmillan & Co., 1883, pp 83 cf.

50. Jacques Lacan: "The mirror stage as formative in the formation of the I, as revealed in psychoanalytic experience." In: *Ecrits—a selection*. Tavistock, London, 1977, pages 2–29.

51. Aelian (Claudius Aelianus): *On the Characteristics of Animals*. Book IV. 30. Translated by A.F. Scholfield. (In 3 vols.) Vol.1 Loeb Classical Library, Harvard University Press, Cambridge, 1958, reprinted 1971.

52. Jean Baudrillard: *La Transparence du Mal*. Galilée, Paris, 1990, page 119.

53. See: *Tono e nagual*, by L. Tanfo. In: Italo Signorini: *Gente di Laguna. Ideologia e Istituzioni Sociali del Huave di San Mateo del Mar*, Milan, 1982, pp. 136–163.

54. Melvin R. Lansky: "Capgras' syndrome and the Significance of Delusions." *Bibliotheca psychiatrica*. Vol. 164, 1986, pages 49–58.

55. Konstantin Mochulsky: *Dostoevsky: His Life and Work*. Translated by Michael A. Minihan. Princeton University Press, 1967, reprinted 1972, page 56.

56. There is an English translation by Margaret Jull Costa, *The Double*. Harcourt, San Diego, 2004.

57. Markidis, M.: "Ego, my double. (The Golyadkin phenomenon)." *Bibliotheca Psychiatrica*. Vol. 164: 1986, pages 136–142.

58. P. Brugger, R. Agosti, M. Regard, H.G. Wieser, and T. Landis: "Heautoscopy, epilepsy and suicide." *Journal of Neurology, Neurosurgery & Psychiatry*. Vol. 57, No. 7 (July); 1994. Pages 838–9.

59. Lara H. Maack and Paul E. Mullen: "The *Doppelgänger*, disintegration and death: a case report." *Psychological Medicine*, Vol. 13, No. 3 (Aug) 1993, pages 651–654.

60. F. Lana Moliner, S. Juan Vidal, I. Pena Garcia: [In Spanish]: "Experience of a double or heautoscopy." *Psychopathological review and case report. Actas Luso-Españolas de Neurología, Psiquiatría y Ciencias Afines*. Vol. 23, No. 6 (Nov-Dec); 1995, pages 314–318.

61. M.J. Fialkov and A. H. Robins: "An unusual case of the Capgras syndrome." *British Journal of Psychiatry*. Vol. 132; 1978 (Apr), pages 403–404.

62. Ted Morgan: *Maugham*. Simon & Schuster, New York, 1986, page 610.

63. Robin Maugham: *Conversations with Willie: The Recollections of W. Somerset Maugham*. Virgin Publishing. 1978

64. Jerome M. Schenck: "W. Somerset Maugham, Capgras syndrome and aging." *New York State Journal of Medicine*. Vol. 92, no. 12 (Dec.); 1992, pages 547–550.

65. Quoted by M. Bussagli: *Bronzi Cinesi*. Milan, 1966, page 128.

66. Cesare Ripa: *Della Novissima Iconologia*. Padova, 1625. See: Public Library of Turin (Biblioteca Civica di Torino 160 B.34).

67. Iconology is said to be the analysis of artistic motifs that tries to

reconstitute the history of the creative imagination. See: Erwin Panofsky: *Essais d'Iconologie. Les thèmes humanistiques dans l'art de la Renaissance.* Gallimard, Paris, 1967. Translated from the English: *Studies in Iconology*, Oxford University Press, 1939.

68. Aelian: *On Animals.* X, 40. translated from the Greek by A.F. Scholfield. Loeb Classical Library, (In 3 vols.)Vol. 2, Harvard University Press, 1959, pages 335–336.

69. Richard de Fourneval: *Le Bestiaire d'Amour.* Edited by C. Hippeau. A. Aubry, Paris, 1860.

70. Quoted by Margaret B. Freeman, in: *The Unicorn Tapestries: the Set of Late Gothic Tapestries at the Cloisters.* New York, Metropolitan Museum of Art, 1976.

71. Bernard d'Astorg: *Le Mythe de la Dame à la Licorne.* Seuil, Paris, 1963.

72. *Miroir tendu, espace clos.* Chapter 4 in: Jean-Pierre Jossua: *La Licorne. Histoire d'un couple.* Éditions du Cerf, Paris, 1994.

73. Palatine Anthology VI, 18. Quoted in: F. Frontisi-Ducroux and Jean-Pierre Vernant: *Dans l'Oeil du Miroir.* Odile Jacob, Paris, 1997, page 54.

74. Diogenes Laertius: *Life of Socrates* (II, 33-35). In: *Lives of Eminent Philosophers.* (In 2 Vols.) Translated from the Greek by R. D. Hicks. Volume I, Chapter 5. Loeb Classical Library, Harvard University Press, Cambridge, 1972, page 165.

75. K. J. Dover: *Greek Homosexuality.* MJF Books, New York, 1989, page 99.

76. Aulus Gellus: *Attic Nights.* Bk. I. v, 1-3. See translation by John C. Rolfe. (In 2 Vols.) Loeb Classical Library, Harvard University Press, Cambridge. Reprinted 1984. Vol. 1, page 29.

77. F. Frontisi-Ducroux and Jean-Pierre Vernant: *Dans l'Oeil du Miroir.* Odile Jacob, Paris, 1997.

78. Octavio Paz: *Risa y Penitencia.* In: *Los Privilegios de la Vista.* 2nd ed. (Vol. 3 of the series *México en la Obra de Octavio Paz*). Fondo de Cultura Económica, Mexico City, 1989, page 99. (Author's translation.)

79. Bonaventure des Périers: *Nouvelle CXXVIII: Des deux jouvenceaux sienois amoureux de deux demoiselles espagnoles*, &c. In: *Conteurs Français du XVIe Siècle.* Gallimard, Bibliothèque de la Pléiade, Paris, 1965, pages 590–2.

80. Act I, sc. 2. Presumably referring to the Isthmus of Corinth, where ships used to be hauled across on rollers.

81. Marie-Françoise Notz: *Perspective et regard dans les Cent Nouvelles Nouvelles.* (Author's translation). In: Michèle Gally and Michel Jourde (eds.): *L'Inscription du Regard. Moyen Age—Renaissance.* Signe ENS Editions, Fontenay/Saint Cloud, 1995, pp. 227–238

82. Marie-Françoise Notz: *Loc cit*, page 236.

83. Maurice Merleau-Ponty: *L'Oeil et l'Esprit*. Gallimard, Paris, 1964, page 14.

84. Jean-Baptiste Porta: *La Physionomie Humaine. Divisée en quatre livres. Enrichie de figures tirées au naturel, où par les signes extérieurs du corps, on voit clairement la complexion, les moeurs et les desseins des hommes, qu'on semble pénétrer jusques au plus profond de leurs Ames. Nouvellement traduite du latin en François par le sieur Riault*. Jean & David Berthelin, printers. Rouen, France, 1655.

85. Michel Foucault: *The Birth of the Clinic: An Archeology of Medical Perception*. Translated from the French by A. M. Sheridan Smith. Vintage Books, 1973, page 110.

86. A. Trousseau: *Clinique Médicale de l'Hôtel-Dieu de Paris*. Vol. 1. J. B. Baillère et Fils, Paris, 1868, pages xxviii-xxix. (Author's translation.)

87. Given the difficulties of transcribing Chinese names to Romanic script, and the confusing custom of the Chinese to take several names, the name of the philosopher appears in Western literature as Lie-Tzu, Lie-dze, Lieh Yu Ku, Lieh Yu k'ao, and Licius. The mentioned story appears in *The Book of Lieh Tzu*, of which there is at least one English translation, by A.C. Graham, published by John Murray, London, 1960.

88. See, for instance: E. A. Murphy: *The Logic of Medicine*. John Hopkins University Press, Baltimore.,1976. Also: A.S. Elstein, N. Kagan, L.S. Shulman, et al.: "Methods and theory in the study of medical enquiry." *Journal of Medical Education*. Vol. 47, 1972, page 85.

89. This investigation was done by Calvin F. Nodine of the University of Pennsylvania, and Elizabeth A. Krupinski, of the University of Arizona, Tucson. Results were presented at the XV Congress of the International Association of Empirical Aesthetics, held in Rome, September 23, 1998. An abstract was posted on the Internet: *<www.ume.maine.edu/~iaea/abwed/html>* Site visited on February 9, 2005.

90. H.L. Kundell, C.F. Nodine, and E.A. Krupinski: "Searching for lung nodules: visual dwell indicates location of false-positive and false-negative decisions." *Investigative Radiology*, 1989, Vol. 24, pages 472–478.

91. H.L. Kundell, C.F. Nadine and L. Toto: "Searching for lung nodules: the guidance for visual scanning." *Investigative Radiology*, 1991, Vol. 26, pages 777–778.

92. J.R. Barrett, E.S. de Paredes, S.J. Dwyer, *et al*: "Unobtrusively tracking eye gaze direction and pupil diameter of mammographers." *Academic Radiology*, 1994, Vol. 1, pages 40–45.

93. Sander L. Gilman: *Picturing Health and Illness. Images of Identity and Difference*. John Hopkins University Press, Baltimore, 1995, page 22.

94. "Charcot artiste." In: *Nouvelle Iconographie de la Salpêtrière.* December, 1898.

95. Charles Richet: *L'Homme et l'Intelligence. Fragments de Physiologie et de Psychologie.* Félix Alcan, Paris, 1884, pages 262–263.

96. Toby Gelfand: "'Mon Cher Docteur Freud': Charcot's unpublished correspondence to Freud (1888-1893)." *Bulletin of the History of Medicine.* Vol. LXII (1988), pages 563–588 (see page 571).

97. F, Raymond and Pierre Janet: *Le syndrome psychastenique de "l'akathisie": impossibilité de s'asseoir.* Nouvelle Iconographie de la Salpêtrière. Vol.15, 1902, pages 241–246. See figure 10.

98. Blaise Pascal: *Pensées*: Pensée # 199 (72 in Brunschvig's system). In: *Oeuvres Complètes.* Seuil, Paris, pages 525–528.

99. Aristotle tells the story and adds a moral in *De Partibus Animalium* (*On the Parts of Animals*), section 645a.

100. It should be remembered that Cajal was a great scientist, and that there was much method in his (apparent) madness. To correct much of the misinformation and prejudiced opinion that exists on Cajal's working methods and tools at his disposal, two authors of the Instituto Cajal of Madrid, Spain, published a historical article on this matter. See: J. De Felipe and E.G. Jones: "Santiago Ramón y Cajal and methods in neuro-histology." *Trends in Neurosciences.* Vol. 15, No. 7, Jul. 1992, pages 237–246.

101. For a chronicle of Spanish neuroscientists exiled and settled in Mexico, see: Augusto Fernandez Guardiola: *Las Neurociencias en el Exilio Español en México.* Fondo de Cultura Económica. Colección Ciencia para Todos. Mexico City, 1997. See also the following website: <http://biblioteca.redescolar.ilce.edu.mx/sites/ciencia/volumen3/ciencia3/153/htm> (Visited Feb. 10, 2005)

102. *Deswegen gab dir Gott des Geistes schärferes Auge / Dass es das leibliche dir zu verbessern tauge. / Wann du mit diesem siehst, zieh jenes auch zu Rat, / Durch beides siehst du recht, wann eines Mängel hat . . .*

This is part of a poem that the dramatist and critic Gothold E. Lessing (1729–1781) placed in the introduction of the first edition of his works in 1753.

103. E.S.M. Tiersma, A.A.W. Peters, H.A. Mooij and G.J. Fleuren: "Visualizing scanning patterns of pathologists in the grading of cervical intraepithelial neoplasia." *Journal of Clinical Pathology* 2003, Vol. 56, pages 677–680.

104. Max Scheler: *Ordo Amoris.* In: *Selected Philosophical Essays.* Translated by David R. Lachterman. Northwestern University Press, Evanston, 1973, pages 98–135.

List of Illustrations

Figure 1. *The Origin of the World*, by Gustave Courbet (1866). Oil on canvas measuring 46 x 55 cm. The lavish, elegant frame enhances the theatricality of the presentation, a characteristic attached to this painting since its creation. Musée d'Orsay, Paris, France. Photo: H. Lewandowski. (Photo Credit: Réunion des Musées Nationaux/Art Resource, N.Y.)

Figure 2. *A Hanging*, redrawn from a print by Annibale Carracci (ca. 1599) kept at the Royal Library of Windsor Castle, England. Credit: Wei Hsueh.

Figure 3. Instrument to detect the power of the eye to set objects in motion. The solenoid is suspended from a thread that comes down from the vertical tube. A magnetized needle oriented north-south (NS) presumably keeps the solenoid on a stable position. The observer's eye is indicated to the right. From *The Lancet*, Vol. 2, July 30, 1921.

Figure 4. *The Holy Family*, also called *The Carpenter's Household*, by Rembrandt van Rijn. Oil on wood. Photo: Arnaudet/Schormans. Louvre Museum, Paris, France. (Photo Credit: Réunion des Musées Nationaux/Art Resource, N. Y.)

Figure 5. Fetal arm and hand protruding through the incised uterus in the course of a surgical procedure on a fetal patient. Photographer: Max Aguilera-Hellweg, Time & Life Pictures. Photo created January 1, 1999. (Photo Credit: Getty Images)

Figure 6. Iconography of *Prudence* according to Cesare Ripa, 1625. To her commonly depicted attributes, a mirror, and a snake, Ripa adds a stag.

Figure 7. *Prudence* according to Hendrick Goltzius (1558–1617). The Janus-like two faced head has become a prominent feature. The serpent is now held directly in her hand. Photo: H. Lewandowski. Musée des Beaux

Arts, Lille, France. (Photo Credit: Réunion des Musées Nationaux/Art Resource, N.Y.)

Figure 8. *Sight* (detail), from the Lady and the Unicorn series of tapestries, executed between 14384 and 1500. Wool and Silk. Musée du Moyen Age (Cluny), Paris, France. (Photo Credit: Réunion des Musées Nationau /Art Resource, N. Y.).

Figure 9. *Old Woman at the Mirror* by Bernardo Strozzi (1581–1644).

Figure 10. Mental patient, adjudged to suffer from "impossibility to sit down," as reported in 1902 in the journal of the Salpêtrière hospital of Paris, work site of the celebrated doctor Jean-Martin Charcot, founder of modern neurology.